Palgrave Studies in Financial Services Technology

Series Editor
Bernardo Nicoletti, Rome, Roma, Italy

The Palgrave Studies in Financial Services Technology series features original research from leading and emerging scholars on contemporary issues and developments in financial services technology. Falling into 4 broad categories: channels, payments, credit, and governance; topics covered include payments, mobile payments, trading and foreign transactions, big data, risk, compliance, and business intelligence to support consumer and commercial financial services. Covering all topics within the life cycle of financial services, from channels to risk management, from security to advanced applications, from information systems to automation, the series also covers the full range of sectors: retail banking, private banking, corporate banking, custody and brokerage, wholesale banking, and insurance companies. Titles within the series will be of value to both academics and those working in the management of financial services.

More information about this series at
https://link.springer.com/bookseries/14627

Bernardo Nicoletti

Beyond Fintech

Bionic Banking

Bernardo Nicoletti
Temple University
Rome, RM, Italy

ISSN 2662-5083   ISSN 2662-5091 (electronic)
Palgrave Studies in Financial Services Technology
ISBN 978-3-030-96216-6   ISBN 978-3-030-96217-3 (eBook)
https://doi.org/10.1007/978-3-030-96217-3

© The Editor(s) (if applicable) and The Author(s), under exclusive license to Springer Nature Switzerland AG 2022

This work is subject to copyright. All rights are solely and exclusively licensed by the Publisher, whether the whole or part of the material is concerned, specifically the rights of translation, reprinting, reuse of illustrations, recitation, broadcasting, reproduction on microfilms or in any other physical way, and transmission or information storage and retrieval, electronic adaptation, computer software, or by similar or dissimilar methodology now known or hereafter developed.

The use of general descriptive names, registered names, trademarks, service marks, etc. in this publication does not imply, even in the absence of a specific statement, that such names are exempt from the relevant protective laws and regulations and therefore free for general use.

The publisher, the authors and the editors are safe to assume that the advice and information in this book are believed to be true and accurate at the date of publication. Neither the publisher nor the authors or the editors give a warranty, expressed or implied, with respect to the material contained herein or for any errors or omissions that may have been made. The publisher remains neutral with regard to jurisdictional claims in published maps and institutional affiliations.

This Palgrave Macmillan imprint is published by the registered company Springer Nature Switzerland AG

The registered company address is: Gewerbestrasse 11, 6330 Cham, Switzerland

Foreword

Over the last 30 years, my research interests have been in human factors engineering. My research started from traditional human factors engineering, then human-computer interaction (HCI) and cognitive engineering. Over the last few years, my research interests have been very much in human-centered artificial intelligence (HCAI), human-AI interaction, and impacts and adoption of AI solutions. When Bernardo asked me to write the foreword on his book on bionic banking, I was perplexed. After reading some chapters of his manuscript, I found it extremely interesting and able to generate challenging ideas.

The book marries very well with the lessons to be learned and actions to be taken from my research. The third wave of AI is characterized by technological enhancement and application plus a human-centered approach, which provides an excellent opportunity for the HCI practitioners to provide integrated HCAI solutions to address emergent challenges. This approach requires a systematic consideration of ethically aligned design, AI technology that fully reflects human intelligence, and human factors design. Specifically, HCI professionals should take a leading role in the human factors design in the HCAI framework by providing explainable, comprehensible AI and useful, usable AI. HCI professionals can also contribute to ethical AI design and AI technological enhancement.

The deep involvement of the HCI community in these areas has yet to be fully realized but is necessary and urgent. In order to provide full disciplinary support for HCAI solutions, the work of the HCI community should include research on human-machine integration/teaming, user interface (UI) modeling and HCI design, transference of psychological theories, enhancement of existing methods, and development of HCI design standards. HCI professionals should proactively participate in AI research and development to increase their influence, enhance their AI knowledge, and integrate methods between the two fields to promote practical cooperation. It is crucial to research the applications of these theories to specific segments, like financial services, as in Bernardo's book.

Human-computer interaction, especially with physical robots, is becoming a trend in the manufacturing industry. However, the development of the services also puts a higher demand for effectiveness and flexibility in the service world. The book by Bernardo moves in this direction by analyzing most of these ideas in the service world of financial institutions rather than in the physical world of manufacturing organizations.

Enterprise management theories about the so-called bionic organization currently face a significant funding gap. Bionic theories have been mainly applied to the enterprise life cycle because of similarities between economic organizations and organisms. The digital transformation has originated relevant advancements in bionics research, which allows discussing bionic organizations for the first time as business realities in which humans and automation, especially robotic process automation systems and artificial intelligence tools, cooperate in executing operations or support decision making.

This book presents the interaction, process, integration, and intelligence (IPII) design implementation for achieving a unified experience in digital solutions that human factors ergonomic professionals deliver. It aims to enhance comprehensively current ergonomics design approaches (i.e., user-centered design (UCD) approach) in delivering digital solutions to financial services organizations. It considers in an integrated way business process design; integration design across data, platform, devices, and applications; and finally, intelligence design that best allocates capabilities between humans and automation.

From the point of view of the financial services digital solutions, the book and the case studies presented on implementing the IPII design approach provide supporting evidence. The book is full of quantitative metrics to demonstrate the return on investment regarding operational and unified experience benefits. Implementation of the IPII design approach requires a mindset change amongst financial services managers and operators. They need to approach design from an end-to-end experience perspective, considering business processes, integration, and intelligent design in the early stages instead of employing the traditional approach that focuses on the interaction design portion of a solution. Additionally, financial service professionals need to seek more opportunities for collaboration across different disciplines.

This book aims to determine how a bionic organization can be defined and its fundamental elements in the case of financial services. Specifically, it investigates the two pillars of bionic enterprises: automation and humans, and the core objectives and outcomes. To provide an exhaustive overview, the book proposes a new conceptualization of the business model of a bionic organization based on the Business Model Canvas framework. Ultimately, the study of bionic organizations aims to discover how they evolved in the post-pandemic phase due to the disruptive events generated by the spread of the pandemic.

My suggestion is to read this book from start to end or go through some chapters, learn the proposed approach, and research or apply it concepts and tools. This reading will help you in your professional and personal life.

November 2021

Wei Xu, Ph.D.
Professor of Human Factors
Engineering/Psychology
Zhejiang University
Hangzhou, China

Contents

1 **Bionic Banking Introduction** 1
   Research Background 1
   Book Objectives 2
   Research Method 2
   Book's Structure 3
   Conclusions 4
   References 6

2 **Bionic Banking** 7
   Introduction 7
   Origin of Bionics 8
   Bionics Fundamentals 9
     Analogies Between Organisms and Organizations 9
   Enterprise Bionic Theories 11
   Bionic Financial Services 13
   Fintech Development 15
   Fintech Categories 19
   New Normal and Organizations 21
     Pandemic Impact 22
     New Normal 23
       Robot and Automation Human Collaboration 25
       Remoteness 25
       Resilience 27
       Resistance 28

	Responsibility	28
	Resilience and New Normal	30
	Agility	31
	Design of a Resilient Bionic Banking	32
	Emergency Management	33
	Characteristics of Resilience	35
	Conclusions	39
	References	39
3	**Bionic Banking Transformation**	45
	Introduction	45
	Bionic Transformation	45
	Birth of Bionic Transformation	45
	Defining Bionic Transformation	47
	Drivers and Impacts of Bionic Transformation	49
	Decision-Making Process	56
	Advancements of Bionic Transformation	59
	Conclusions	61
	References	62
4	**Bionic Banking Business Model**	65
	Introduction	65
	Business Model Canvas (BMC)	65
	An Extended Hai Framework	68
	Bionic Banking BMC	70
	Philosophy	71
	Vision	71
	Mission	71
	Enablers	72
	Outcomes	72
	Customer Value Proposition	74
	Customers Proximity	75
	Place and Distribution Accesses	78
	Partition of the Market	81
	Processes	83
	Platforms	84
	Augmented Intelligence	86
	Machine Learning	89
	Cloud Computing	90
	Data Science	91

	Robotic Process Automation (RPA)	92
	RPA and Banking	95
	Benefits of RPA	96
	Persons	98
	Partners	103
	Pricing and Revenues	106
	Payments and Investments	107
	Protection	109
	Cyber-Security	109
	Fraud	111
	Compliance	113
	Conclusions	113
	References	116
5	**Bionic Banking Life Cycle**	123
	Introduction	123
	Bionic Banking Across the Customer Life Cycle	123
	Customer Acquisition	126
	Credit Decisioning	127
	Monitoring and Collection	129
	Deepening Relationships: Wealth Management	131
	Intelligent Servicing	136
	Bionic Insurer	141
	Conclusions	143
	References	144
6	**Bionic Banking Project**	149
	Introduction	149
	Human-Automation Collaboration (HAC) Project	150
	Human-Automation Collaboration Models	151
	Proactive Human-Automation Collaboration	153
	Inter-Collaboration Cognition	154
	Temporal Collaboration	155
	Self-Organizing Teamwork	156
	Critical Success Factors of Bionic Banking	157
	Critical Success Factors for Bionic Banking	157
	Collaboration	159
	Complementarity	160
	Confidence	161
	Competence	161

	Customization	162
	Cognition	162
	Contribution	162
	Clarity	164
	Creatural (Humanness)	164
	Significant Challenges	164
	Innovation Methods	165
	Innovation Processes	166
	Design Thinking	167
	Design Thinking Method	168
	Lean and Bionic Transformation	169
	Research Method	170
	Lean and Bionic Transformation	171
	Define	171
	Discover	175
	Design	176
	Develop	180
	Deconstruct	181
	Deploy	182
	Diffuse and Operations	183
	Agile	185
	Innovation Acceptance Model	186
	IAM Model	188
	Conclusions	190
	References	192
7	**Bionic Banking Conclusions**	203
	Main Findings	203
	Future Research	206
	References	207
Glossary		209
References		233
Index		265

Acronyms

AI	Artificial Intelligence or Augmented Intelligence in this book
AMS	Adverse Media Screening
ANN	Artificial Neural Network
API	Application Programming Interface
B2B	Business-to-Business
B2C	Business-to-Customer
BATX's	Baidu, Alibaba, Tencent, and Xiaomi
BBS	Bionic Banking System
BCG	Boston Consulting Group
BI	Business Intelligence
BLCP	Benefits, Limitations, Challenges, and best Practice
BMC	Business model Canvas
BT	Bionic Transformation
CLV	Customer Lifetime Value
COE	Center of Excellence
CRM	Customer Relationship Management
CRPA	Cognitive Robotic Process Automation
CtQ	Critical to Quality
CX	Customer Experience
DB	Digital Banking
DT	Design Thinking
E2E experience	End-to-End Experience
EBITDA	Earnings Before Interests Taxes Depreciation and Amortization
ERP	Enterprise Resource Planning
ES	Expert System

xiii

EU	European Union
GDP	Gross Domestic Product
HAC	Human-Automation Collaboration
HAI	Human-Automation Interaction
HATI	Human-Automation Team Interaction
HCAI	Human-Centered AI
HCD	Human-Centered Design
HCM	Human Capability Management
HD	High Definition
HFE	Human Factors/Ergonomics
HR	Human Resources
HRI	Human Robot Interaction
IaaS	Infrastructure-as-a-Service
ICT	Information and Communication Technologies
IEA	International Ergonomics Association
IEEE	Institute of Electrical and Electronics Engineers
IoT	Internet of Things
IPA	Intelligent Process Automation
IPDP	Innovative Product Development Process
IPII	Interaction, Process, Integration, and Intelligence
IPO	Initial Public Offers
IS	Information System
ISO	International Organization for Standardization
IVP	Innovative Value Propositions
JPEG	Joint Photographic Experts Group
KBI	Key Behavioral Indicator
KPI	Key Performance Indicator
LPD	Lean Product Development
MiFID	Markets in Financial Instruments Directive
MIT	Massachusetts Institute of Technology
ML	Machine Learning
MRP	Material Requirements Planning
NLP	Natural Language Processing
OCR	Optical Character Recognition
OTP	One Time Password
PaaS	Platform-as-a-Service
PFO	Product Feedback-Oriented
PML	Project Management Lifecycle
PoC	Proof of Concept
PPE	Personal Protection Equipment
PPI	Processes, Protocols, and Infrastructures
PSO	Product Sharing-Oriented
PSS	Product Service System

PUO	Product Use-Optimization
QFD	Quality Function Deployment
R&D	Research and Development
RPA	Robotic Process Automation
RRSP	Registered Retirement Savings Plan
SaaS	Software-as-a-Service
SMACIT	Social, Mobile, Analytics, Cloud and to the Internet of Things (IoT) Technologies
SME	Small Medium-sized Enterprises or Subject Matter Experts
SMS	Short Message Service
STP	Straight Through Processing
TCM	Transition Change Management
TRIZ	Theory of Inventive Problem Solving
UAO	User Activity-Oriented
UC	University of California
UCD	User-Centered Design
UI	User Interface
UX	User Experience
UXD	User Experience Design
VPN	Virtual Private Network
VR	Virtual Reality
WOZ	Wizard of Oz

List of Figures

Fig. 2.1	Waves of fintech organizations (Adapted from www.digitalinsuranceagenda.com/thought-leadership/the-four-waves-of-insurtech/)	16
Fig. 2.2	New normal	24
Fig. 2.3	The cycle of risk management	34
Fig. 2.4	The essential characteristics of resilience	36
Fig. 4.1	Modified business model canvas	67
Fig. 4.2	Human automation integration framework (*Source* Elaboration of the Author from Xu [2019])	68
Fig. 4.3	Operational bionic model	69
Fig. 4.4	Outcomes and enablers of a bionic enterprise	70
Fig. 4.5	Support from the platforms	85
Fig. 4.6	Cognitive platforms	86
Fig. 4.7	A continuum of the bionic approach	88
Fig. 4.8	Types of financial frauds	111
Fig. 4.9	Bionic business model canvas	115
Fig. 5.1	Customer life cycle automation	124
Fig. 5.2	Types of robo-advisors	134
Fig. 6.1	The 7D lean and bionic transformation model	172
Fig. 6.2	A Conceptual view to synergies between HAI Systems and user centered design (Elaboration of the Author on Pizzagalli et al., 2021)	173
Fig. 6.3	Example of RATER assessment	178

Fig. 6.4	Schema of a by design method	184
Fig. 6.5	Agile bionic transformation framework (7i)	187
Fig. 6.6	Innovation acceptance model	189

LIST OF TABLES

Table 3.1	Definitions of digital transformation	48
Table 3.2	Development of BBS	60
Table 6.1	Characteristics of big data	163

CHAPTER 1

Bionic Banking Introduction

RESEARCH BACKGROUND

This book provides an exhaustive explanation of the theory of bionic enterprise. The context of the research is mainly related to the organization and management of bionic banking. This research field is vast and comprises various interrelated academic disciplines such as economics, organizational studies, automation, and business strategy. Because of this, the research has many application areas. In particular, it refers to the management and administration of an innovative form of organization. The multidisciplinary nature is also due to the continuous reference to emerging solutions, jobs, and automation management.

It is not possible to identify a specific targeted financial sector for the practical application of this book since the interdisciplinary character of the research allows to extend the main findings, resulting from the analysis, to every industry and market. The book directly refers to the banking and insurance industry because of the characteristics of the financial sector, which suit particularly to a bionic transformation. The demonstration of this characteristic also comes from the large availability of official information, periodically published by financial institutions to increase public trust in them. This characteristic is fundamental to the sector.

The topic selected is relevant for scholars because of a gap in management and organizational studies about bionic enterprises. In particular,

---

© The Author(s), under exclusive license to Springer Nature Switzerland AG 2022
B. Nicoletti, *Beyond Fintech*, Palgrave Studies in Financial Services Technology, https://doi.org/10.1007/978-3-030-96217-3_1

the academic literature focuses on applying "bionics" to an economic organization's life cycle. This book fills this gap by presenting the critical pillars of the bionic enterprise theory and developing a business model peculiar to this innovative organizational reality for financial institutions. The business model developed is considered in this book for real applications in several countries. In this way, it is possible to get an experimental confirmation of the soundness of the approach.

This analysis contributes to a big step forward to the existing knowledge on the bionic enterprises published by Boston Consulting Group in 2018 by raising criticisms, generating improvements, and demonstrating the existence of such a typology of organizations with the illustration of real-world case studies (Aré et al., 2019).

Book Objectives

This book explores the organizational reality of bionic banking. The main question that the author has answered is *what is bionic banking, and how it should be structured?*

For a more detailed description of the objective of this book, it is possible to divide this main question into sub-questions:

Q1: *Which are the main characteristic elements of bionic banking?*
Q2: *What are the outcomes that bionic banking delivers into the market?*
Q3. *Which are the main components of the business model of bionic banking?*
Q4. *Is there evidence of the existence of bionic banking?*
Q5. *How will bionic transformation evolve in this turbulent time?*

Research Method

The approach used to execute this research is a mix of qualitative and descriptive methods. The qualitative approach collects and extends available models on the topic, develops different research questions, and acquires evidence to answer the research questions. The descriptive method selected for the book allows to describe the existing theory and to discover new facts and models about it.

For combining these two methodologies, the approach used is a constructivist learning approach (Savery et al., 1995). Constructivism helps to increase the existing knowledge about a phenomenon or a specific research field. According to the constructivist theory, the initial knowledge is local, not universal, and consequently, from this, it is possible to extract a general conceptualization globally applicable.

The completion of the book required collecting several related information and data. The information analyzed has been extracted from academic publications and online papers, mainly from the personal research and case studies. In particular, case studies reporting real-work examples are helpful to determine how bionic banking operates and determine which are the main components of a bionic transformation. With this objective, it has been necessary to collect official documentation from the organizations involved and execute "covert" observations of how they operate. These case studies are the basis for building theoretical models applicable to the specific business model canvas. This approach has generated a series of practical rules that under particular circumstances can be applied as a method to support the bionic transformation.

Book's Structure

This section briefly illustrates the book's structure and gives information about the main contents discussed in each chapter.

Chapter 2 reports the fundamentals of the bionic theory. It defines the bionic research field by highlighting the multidisciplinary nature of the subject and the difference with other related disciplines. This chapter lists some of the significant bionics' applications in management science, especially enterprise management. To this extent, the chapter analyzes some relevant Japanese theories and the relative Chinese scholars' criticisms. The chapter also describes the New Normal emerging after the pandemic for organizations to reshape their operating and business model to survive and, in best cases, thrive.

Chapter 3 supports how bionic banking can evolve and be at the base of a bionic transformation. At the start, digital transformation is examined and defined. This chapter proposes a definition for the bionic transformation extracted from the literature available for digital transformation. It reports the main drivers of bionic transformation and examines this phenomenon by dividing it into three main phases. For each of the phases of the digital transformation, the chapter identifies the impact on the business model. The last section of Chapter 3 analyzes the advancements in bionics research with the advent of bionic transformation.

Chapter 4 presents the bionic life cycle. It first defines the paradigm of bionics based on the interdependence of persons and automation. Secondly, it focuses on identifying the main factors that make a financial institution bionic. Thirdly, it describes the outcomes delivered by this hybrid organization for what concerns its operations, the main value propositions, and especially the relationship with customers.

Chapter 5 answers the main research question of the book about the structure of bionic banking. Using the analytic tool Business Model Canvas (BMC), this chapter identifies the nine fundamental components of a business model (Osterwalder et al., 2010), to which the author adds three additional ones (Nicoletti 2021a). These twelve building blocks create the bionic business model as denominated in this book.

Once defined what bionic banking is and its main structural components, Chapter 6 presents the characteristics of a bionic transformation project. The case studies proposed in this chapter belong to the financial industry. Their selection is for the presence of many of the characteristics and models analyzed in the previous chapters.

Chapter 7 presents the conclusions summarizing the answers to the research questions. It also specifies the type of future research on the subject.

Conclusions

Just after the crisis in which emergency measures are no longer necessary, bionic banking must reorganize its operations, processes, and management strategies based on the changes experienced. If necessary, the organization must adapt to the post-pandemic market, social, and environmental disruptions (Nicoletti 2021b). Eventually, it is desirable to perform an ex-post analysis and assessment of the approach taken during the emergency and, notably, the crisis management plan to establish whether it has adequately worked.

This book identifies the main consequences of the crisis, which have become fundamental in the core operations of organizations for the post-pandemic phase. From the considerations above, it is possible to derive the lessons learned by organizations which can translate into objectives to implement in the shortest possible time for bionic banking. Firstly, to prepare for future critical events, bionic businesses need to implement crisis management practices. These initiatives aim to grant business continuity of core operations, save lives and assets, and learn how to recover after being hit by disruptive events.

In addition to crisis management plans, bionic organizations need to include in their operative strategy the remote work modality. Remote work has spread during the lockdown period in which the recurring imperative was to "stay at home." However, remote does not refer only to the way work is carried out. It should be a new modality for offering different services, remote banking, and products such as wealth management.

The continuous increase in technology, the internet, and innovative tools expose organizations to information security risks. During the pandemic crisis, cyber-attacks damaged many organizations, and consequently, it is necessary to consider cyber security as one of the main concerns for the "New Normal."

In conclusion, it is possible to say that bionic organizations need to include in their business and operating model the three factors previously discussed—crisis management practices, remote modality, and cybersecurity strategies—that have been fundamental during the pandemic for organizations to remain sustainable.

The book provides an overall description of bionic transformation. Since there is no unanimous definition of bionic transformation, the first section identifies an appropriate theorization of this phenomenon. This conceptualization determines Bionic Transformation (BT) drivers, introducing advanced solutions to cope with the global shift of competition and customer preferences changes. The analysis underlines that digitization is not the only impact of bionic transformation. BT affects the organization's core business model, the Customer Experience (CX) and engagement in the value creation process, and the overall business model. In summary, the outcome of BT is a disruptive modification of the original business model.

The implication for practice is that it is necessary to consider the micro-, meso-, and macro-levels for coping with the disruptive changes brought about by the bionic transformation (Oosthuizen 2021). On the micro-level, instead of individuals wasting time worrying about technological unemployment, they should instead develop a resilience-based coping strategy and reskill themselves to be ready for their new role (Hillmann et al., 2021). They need to choose a new role to take advantage of the fourth industrial revolution (Noble 2020). On the meso-level, organizations should adopt a strategic transformational approach to empower operators in the context of the bionic transformation. On the macro-level, governments should direct bionic change initiatives (Steyn 2020). Governments should mobilize organizations to arrange skills training courses and assist citizens in adapting modern innovations.

References

Aré, L., Bailey, A., Hutchinson, R., & Rose, J. (2019). The bionic company. *Boston Consulting Group-BCG. Featured Insights*.

Hillmann, J., & Guenther, E. (2021). Organizational resilience: A valuable construct for management research? *International Journal of Management Reviews, 23*(1), 7–44.

Nicoletti, B. (2021a). *Banking 5.0*. Springer.

Nicoletti, B. (2021b). Introduction. In E. Lechman, & A. Marszk (Eds.), *The digital disruption of financial services: International perspectives*. Routledge.

Noble, E. (2020). The stages of industrial revolution and its impact on jobs. *The South African Institute of Chartered Accountants*.

Oosthuizen, R. M. (2021). The fourth industrial revolution: A resilience-based coping strategy for disruptive change. *Agile coping in the digital workplace* (pp. 11–34). Springer.

Osterwalder, A., Pigneur, Y., & Clark, T. (2010). *Business model generation*. John Wiley & Sons.

Savery, J. R., & Duffy, T. M. (1995). Problem based learning: An instructional model and its constructivist framework. *Educational Technology, 35*(5), 31–38.

Steyn, P. (2020). *Get educated for industry 4.0. Business Day Focus 4.0*. Cold Press Media (Pty) Ltd for Arena Holdings.

CHAPTER 2

Bionic Banking

INTRODUCTION

This chapter presents the most recent findings in bionic research based on the innovative trends introduced by bionic transformation (BT). In this sense, BT contributes to the development of bionic operating systems, bio-inspired product design practices. It leads to a significant transformation of the enterprise system defined bionic enterprise. The following chapters explore some of the critical determinants of bionic banking. This chapter presents a history of bionics and starts by describing how Japanese researchers launched this new field of research, the criticisms raised by Chinese scholars, and the main findings resulting from these initial critics.

Improving the innovation process provides a competitive advantage in banking, as required by today's challenging times. Combining humans and automation helps make organizations faster and more efficient than the competitors, thus creating the basis for competitiveness and future success. In this context, the transfer and application of bionic transformation is an appropriate approach to face these challenges.

Bionic transformation is essential to innovate processes, organizations, and business models. This extension might require modifications to make it successful.

This chapter overviews the main bionic theories following the introduction of the new concept. First and foremost, it is necessary to specify what is intended for bionics since what is commonly associated with this concept refers to robots and artificial body parts. Because of this, to avoid misconceptions, it is essential to distinguish between bionics and biomimetics.

Due to their capabilities, robots also increasingly act as collaborators of human labor (Decker et al., 2017). Robots and automation, in general, do not necessarily replace human labor but complement it and, in many areas, make it more productive. This chapter elaborates on these considerations and demonstrates how technical progress can enable a transition from industrial to services automation and a shift in the relationship between humans and automation from a formerly substitutional to a complementary one. These considerations connect with the so-called capital-skill complementarity hypothesis, which addresses the relationship between physical capital and different types of skills (Beltrán-Martín et al., 2008).

Until now, there has not been a complete presentation of a model for the New Normal. The objective of this chapter is to contribute to this direction, especially for the financial services. The human-automation collaboration addresses both challenges and opportunities for human labor resulting from technological change.

Origin of Bionics

The word "bionics" derives from the Greek word bios (life) and the ending of the word "electronic." It thus basically refers to an association between biology and electronics. Since the 1960s, scholars have started to pursue studies in the research field of bionics. Jack Steele, Colonel of the USA Aerospace Division, in 1958 defined bionics as "the science of systems whose foundation is based on living systems, or which have characteristics of living systems, or which resemble these" (Roth, 1983).

Jack Steel in 1950 promoted bionics as a social science during a seminar in Dayton, Ohio. When he first coined the term, he referred to engineering studying living organisms. This discipline is called biomimetics. It creates artificial products by synthesizing and imitating biological living entities or structures, functions, and composition. According to literature, robotics is one of biomimetics' largest areas of interest (King, 2013). While for what concerns bionics, it is generally considered a multidisciplinary subject which deals with modeling engineering systems that display a set of features coming from similar biological systems. Recently this practice has been widely used in augmented intelligence.[1] Engineers have observed and abstracted human problem-solving processes and have implemented them on software applications.

BIONICS FUNDAMENTALS

Analogies Between Organisms and Organizations

This book focuses on the application of bionic theories to business management. For the first time in 1952, Edith Tilton Penrose pointed out in her paper "*Biological analogies in the theory of the organization*" (Penrose, 1952) about the similarity between enterprises and living beings. She affirmed that the most widely agreed-upon resemblance between human beings and organizations regards their life cycle. Like humans, also organizations experience a growth process in their lives, commonly divided into phases: birth, growth, maturity, decline, and death.

Japanese and Chinese scholars in the 1960s developed some studies regarding bionics applied to enterprise management. According to them, the study of economic systems and processes from a bionic point of view had similarities between organisms and organizations.

Enterprise life cycle is just one of the main drivers of the bionic theory. Another characteristic shared by humans and enterprises is the interaction with the external environment. As a result, this interaction affects their behaviors and processes. Supporters of organizational ecology theory, such as Aldrich and Wiedenmayer, spent significant efforts sustaining that environmental social, economic, political, factors and events are similar (Aldrich & Wiedenmayer, 2019). Changes in the external ecosystem produce variations within the organization (Clegg & Hardy, 1999). This situation is because environments own the necessary resources for running an organization. In this sense, it is possible to consider the environment as a "resource controller" (Aldrich, 1979).

Starting from representing the environment as a resource controller, scholars have noticed that the organisms belonging to the same ecosystem need to share the same resources. Therefore, resources are limited. Aldrich wrote in his book "*Organizations and Environments*" that six

---

[1] In the spirit of bionics uses the term Augmented intelligence (AI) rather than Artificial intelligence.

dimensions of environments affect the distribution of resources and availability to resources: environmental capacity, environmental homogeneity–heterogeneity, environmental stability–instability, environmental concentration–dispersion, domain consensus–dissensus, and turbulence (Aldrich, 1979). Since the resources are limited, only the fittest organization can survive (Winter, 1964). This concept comes from Charles Darwin's environmental-driven natural selection principles (Darwin, 2004). The economic phenomenon that corresponds to the "struggle to survival" among living organisms is competition among organizations. Like in natural selection, the individuals unable to adapt to a changing environment will eventually disappear. Organizations that fail in competing with the others within a sector succumb.

Literature has discussed adaptation. There is a dispute between determinists and voluntarists (Çera et al., 2019). Scholars have agreed that adaptation to the environment is necessary because the external ecosystem of economic agents is continuously changing. A practical example of ecosystem variations is the presence of new entrants in the market. The new entrants represent a threat for the already existing organizations (This is the case of fintech organizations in the financial services (Nicoletti, 2017)). To not exit the market, organizations require changes, thus, to react to environmental variations. Adaptive changes of the main components of an organization are fundamental to conform to the evolving external environment. Otherwise, evolution would prevail, and the organizations would not survive for a long time. These assumptions lead to identifying another similarity between humans and economic organizations: the need for adaptation and struggle to survive.

A structural aspect that characterizes both organisms and organizations is the interdependence among parts: that is, departments, business units, divisions, responsibility centers for what concerns organizations, and organs, apparatus, tissues for humans. Organizations are generally complex organizations made of "components." These logical units are self-functioning because they have independent means, such as HR, financial, and other resources or plants. The different parts of an economic organization are interdependent because they collaborate in pursuing the same object, that is, the main business goals based on the vision and mission of the organization. Cooperation is necessary to make the organization sustainable and effective. In this perspective, various organization functions share a unified strategy designed by the top management level.

A broadly discussed topic in the literature related to behavioral economics regards the *"bounded rationality,"* a theory developed by Herbert Simon in 1982 (Simon, 1997). This theory applies to the study of persons' cognitive capabilities. It deals with the conception that living beings have limited rationality regarding knowledge and information when making decisions. Although individuals try to optimize the decision-making process and make it as efficient as possible, their limits, which concern discovering and developing alternatives, persist. Simon adapted the concept of bounded rationality to economics (Cristofaro, 2017). It is possible to extend it to economic organizations since individuals are the decision-maker agents in the business. Enterprises are run, designed, controlled, and managed by humans. It is possible to state that a further analogy between humans and enterprises is that both are rationally bound beings.

ENTERPRISE BIONIC THEORIES

Starting from these assumptions, scholars have applied bionics to organizations. They developed theories about improving the enterprise system based on what they had observed in biological systems.

Japanese research on enterprise bionics aimed to develop a quantitative model to measure an organization's age. It reflects the speed of development, competitive capacity, operating capability, and economic benefit of an enterprise. It is a quantitative index of enterprise vitality (Jiali et al., 2009). They built this index as a synthetic measure of three variables (Liu et al., 2013):

- The operators' average age represents the level of management and innovation ability of the whole organization.
- The equipment age is an indicator of the technology level of operations.
- The average sales growth rate measures the growth of the organization and its profitability.

The main merit of this model is the nature of the data at its basis. Enterprise reports and statistics can provide this information. Chinese scholars challenged the model claiming that this study lacks qualitative evaluation. Furthermore, from a statistical point of view, the Japanese index is unreliable since it does not consider measures such as the organization's competitive ability and economic profit.

In the 2000s, Chinese researchers developed improvements to this organization age model. Some of these studies lack empirical evidence, such as the one published by Xu et al. (2009). What is common to all of them is the inclusion of additional variables—to the three considered in the Japanese model to define the organization age of an enterprise more accurately. For example, the Chinese approach suggests extrapolating additional information from the Research and Development (R&D) expenses and the capital earnings rate.

Chinese studies also devoted efforts to the theoretical formulation of enterprise bionic. These studies focused on distinguishing three main aspects: enterprise life cycle, biological age, and commercial age (Lihua et al., 2010). These studies structure the organization's life into five phases from the foundation until its disappearance. The analysis of the enterprise life span is not from a quantitative perspective but a qualitative one. The study aims to identify the practical strategies the organization must undertake to remain sustainable over the different moments of its life cycle. Furong and Yanmei (2001), in their publication "Enterprise Bionics," identified the factors that most impact the life of enterprises: management and innovation capacity, living environment, product life cycle, and technology life cycle.

The biological age of an organization is the quantitative measure of its longevity. Broadly speaking is the duration of the life of an organization. This measure has become crucial in bionics when studying how to become a "long-live fintech" and trying to increase the life expectancy of an organization (Lihua et al., 2010). Arie de Geus (1997) studied long-living organizations to demonstrate that 30 organizations with about a century of history presented four common characteristics:

- They did not invest their capital in high-risk opportunities.
- They were good at adapting to the changing external environment.
- They presented a strong identity even if in some cases they were highly diversified organizations, such as General Electric and Unilever.
- They worked toward innovation.

The concept of commercial age connects with the comprehension of *enterprise vitality* theories developed by Chinese scholars. According to them, organization vitality is related to the operating performance of the organization. It is the outcome of three determinants: the enterprise growth ability, the survival capacity, and the regeneration competence of the organization (Liu et al., 2013). From these studies emerged that organization correlates positively with enterprise vitality. This consideration means that when an organization's age is lower than 30 years, the energy tends to increase until reaching a maximum level that corresponds to 40 years of the organization's life. While if the organization's age is greater than 40 years, then there is a decrease in the enterprise vitality.

Bionic Financial Services

This book interprets bionic in a different way to biometrics. The environment is more and more turbulent and challenging to predict. On the other hand, more and more organizations analyze new business models to perform their functions and processes essential to their operations. The motivations are simple:

- Add value to the customer.
- Focus on the organization's core business.
- Gain in flexibility.

In this scenario, bionic organizations represent an interesting case. This term refers to organizations based on the collaboration between persons and automation to run their processes or subprocesses. In recent years, there has been an increasing interest in this business model. Many service organizations are of this type because, in many services, the customer (usually a human) and the organization operators are in the loop. The trend is moving from one vertical enterprise to a highly integrated system of networked enterprises. This model is typical of an ecosystem.

Not much has been written and said on this model. In the past, the attention of scholars has been mainly on the interaction between industrial robots and humans.

Banking is again evolving and seeking a new equilibrium due to digital transformation under the push of significant events such as the 2008 global financial crisis and the 2020 pandemic. Five factors drive the need for financial institutions' evolution toward bionics (Aré et al., 2019):

- Financial institutions pay greater attention to regulatory compliance. Because of the losses experienced during the economic recession, regulators asked for more stability, customer protection, and visibility in operations.
- Digital acceleration caused traditional banking value networks changes, such as introducing new solutions that make processes execution more direct, faster, cheaper, and more accurate.
- Along with the digital revolution, financial institutions are encouraged to modify how they operate by changing customers' behaviors. Customers have clear service expectations. They ask for a customer-centric approach and robust product/service customization and innovation.
- Traditional financial institutions are generally considered consolidated realities. Today, new competitors threaten them, built on innovative business models, functioning as fintech organizations and digital-payment providers.
- Lastly, these organizations operate in a multispeed world wherein new industries, markets, and strategies come into view every day, and for this reason, banking needs to evolve to keep pace.

Each financial institution is characterized by a different starting point when accessing the path to become bionic. It is possible to discuss some interconnected elements these organizations have in common.

- Bionic banking can harmonize digital with physical experience. It distributes products and services through a combination of personal interactions and technological solutions through data-driven analyses, digital communication accesses, automation, and innovative interfaces.
- This collaboration between the people and automation reflects the value proposition created by bionic banking. On the one hand, customers nowadays are interested in buying easy-to-use financial services, which are highly accessible and secure. On the other hand, they ask for an excellent level of personalization of the banking service at a fair price. Bionic banking has to extrapolate and process

information acquired from data to understand customers' needs in advance, and at the same time, their operators need to be comprehensive. As mentioned in the article *"How banks are harnessing artificial intelligence,"* "Some financial institutions are using Artificial Intelligence or Augmented Intelligence (AI) to leverage one of their most valuable resources: customer data. These data may include emails sent to an advisor, financial transactions, and the number of times a customer has signed into an online account" (Collie, 2021).

- The customer-centric service approach is related to providing a superior experience and persons and digital-enabled value propositions. Bionic banking has the opportunity to use design thinking tools such as building a customer journey to assure the best service journey and offering and building long-term relationships (Gruber et al., 2015).

FINTECH DEVELOPMENT

The Financial Stability Board defines financial technology (Fintech) as "technology-enabled innovation in financial services" (Atanasova et al., 2020). At the 2015 World Economic Forum, experts proposed a taxonomy for financial services (Bi et al., 2020). They are in several major categories: payments, deposits and lending, market provisioning, capital raising, insurance, and investment management. Fintech organizations are present in all these categories. Their presence not equally distributed has changed over time.

There are four waves in the development of fintech organizations (Fig. 2.1) (adapted by the author from Peverelli & de Feniks, 2019).

In the first wave, around 2016, fintech organizations were mainly challengers and disruptors. New entrants were attacking the established order. The mantra was disruption. New entrants took the lead in intelligent and innovative solutions and data, designing innovative solutions that solved customers' dissatisfaction with traditional financial institutions. Their focus on fewer frictions and new service levels has changed the expectations of customers. New entrants set new standards.

The second wave's value, the enablers, is characterized by the impact on traditional financial institutions' top and bottom lines. Many fintech organizations explore the potential of new data streams to improve pricing, automate credit scoring, and reduce fraud. They launch all sorts of new proactive services, especially in the online and mobility space.

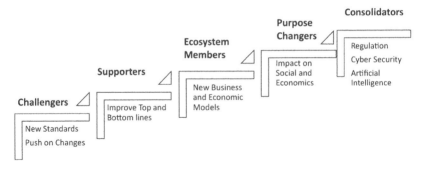

Fig. 2.1 Waves of fintech organizations (Adapted from www.digitalinsuranceagenda.com/thought-leadership/the-four-waves-of-insurtech/)

Many traditional financial institutions realize that partnering with fintech organizations is vital to accelerate innovation.

The third wave characteristic is ecosystems beyond banking. The mantra is about increasing relevancy and opening. More fintech organizations realize that the most effective way to reach customers is to be part of essential platforms and ecosystems (Deloitte, 2020). These platforms are not only platforms around the home, mobility, work, and health. In the case of individuals, these platforms are around significant life events such as study, weddings, birth, divorce, and retirement. In the case of commercial banking, these platforms are around transportation, procurement, banking, and so on. All those events require significant financial and risk decisions. More fintech organizations partner in financial ecosystems with traditional financial institutions or other fintech organizations to satisfy these market requirements.

The pandemic generated the fourth wave (Deloitte, 2020). It created uncertainty about everything. Many fintech organizations have been under stress on several fronts (Deloitte, 2020). It was already becoming not easy to get funds for fintech organizations, especially for some early stage ventures. Many investors preferred to focus on established fintech organizations with proven business models. Interest rate cuts and the economic slowdown have changed the scenario in which to act. Fintech organizations were putting the basis for new business models. The fourth wave sees fintech organizations as social challengers. They can grab the opportunity to increase their social and economic impact and position themselves as a Force for Good (Taddeo & Floridi, 2018). More and more fintech organizations set up the mission to tackle critical global challenges: applying new sustainable solutions with significant social and economic impact.

The pandemic also created new opportunities for some fintech organizations. For example, as social isolation became common globally, this situation generated considerable growth in online financial services and e-commerce. Forty-two percent of respondents surveyed in 2020 said they used at least one fintech organization (Krivkovich et al., 2020). More than six percent of all financial decision-makers surveyed became fintech customers since the start of the pandemic. The fintech organization sector, based on innovation, can generate new and transformative solutions. The added value of the fourth wave is different from the earlier waves. The possibilities to increase banking's social and economic impact with innovative solutions seem almost endless.

Given their differentiated capabilities, namely adaptability and innovation, many fintech organizations were well-positioned to survive the crisis and contribute to the organization and society in meaningful ways. Adversity inspires creativity.

It is interesting to analyze some of the trends at the base of the future fintech waves.

- Investments in the payments space will be a hot subject worldwide, particularly in less mature markets (Mehrotra & Menon, 2021). Prominent payments players will likely consolidate to drive global scale in a situation of new mega Mergers and Acquisitions (M&A) deals.
- Maintaining operational resilience is top of mind as well (Nicoletti, 2016). Lending fintech organizations are being overwhelmed with customer requests for tolerance and relief. They secure the small organization loans established by the pandemic aid, comfort, and economic security act, implemented in many countries.[2] Payment- and wealth-focused fintech organizations' expand or invest in added resources to withstand their systems' stress from higher transaction volumes. These actions are especially challenging for fintech organizations that depend on transaction volumes for revenue and were thus cash-starved at the time of the pandemic (Pollari, 2021),

---

[2] An example is the CARES Act in the USA, but similar programs are present in many countries. home.treasury.gov/policy-issues/cares. Accessed 20 October 2021.

- Open banking (generalizable in open finance (Kwasniok et al., 2021)) offers customers the opportunity to manage bank accounts belonging to different financial institutions inside their online or mobile banking applications. Open finance can create substantial developments with the opening of access to financial data to more organizations.
- M&A activity may grow again, driven by incumbents looking to accelerate their acquisition of digital capabilities and by fintech organizations looking to scale as they try to grow globally or extend to nearby sectors.[3] Banks are more likely to form alliances with fintech organizations when they pursue a well-defined digital strategy and/or employ a Chief Digital Officer (Khatik, 2021). Markets react more strongly if digital banks rather than traditional banks announce a bank-fintech alliance. Alliances may be a product-related collaboration between the financial institutions and the fintech organization. Financial institutions most often cooperate with fintech organizations providing payment services (Elsaid, 2021).
- There will be strong growth in embedded finance (for example, buy now and pay later programs, embedded insurance options, and so on), banking-as-a-service offerings, and related partnerships.
- While the USA should continue to dominate fintech investment globally, fintech hubs will likely continue to evolve and grow significantly in Central and North Asia and South America.
- Given the successful Initial Public Offers (IPOs) of many tech unicorns in 2020, IPOs will likely be on the agenda for many mature fintech unicorns in the years to come. Many local exchanges are also making themselves much attractive for technology listings to compete with NASDAQ.
- The evolution of digital ledger technologies combined with stablecoins and increasing interest in central bank digital currencies will open up exciting opportunities in the cross-border payments space and not only (Cunha et al., 2021). This change might even lead to a digital disruption (Nicoletti, 2021).

---

[3] home.kpmg/xx/en/home/insights/2021/02/top-fintech-trends-in-h1-2021.html. Accessed 22 August 2021.

The fintech work is changing; still, it is necessary to consider that most fintech organizations still realize the past waves' promises.

Fintech Categories

Ian Martin presented an exciting categorization of fintech organizations. It is possible to update its initial seven categories, thanks to recent developments in this way (Gakman, 2017; Ghahroud et al., 2021):

- Lending: Fintech organizations are changing the lending processes. Customers do not need to turn to financial institutions to borrow money. Many fintech organizations are now making loans directly to customers. Customers can request loans online and get approval quickly. Fintech organization lenders assess borrowers' creditworthiness with an automatic underwriting process.
- Payments: Fintech organizations in the payment category let customers send money to each other without turning to financial institutions. Financial institutions tend to charge excessive fees for simple payments like peer-to-peer transfers. Fintech organizations let individuals send money quickly and cost-effectively. Solutions like blockchain make it possible for these organizations to process payments more cost-effectively than traditional financial institutions. In this respect, some fintech organizations are active with electronic wallets or e-wallets. They allow individuals to track their spending, benefit more from their income, handle transactions, and much more. An electronic wallet that follows the user's cash flow (expenses and income) provides different statistics and allows the user to set a budget for a shopping list (for example, dresses) and recommend the best choice.
- International Money Transfers: Traditionally, international money transfers are costly. Financial institutions and traditional money transfer organizations charge up to eight percent in fees. For large money transfers, these fees add up quickly. Standard transfers are slow. Fintech organizations in this category are offering faster and cheaper international money transfers.
- Personal Finance: In the past, customers needed to talk to financial advisors at financial institutions to get personal finance advice. To budget their finances, they needed spreadsheets or the back of an envelope. Now, there are plenty of robo-advisors that can offer

advice and help with financial budgeting. Customers can get personal finance advice anywhere, at any time, with hybrid (human and robot) applications. There are also fintech organizations providing pension or investment advice.
- Crowdfunding (or business equity finance): Crowdfunding is a solution to support a large number of individuals to finance a new business venture through a technology platform collectively (Bouncken et al., 2015). Over the past years, crowdfunding has risen rapidly as a popular way of funding a wide range of activities, including business ventures, personal loans, and charity projects (Ma & Liu, 2017). The current crowdfunding business model consists of three players: the project proposers who provide the original idea that requires external finance, potential investors interested in the idea, and an internet platform that brings all parties together to launch the business venture. According to crowdexpert.com, the global crowdfunding industry raised an estimated total of $34 billion in 2015 (Ma & Liu, 2017).
- Equity Financing: Fintech organizations are transforming equity financing. Organizations in this category of the fintech market are making it easy for businesses to raise money. Some organizations work to connect accredited investors with vetted start-ups. Others use a crowdfunding model and let anyone invest in new ventures. These organizations simplify the fundraising process for businesses. Virtual fundraising is also easier for investors since everything is with online processing.
- Retail Banking: Retail banking is another category of the financial technology market. Traditional financial institutions charge high fees. Organizations in this category present an alternative for individuals. These organizations also have the opportunity to reach underbanked or unbanked customers or small businesses. Consumers who cannot get approved for a credit card—or do not want one—can get prepaid cards from fintech organizations.
- Insurance: Fintech organizations have branched out into the insurance market with the so-called insurtech organizations. Many organizations in this category are focusing on distribution. They are using new technologies like apps to reach customers poorly served by insurance. They are also more flexible than traditional insurers. For example, people who want to borrow a friend's vehicle can buy vehicle insurance for just a few hours. Since the insurance market

is highly regulated, organizations tend to partner with traditional insurance organizations.
- Regulations: The term regtech organizations (REGulatory TECHnology) refers to the technological solutions developed to support the management and regulatory compliance monitoring. Regtech organizations are part of the fintech organization world (Nicoletti, 2017). Regtech organizations are often startups characterized by lean business models and innovative solutions. The regulatory changes and technological developments following the 2008 global financial crisis fundamentally changed the nature of financial markets, services, and institutions. At the juncture of these two phenomena, regtech organizations aim to use new solutions, mainly based on humans and automation, in the context of regulatory monitoring, reporting, and compliance. Regtech organizations to date have focused on the digitization of manual reporting and compliance processes, for example, in the context of know-your-customer requirements. This approach offers tremendous cost savings to the financial services industry and regulators. The potential of regtech organizations is far more significant. It could enable a close to a real-time, based on human-automation collaboration and a proportionate regulatory regime that identifies and addresses risk while facilitating more efficient regulatory compliance (Arner et al., 2016).

New Normal and Organizations

The global health crisis has led to modifying the routines and behaviors of individuals because of restriction and isolation. It has also impacted the operating and business models of organizations. The period that follows the pandemic in which people abandon their old behaviors is called "New Normal." According to Forbes: "in a business sense, the new normal is how we usher in a new way of working, taking lessons from the past months and deciding what to keep and what to throw out" (Tomsett, 2011). Therefore, organizations must consider new factors, trends, and practices to adapt to this changing scenario and include them in their daily operations.

Pandemic Impact

In December 2019, some cases of an unknown infection appeared in Wuhan, China. This disease is called Coronavirus, a pandemic. Because of its high transmission rate, Coronavirus rapidly spread from China to the entire world. National governments introduced movement and travel restrictions within each country and outside. In most of the cases, governments proclaimed *lockdowns*. Lockdown measures are "stay-at-home" restrictive policies that limit citizens from freely moving in a specific area or leaving it.

China was one of the first countries to contain the spread of the virus in spring 2020, thanks to an intense contact tracing activity driven by the government.

The global health crisis lasted more than one year, and it hit the global economics. In its executive summary about the pandemic, the International Trade Center stated the impact of the pandemic on the business in this way: "the pandemic is an unprecedented global crisis, affecting health and economic welfare across the globe. It is primarily a health crisis, with governments worldwide taking measures to prevent the spread of the virus. The pandemic has also resulted in a planet-wide economic slowdown, affecting trade, investment, growth, and employment. The World Trade Organization estimates that world merchandise trade in 2020 fell sharply, between 13 and 32%. Estimated global losses in Gross Domestic Product (GDP) growth hover around five percentage points" (International Trade Centre, 2020).

One of the first industries affected by the spread of the pandemic was travel and tourism. Governments imposed travel restrictions both among countries and within them. Travel declined and there was a suspension of national and international flights.

The New Normal will not look like any in the years preceding the pandemic that changed many socio-economic situations worldwide. In their paper, Buheji and Ahmed (2020) explore the possibilities of the socio-economic spillovers expected in an unprecedented pandemic, studying their importance and how to deal with them to eliminate their opportunity cost on the following normal. This paper synthesized the type of spillovers in the New Normal and its future socio-economic challenges. It presented how to enhance the readiness for the coming era. The main implication of this work is that it would change the way any future pandemic or global emergency spillovers are evaluated or dealt with.

The pandemic outbreaks led many countries to impose travel restrictions and movement controls. The small business sector was directly affected by the movement's control order. Fabeil et al. (2020) found that the impact is more significant among micro-enterprises than its larger counterparts. Entrepreneurs experience business cancellation or closure and reduced income due to several supporting sectors such as retails and transportation. There is still a lack of study on the impact of a pandemic outbreak on financial institutions, especially in business continuity and recovery strategy. This book aims to create effective business models through the human–robot collaboration for financial institutions to thrive during and after a crisis.

Pandemic has disrupted lives and the economy. Nah and Siau (2020) outline approaches in which information technology can support business strategies to enhance resilience by coping with, adapting to, and recovering from adversity resulting from the pandemic. They discuss how information technology such as digital supply chain, data analytics, augmented intelligence, machine learning, robotics, digital commerce, and the Internet of Things (IoT) can enhance resilience and continuity of business in close collaboration and support of humans.

New Normal

There are already signs of how the organizations will change after the shock of the pandemic. This chapter defines the possible transformation as the five Rs, connected with five Ss (Fig. 2.2).

- Responsibility means taking practical actions in the organizational environment, especially from the sustainability point of view.
- Remoteness is the system with remote working, the remote commerce, the remote of every possible activity. Network management is essential in this respect.
- Resistance is the awareness and the actions on cyber-security increasing threat and need of management.
- Resilience is the capability to assure stability and continuity notwithstanding the happening of external changes also drastic. It is the move from "just in time" to "just in case" (Brakman et al., 2020).
- Robot-Person collaboration is the change in the work design based on practical, efficient, ethical, and economic sharing and collaboration between humans and automation and work sharing.

Fig. 2.2 New normal

These changes have a significant effect also on financial institutions. Information and communication technologies (ICT) and Operations Technologies (OT) can support all these aspects. Automation-human interactions can help many of these transformations. They are a powerful way for improving processes securely.

Blockchain solutions can help share data across organizations securely and trustfully, especially among customers, organizations, partners, and regulators (Guo & Liang, 2016).

BCG found that between February and June 2020, mobile banking usage grew by 34%, while banking at branches declined by 12% (Erlebach et al., 2020). Younger customers are increasingly willing to go all-digital, as are a significant share of older account holders.

Robot and Automation Human Collaboration
The New Normal requires less dependence on humans. The use of automation can help in this respect. This requirement is undoubtedly actual in the case of manufacturing. Robotic process automation can also help in the case of service organizations. Robotic process automation (RPA) is a technology capable of automating or augmenting human activities. Its use allows carrying out some activities with the digital workforce and no more than the human ones. For example, RPA can help transfer data from multiple sources to new storage, such as the organization's Enterprise Resource Planning (ERP) systems or supply chain management systems and perform all those activities that organizations carry out daily to monitor and manage their activities. RPA offers critical benefits such as improved task execution and greater accuracy and guarantees a better customer experience. Introducing this solution is a relatively fast and low-risk activity since it accesses existing ICT applications in a non-invasive mode (Madakam et al., 2019).

Remoteness
During the pandemic, the restrictions imposed by governments forced thousands of operators and organizations to change their way of working. To keep operating in lockdown periods, many organizations introduced the "work remotely" formula. Remote work has been considered an immediate short-term solution. In a few days, professional operators had to recreate their offices inside their homes and switch to "teleworking" as organizations had to make available the appropriate Information and Communication Technologies (ICT) infrastructure and the necessary technological tools. Before the pandemic, only 5.4% of EU operators had already experienced remote working. In contrast, for USA office operators, the statistics are around 5% (The European Commission's science and knowledge service, Joint Research Centre, 2020: Levanon, 2020).

On the one hand, remote work was the best solution to grant business continuity in the short term. The majority of the organizations were satisfied with this new working modality since they did not experience decreased productivity (Maurer, 2020). For example, the phenomena of absenteeism, delays, and frequent breaks did not occur to the same degree as for "in-person" work. Many organizations preferred work from home even after the end of lockdown because of the benefit of reducing overhead expenses such as offices, utilities, travel, and supplies.

Remote work represented a challenge for many organizations without an efficient decentralized ICT infrastructure. The decentralized infrastructure allows operators to work independently from their home or wherever they prefer simply through an adequate internet connection using internet and video-conference tools. Virtual private connection (VPN) provided by the business and authentication mechanisms such as VPN tokens or multi-factor authentication can improve security for the organization.

Another consequence of remote working for organizations concerns leadership practices. Leaders have no more opportunity to manage their teams through face-to-face interactions. To exercise leadership, managers may support their operators through daily calls and video conferences to discuss the key issues or results achieved. In this context, leaders understood that monitoring each operator's output by assigning them daily or weekly objectives is better than controlling how many hours they have worked.

On the other hand, remote work has changed operators' daily routines. In this sense, some issues arise when considering remote work from an operator's perspective. Many operators have experienced a sense of self-isolation in lockdown periods, psychological distress, also caused by the uncertainty associated with the health emergency. To face a sense of loneliness, many organizations have organized internal virtual events such as "Zoom coffee breaks" in which it is possible to socialize with other colleagues and perceive corporate culture. Secondly, many operators have experienced problems in working from home because of technical issues. The level of technology implemented in an operator's home varies. It is not comparable to the technological tools available in the offices. In addition to this, sometimes technical issues may be related to inadequate or unreliable signals for the internet connection. This situation often depends on the operators' geographical area (Lusinski, 2019) rather than on the equipment.

At the same time, remote operators have experienced more significant distractions, miscommunication, team building difficulties, and work-life balance. Regarding the latter, before the pandemic, every operator had found a balance between work and personal life interests, which may be related to hobbies, family, self-care, and other needs. With the spread of the pandemic and the introduction of remote working modalities, a blurred line has separated personal and professional life.

Nevertheless, the remote modality has not exclusively affected the way of working. Indeed, starting from spring 2020, many organizations have started offering more services remotely through online access. E-commerce, customer service, and online banking are practical examples of remote modality services.

Due to global health emergencies, remote working has become a widespread "attitude" both in the professional and personal life habits. According to Ernst & Young, remote working will remain present in the New Normal after the pandemic because, in many cases, it brings greater flexibility to organizations in terms of expenses by not affecting productivity. It offers new job opportunities to operators who are no more bound to a specific workplace (EY Belgium, 2020).

Resilience
Along with robotic process automation, bionic operations can resist unwanted changes thanks to business *resilience*. According to IBM, operational resilience is: "the ability of an organization's business operations to adapt and respond to internal or external dynamic changes rapidly—opportunities, demands, disruptions or threats, and continue operations with limited impact to the business" (Finextra, 2016; Ralston & Blackhurst, 2020). These unexpected events have an exogenous origin and come from the variable and uncertain political, economic, social, and environmental factors. These events could disrupt financial organizations' value chains and operations, compromising the ability to remain operative even in the long term. In this sense, resilience encompasses two main strengths: resisting traumatic changes and recovering and reorganizing after being overwhelmed.

Resilience is an essential subject for two reasons. Organizations should analyze their capabilities better to reduce the probability of the risks and especially their potential impact. Besides, to defend their reputation, financial institutions should assure maximum resilience in such a way to be able to provide their services under any foreseeable conditions and events (Bitter et al., 2017). As a matter of fact, after the pandemic, what was "just in time" has become "just in case." In other words, it is essential to prepare for some unknown event that can endanger the existence itself of the financial institution (Brakman et al., 2020).

Due to the hybrid identity of bionic organizations, the processes and tasks performed works on a collaboration between persons and automation. To better describe this collaboration type, it is necessary to investigate the automation exploited by bionic organizations. For what concerns bionic organizations, the coexistence of both automation and humans provides the organization a high level of flexibility and improves its resilience. In disruptive events, person components can replace automation and/or vice versa to continue operating. For example, the workforce can substitute virtual robots by executing tasks in a virtual model due to an information system breakdown. On the other side, the automation of processes such as service distribution allows businesses to continue addressing customers' requests even in adverse working conditions for persons.

Another characteristic that is strictly related to resilience and the ability to adapt to change is the *agility* of business processes. Organization agility is the ability to modify operations in response to external changes or change inputs or even how outputs are delivered. An agile organization can anticipate changes through forecasting, planning, and taking consequent decisions to act. In this sense, hybrid organizations, where intelligent automation and humans collaborate, have the opportunity to conduct predictive analysis exploiting AI techniques. Once predicted the changes, people can evaluate the different alternatives necessary to react to them.

Resistance
Pandemic has created new challenges for organizations to adapt to their operations to a context in which working from home has become the New Normal. To do so, organizations need to accelerate their digital evolution in short periods. Solutions in the workplace are evolving at high speed, affecting all business areas, from internal and external communication to evaluating and analyzing data and performance. The speed at which these technologies emerge, combined with disruptive operations and processes, generates some risks. In this scenario, cyber-security becomes an additional concern to cope in an integrated and complete way.

Responsibility
To remain sustainable in times of crisis, organizations should have a consolidated crisis management strategy. Crisis management is fundamental to anticipate market or environmental threats, understand how to minimize crisis impact on business continuity, and ultimately recover from possible disasters. All organizations need to implement crisis management practices in the New Normal. A crisis management plan considers external

and internal threats, which can be various and from various sources such as natural crises, thefts, terroristic attacks, and data breaches. The peculiarity that these events have in common is that they are unplanned and unpredictable. Problems originate from a single or a set of circumstances that impact organizations' ability to operate, bring negative changes in society and the external environment, and affect the population and/or internal workforce well-being and brand reputation.

Crisis management is the process of coordinating actions to face a crisis in a fast, effective, and non-invasive way. These actions tend to minimize the risks of profitability loss, supply chain and operations disruption, and damages on tangible and intangible assets. Decisions made in times of crisis to take appropriate protection measures depend on the uncertainty of the occurring events and sometimes result from emergencies. It is necessary to develop crisis management plans for dealing with critical events (Sapriel, 2003).

Crisis management plans are documents that define guidelines and approaches to be taken internally by the organization to react and recover. This prospectus is in advance. Risk analysis assesses the main events that threaten the organization and to which extent the organization is well prepared to act. A crisis management plan should include:

- Crisis definition and alert criteria.
- Description of priorities (saving lives and assets, minimizing the impact on operations, protecting brand reputation, and so on).
- Area and period of validity of the plan.
- Crisis management team.
- Business continuity plan.
- Actions to remediate and possibly recover what could be lost or damaged,

Developing a business continuity plan is part of crisis management practice. It is integrated within crisis management plans because it gives basic information about how to continue operations which may not necessarily concern the traditional way to do business but may be related to innovative technologies, business models, and strategies. A business continuity plan is the core of business resilience.

In addition to developing a plan, crisis management practices relate to all those activities performed during emergencies, such as crisis communication to stakeholders, coordination with government and authorities if required, controlling and monitoring the overall situation, and supporting customers, operators, and partners.

Resilience and New Normal

This chapter considers the characteristics of bionic banking. It details a critical aspect of the New Normal connected with the operational risks: the Basel Accord for financial services defines operational risks like losses due to inadequacy or failures of processes, human resources, internal systems, or external events. This chapter examines how bionic banking can help in managing these operational risks.

Several papers have in the past underlined the importance of resilience. Carrozzi (2009) emphasized that essential services such as energy, transport, healthcare, or banking occur through complex infrastructures in which procurement and operations play a crucial role. If not adequately governed due to various severity and origin events, these aspects can cause instability in the provision of services. The possible consequences can have a high or very high impact on the organizations and, in some cases, on the entire community. Carrozzi's L. thesis highlights the key drivers and best practices for the proper governance of continuity and maintaining service levels of critical services, with specific reference to critical information infrastructure protection.

Turner and Kutsch (2015) analyzed answers to questions such as which analysis is necessary beyond the risk horizon, how to interpret those entities that cannot be quantified or qualified with confidence, and how to prepare better for unknown effects. Their paper analyzes how to contain the unknown in a timelier and appropriate manner. They describe which practices could be defined to reach a state of reliable, although not perfect, resilience. These practices should allow dealing with risk, uncertainty, and complexity effectively.

The aim of the collection of articles presented in the Technology Innovation Management Review (2015) issue was to highlight the significance of resilience and develop a shared understanding of the definition, theory, and managerial implications of cyber-risk and cyber-resilience in operations. This collection of articles seeks to establish a plan for future research that provides solutions to the challenges, develops a cyber-resilience strategy, the tools, and methods to respond to cyber-attacks, and presents case studies of best practices.

The pandemic has induced a deep economic crisis that may provoke another financial crisis. Financial institutions have been a source of resilience in the middle of the financial turmoil over the past years (Carletti et al., 2020). Thanks to significant reforms after the crisis of 2008, the much better capitalized and more liquid financial institutions were not under immediate stress during the pandemic. They are helping to support the real sector's financing needs.

The pandemic's lessons are to be ready for large-scale disasters, severely impacting services, including banking. Financial institutions could come under stress. Large-scale insolvencies among organizations may arise. A wave of bankruptcies among households may follow (Carletti et al., 2020). Financial institutions could eventually get caught up, with pressures to exceed those envisioned in many scenarios.

Agility
Resilience refers to the ability of a material to deform elastically, to bend opposite to stress without becoming distorted permanently. This situation is what financial institutions need to meet the growing challenges of socio-economic environments. Resilience in bionic banking is the ability to continue to provide services by a collaboration between automation (such as robots or AI) and humans. In this way, financial services should adapt to the conditions of use and resist external events to ensure the availability of the services. These two separate actors, automation and humans, can assure resource backup in case of unexpected events.

All the previous resilience characteristics require an approach based on a few words: financial institutions must be agile. This aspect is essential for increasing the flexibility of a financial institution to deal with unexpected events (Waters, 2011).

Agility is an organization's ability to recognize opportunities and threats, seize them by rapidly recombining or introducing digital solutions, assets, and existing human knowledge. Agility is commonly associated with being flexible and immediately adapting to changes in the external environment. This capability is central in high digitally transformed markets because of frequent unexpected customer preference changes, intensified competition, and the increasing need for structural changes inside the organization. Regarding the flexibility of the organizational structure, self-managing agile teams characterize organizations that successfully implement bionic transformation processes. Organizations, built upon a more standardized and hierarchical structure, were more susceptible to have success (Simpson, 2017).

The best way to increase flexibility is to have an agile organization. Agility means that operations are flexible enough to operate effectively, efficiently, economically, and ethically (compliant with laws and regulations) with rapidly changing conditions. For example, rather than increasing the number of resources for making banking capable of dealing with unexpectedly high demand, an organization can use flexible operations to improve deployment and deliver additional services with short lead times. It is often challenging to forecast the details of events that might follow risks, so agility is often the best response.

Agility can be achieved in several ways, such as short lead times, so that the completion of all changes is fast, making it possible to recover quickly from disruptions. It is possible to take actions such as:

- Rapid rescheduling of operations, diverting work and resources away from branches or surplus areas and toward areas with shortages.
- Moving operations between different operators when the risks to one place increase.
- Concurrent development to speed up new methods and products.
- Flexible vendors, using multiple sources with various features to meet differing needs, types of contracts, and spot markets.

Design of a Resilient Bionic Banking
To analyze the principles of the design of resilient bionic banking is interesting to follow what is necessary for other operations and make the appropriate changes (Waters, 2011).

The design of resilient banking requires a fully integrated approach (Kleindorfer & Saad, 2005). Several basic principles are involved with this move, such as the need for careful design, agile operations, visibility, relationships with customers and vendors, culture, and the like.

It is essential to take a strategic view in common with all major initiatives. Resilience needs commitment from senior managers who are aware of the issues and can allocate their resources. Bionic banking is a strategic initiative that can have substantial effects on an organization and its run.

With poor risk management, there is less chance that an organization will survive in the long term.

The first concept in resilience is that the fundamental processes work correctly. Suppose the organization adopting bionic banking does not have such properly organized processes, in that case, the management must take the responsibility to make them proper while transitioning in the challenging move toward collaboration. Only when everything is working internally, can managers expand their scope to consider other members of the process. Bionic can help in this respect since automation requires careful planning and assurance of a proper organization.

The following concept is to understand the idea of bionic banking risks. Before they can successfully plan for risk along a process, operators and customers must know what they are studying. In other words, they must understand the concept of risk—and the members, roles, links, interactions, objectives, forces, dynamics, power, and all the other elements that form the complex web of a service value network.

Then, they can combine these two concepts in the integrated function of resilience management involving both humans and automation.

A process is only as strong as its weakest link. Disruption at any point in a process causes problems for the whole flow. It is necessary to identify risks throughout the process to find the weakest parts. There are always weak spots in the process. These might include single paths, links with long lead times, humans facing specific risks, those unwilling to share information, automation that does not manage risks appropriately, and so on. Sometimes it is possible to create parallel paths around dangerous components. This approach may not be easy, for example, there might be only one robotic process automation to collaborate with humans. Managers must be cautious of the risks in vulnerable areas, mainly when these areas are outside their control. Then they might take steps to reduce the consequences of the risks or try to influence the managers responsible by including them in the risk management process. They can also redesign the chain to bypass the area of weakness (Handfield, 2019; Kunreuther & Heal, 2004).

Emergency Management
Resilience also requires an effective, efficient, and economic management of emergencies. When a risky event occurs, flexible operations, either based on humans or automation, can avoid its worst effects, and continue to work usually. Sometimes the consequences are too severe for even the

most flexible operations to deal with. The alternative is to build contingency plans for emergencies. These are used as a last resort when all other aspects of risk management have failed, and they work based on that. If the organization does not know what could happen, the best plan is to be ready for anything "just in case" (Nicholson et al., 2019).

The features of a risk management plan are in Fig. 2.3. The management must request that the service operations have the capability throughout the entire cycle. The operators, including automation, must improve their characteristics to manage the risks and the disasters. This capability depends on dealing appropriately with the potential malfunctions of the bionic processes and their subprocesses.

The first thing to do in case of an emergency is to re-establish the service. Very often, this requires finding a workaround rather than solving once and for all the problems. In the case of bionic systems, this might be to replace broken automation with humans. Once applied the

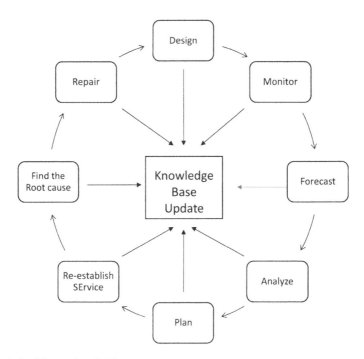

Fig. 2.3 The cycle of risk management

workaround, it is necessary to test if it works well or not. If the test is positive, one can start resuming the service at the usual or a reduced rate.

The following action is finding the root causes of the incidents. A root cause is a factor that causes a nonconformance and should be permanently eliminated through process improvement (Andersen & Fagerhaug, 2006). Root Cause Analysis (RCA) is a term that describes a wide range of approaches, tools, and techniques used to uncover the deep causes of problems.

Once found the root cause, it is necessary to fix the problem permanently. Once done this activity, it usually is possible to restore a reliable process fully. Before applying the fix, it is necessary to test it.

It is essential to create and update a knowledge base of all the known incidents and find a workaround and fix the incidents. This action is critical to improving the system's resilience in rapid re-establishment in case of known errors. There are many different ways to organize such a knowledge base. One simple but effective way is to manage it with a wiki. A wiki is an (internet or intranet) website allowing collaborative modifications of its content and structure directly from the web browser (Encyclopaedia Britannica, 2007). In a typical wiki, the text is written using a simplified markup language (known as "wiki markup") and often edited with the help of a rich text editor.

Characteristics of Resilience

Some characteristics are essential for ensuring the resilience of bionic banking. They are distinct, but in fact, they are interconnected. Some authors have considered them for resilience in general (Gulati, 2013; Nicoletti, 2016; Waters, 2011). This chapter generalizes them in bionic banking and refers to them as the nine Cs (Fig. 2.4).

- **Commitment**. This characteristic refers to the delight of the customer. It starts with the minimum obligations to the customer for the services or the contract with the vendors. The fundamental objective is the delight of the customer. The commitment to the customer is the base of the other characteristics, which must be spelled out and defined in the processes.
- **Command**. The command is vital for risk management. The organization must have effective leadership, both internally and on the vendor side. The management must be able to make decisions before, during, and after a disaster. It must also be efficient, and therefore be able to intervene with timeliness and economics. It is

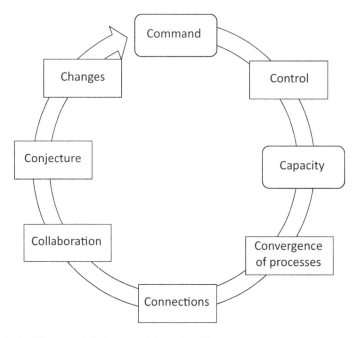

Fig. 2.4 The essential characteristics of resilience

essential to manage the risks and the potential emergencies, considering the customer's delight and the organization's profitability.
- **Control.** Control is the ability to have sound governance of bionic banking. It implies a solid and detailed plan and implementation. It must also take into account the imponderables. It must include the "what if" and then consider the management of what might happen ("just in case").
- **Conjecture.** Conjecture implies the capacity to forecast or anticipate the occurrence of a disaster. It is important to consider risks by design. Prevention is better than cure (Lund & Lund, 1996). To be more specific, the best options for mitigation are on preventing a harmful event, then reducing its consequences if it does happen, remediating for damages after it has happened, and especially learning from what has happened to manage risks better in the future. The customers and vendors should explicitly include the effects of risks in their decisions. They will focus on leanness,

efficiency, or other goals that might inadvertently increase vulnerability if they ignore risk. The best design needs a balance between resilience and standard measures of efficiency. For example, a single path through any activity in the process creates a vulnerable point. If anything happens at this point, the whole process is at risk. To avoid such risks is necessary to design a process with parallel paths (automation and humans). In this way, it is possible to divert the flows from a disrupted path to the one that usually keeps working. This approach involves continuous monitoring of the services that must be resilient.
- **Capacity**. Often, organizations push on being lean and, consequently, reducing waste, such as overcapacity or quantity of resources. This approach is acceptable, but it cannot go overboard in ensuring resilience and being too lean. It is undoubtedly helpful to have some spare capacity available in case of emergency.
- **Collaboration.** One of the most critical ways to ensure a resilient process is through partnership. Several members work together to solve mutual problems even if they might belong to different organizations. Without a basic level of cooperation, it is almost impossible to progress toward an objective of integrated processes. Collaboration can take many forms. It could range from informal discussions to strategic alliances. The most common conditions to share information are to increase visibility—with more formal arrangements of collaborative planning, forecasting, resourcing, and synchronized actions. There are various reasons why collaboration is difficult to achieve, but methods exist, and managers need to use them. Sharing information throughout the entire process is the basis of visibility, which means the extent to which one member working on an activity can see what is happening at all points in the flow. This information typically includes demands, seasonality, promotions, new service introductions, industry, market conditions, operations, procurement schedules, performance, risks, unexpected events, lost sales, and other relevant information. Many aspects of collaboration in the process should be in a correct automation relationship management. This term is an umbrella for procedures that allow an organization to cultivate new automation, lean existing processes, reduce interruptions by spreading business among vendors and locations, and manage risks with sole sources. The sharing of ideas, methods, and information is a core part of service management. This approach is the only way that members of the process can identify mutual risks

and design effective ways of dealing with them, gaining synergies from the collaboration. Managers can learn valuable lessons from working with others on their joint problems, so they should not approach automation with well-defined and inflexible ideas. Still, they should go in a spirit of exploration. The best ideas will emerge from a collaborative approach, combining ideas and experiences to learn new ideas and methods that they can use within their organizations. Perhaps the best answer is somewhere between these two extremes, where managers progress on their risk management and then look to improve and consolidate their methods using inputs from other organizations.

- **Convergence of processes.** Visibility benefits risk management, but it can also lead to other uses, including the intersection of operations. In other words, operations tend to converge to expected standards, and they are the usual ways of working. Other initiatives have the same effect, particularly quality assurance, and risk management. Automation standardization can help very much. Standardized processes, the same subprocesses used in different banking operations, reduce the need for resources, delivery problems, work in progress, number of vendors, and the like. The critical point for agility is that operations can switch from one service to another without waiting for new resources. Standardized procedures for different processes can switch seamlessly between products, with cross-trained operators or flexible automation moving to areas of shortage.
- **Connections.** Resilience requires flexible but effective relationships, capable of acting in support of events not anticipated. The relationships or networks are automation or human capacity to allow continuity using a backup if necessary. The relationships are also of a business type, with the possibility of resorting to other organizations' resources to enable continuity in providing the services in emergency conditions.
- **Changes**. Change management requires agility. The agile organization focuses on its "non-negotiable." The organization need to create the right mix of necessary formal procedures with agility and speed that distinguish the frontline innovators.

The more distant future is digital resilience (Kaplan, 2015) or resilience by design (Di Orio et al., 2020), that is, the ability to design customer applications, business processes, technology architectures, and cybersecurity defenses with the protection of critical information assets in mind (Fig. 2.4).

Conclusions

The concept of ionic has evolved. This book considers bionics as a hybridization of humans and automation, collaborating to reach the vision of the enterprises. It is a fundamental approach for the organizations' transformation. Fintech organizations have evolved. Now they are more and more inclined toward bionic and sustainability, becoming bionic financial services. The New Normal have stressed the importance of bionic, from several points of view: robot and automation, remoteness, resistance, responsibility, but above all resilience. Resilience requires agility. The chapter has considered the design of resilient bionic banking.

The following chapters cover these topics with bionic banking transformation.

References

Aldrich, H. E. (1979). *Organizations and environments*. Cornell University.

Aldrich, H. E., & Wiedenmayer, G. (2019). From traits to rates: An ecological perspective on organizational foundings. In *Seminal Ideas for the Next Twenty-Five Years of Advances*. Emerald Publishing Limited.

Andersen, B., & Fagerhaug, T. (2006). *Root cause analysis: Simplified tools and techniques*. ASQ Quality Press.

Aré, L., Bailey, A., Hutchinson, R., & Rose, J. (2019). *The bionic company*. Boston Consulting Group-BCG. Featured Insights.

Arner, D. W., Barberis, J. N., & Buckley, R. P. (2016). *The emergence of RegTech 2.0: From know your customer to know your data* (KPMG Paper).

Atanasova, P., Wright, D., & Augenstein, I. (2020). Generating label cohesive and well-formed adversarial claims. *arXiv preprint*:2009.08205.

Beltrán-Martín, I., Roca-Puig, V., Escrig-Tena, A., & Bou-Llusar, J. C. (2008). Human resource flexibility as a mediating variable between high performance work systems and performance. *Journal of Management, 34*(5), 1009–1044.

Bi, Y., Song, L., Yao, M., Wu, Z., Wang, J., & Xiao, J. (2020, July). DCDIR: A deep cross-domain recommendation system for cold start users in insurance domain. In *Proceedings of the 43rd International ACM SIGIR Conference on Research and Development in Information Retrieval* (pp. 1661–1664).

Bouncken, R. B., Komorek, M., & Kraus, S. (2015). Crowdfunding: The current state of research. *International Business & Economics Research Journal (IBER), 14*(3), 407–416.

Brakman, S., Garretsen, H., & van Witteloostuijn, A. (2020). The turn from just-in-time to just-in-case globalization in and after times of Covid-19: An essay on the risk re-appraisal of borders and buffers. *Social Sciences & Humanities Open, 2*(1), 100034.

Buheji, M., & Ahmed, D. (2020). *Planning for the 'new normal'*. Bahrain. CO Founder of the International Inspiration Economy Project.

Carletti, E., Claessens, S., Fatás, A., & Vives, X. (2020). *Post-Covid-19 world*. Centre for Economic Policy Research.

Carrozzi, L. (2009). *Procurement Management per la Protezione delle Infrastrutture Critiche*. Tesi Master in Procurement Management, Università di Tor Vergata, Rome, Italy.

Çera, G., Belas, J., & Zapletalíková, E. (2019). Explaining business failure through determinist and voluntarist perspectives. *Serbian Journal of Management*.

Clegg, S. R., & Hardy, C. (1999). *Studying organization theory and method* (p. 1). Sage Publications Ltd.

Collie, F. (2021). *How banks are harnessing artificial intelligence*. IE Investment Executive.

Cristofaro, M. (2017). Herbert Simon's bounded rationality: Its historical evolution in management and cross-fertilizing contribution. *Journal of Management History*.

Cunha, P. R., Melo, P., & Sebastião, H. (2021). From bitcoin to central bank digital currencies: Making sense of the digital money revolution. *Future Internet, 13*(7), 165.

Darwin, C. (2004). *On the origin of species, 1859*. Routledge.

Decker, M., Fischer, M., & Ott, I. (2017). Service robotics and human labor: A first technology assessment of substitution and cooperation. *Robotics and Autonomous Systems, 87*, 348–354.

Deloitte Development LLC. (2020). *The social enterprise at work: Paradox as a path forward*. 2020. Deloitte Global Human Capital trends.

Di Orio, G., Brito, G., Maló, P., Sadu, A., Wirtz, N., & Monti, A. (2020). A Cyber-Physical Approach to Resilience and Robustness by Design. *International Journal of Advanced Computer Science and Applications*.

Elsaid, H. M. (2021). A review of literature directions regarding the impact of fintech firms on the banking industry. *Qualitative Research in Financial Markets*.

Encyclopedia Britannica. (2007). *Encyclopedia Britannica*. London, UK.

Erlebach, J., Pauly, M., Du Croo De Jongh, L., & Strauß, M. (2020, November). *The sun is setting on traditional banking* (BCG Paper).

EY Belgium. (2020, April). *Why remote working will be the new normal, even after the pandemic.* Multidisciplinary Professional Services Organization.

Fabeil, N. F., Pazim, K. H., & Langgat, J. (2020). The impact of Covid-19 pandemic crisis on micro-enterprises: Entrepreneurs' perspective on business continuity and recovery strategy. *Journal of Economics and Business, 3*(2).

Finextra IBM. (2016). *How to get ahead on operational resilience: Strategies for financial institutions.* Finextra Research Ltd.

Furong, H., & Yanmei, X. (2001). *Enterprise bionics.* Enterprise Management Press.

Gakman, C. (2017). *Understanding FinTech categories.* The Ian Martin Group.

Ghahroud, M. L., Jafari, F., & Maghsoodi, J. (2021). Review of the Fintech categories and the most famous Fintech startups. *Journal of FinTech and Artificial Intelligence, 1*(1), 7–7.

Gruber, M., De Leon, N., George, G., & Thompson, P. (2015). Managing by design: From the editors. *Academy of Management Journal, 58*(1), 1–7.

Gulati, R. (2013). *Reorganize for resilience: Putting customers at the center of your business.* Harvard Business Review Press.

Guo, Y., & Liang, C. (2016). Blockchain application and outlook in the banking industry. *Financial Innovation, 2*(1), 1–12.

Handfield, R. (2019). Shifts in buyer-seller relationships: A retrospective on. *Industrial Marketing Management, 83*, 194–206.

International Trade Centre. (2020). *The pandemic: The great lockdown and its impact on small business.* International Trade Centre.

Jiali, Y., Wenming, L., & Yanmei, X. (2009). Evaluation of enterprise vitality and model of enterprise commercial age. In *International Conference on Management Science & Engineering.* IEEE, New York, NY.

Kaplan, J. M., Bailey, T., O'Halloran, D., Marcus, A., & Rezek, C. (2015), *Beyond cybersecurity: Protecting your digital business.* John Wiley & Sons, Hoboken, NJ.

Khatik, R. K. (2021). Role of digital banking in strategic alliance and FinTech. *International Journal of Research and Analysis in Commerce and Management, 1*(1), 10–10.

King, R. S. (2013). *BiLBIQ: A biologically inspired robot with walking and rolling locomotion.* Springer.

Kleindorfer, P. R., & Saad, G. H. (2005). Managing disruption risks in supply chains. *Production and Operations Management, 14*(1), 53–68.

Krivkovich, A., White, O., Zac Townsend, Z., & Euart, J. (2020, December). *How US customers' attitudes to fintech are shifting during the pandemic.* McKinsey Paper.

Kunreuther, H., & Heal, G. (2004). Interdependent security: The case of identical agents. *Journal of Risk and Uncertainty, 23*(2), 103–120.

Kwasniok, S., Kretz, J., & Kettnaker, F. (2021). Plattformentwicklungen im Versicherungsmarkt–Von Open Banking zu Open Finance. *Digitale Ökosysteme: Strategien, KI, Plattformen*, 437.

Levanon, G. (2020, November). Remote work: The biggest legacy of the pandemic. *Forbes*.

Lihua, W., Wandui, M., Yu, L., et al. (2010). *Research on enterprise bionic and ERP application*. IEEE Publisher.

Liu, L., Xu, Y., Huang, L., & Yao, X. (2013) Research on the improvement of business age model. In W. E. Wong & T. Ma (Eds.), *Emerging technologies for information systems, computing, and management*. Lecture notes in electrical engineering, 236 (pp. 1239–1250). Springer.

Lund, M. S., & Lund, M. (1996). *Preventing violent conflicts: A strategy for preventive diplomacy*. United States Institute of Peace Press.

Lusinski, N. (2019, October). *9 of the most challenging things about working remotely, according to people who do it*. Business Insider.

Ma, Y., & Liu, D. (2017). Introduction to the special issue on Crowdfunding and FinTech. *Financial Innovation*, 3(8).

Madakam, S., Holmukhe, R. M., & Jaiswal, D. K. (2019). The future digital work force: Robotic process automation (RPA). *JISTEM-Journal of Information Systems and Technology Management*, 16.

Maurer, R. (2020, September). *Study finds productivity not deterred by shift to remote work*. SHRM.

Mehrotra, A., & Menon, S. (2021, January). Second round of FinTech-Trends and challenges. In *2021 2nd International Conference on Computation, Automation and Knowledge Management (ICCAKM)* (pp. 243–248). IEEE.

Nah, F. F. H., & Siau, K. (2020, July). Covid-19 pandemic–role of technology in transforming business to the new normal. In *International Conference on Human-Computer Interaction* (pp. 585–600). Springer.

Nicholson, K. P., Pagowsky, N., & Seale, M. (2019). Just-in-time or just-in-case? Time, learning analytics, and the academic library. *Library Trends*, 68(1), 54–75.

Nicoletti, B. (2016). Resilience & outsourcing. *PMWORLD*, 2, 16.

Nicoletti, B. (2017). *Future of FinTech*. Palgrave Macmillan.

Nicoletti, B. (2021). Introduction. In Lechman, E., & Marszk, A. (Eds.), *The digital disruption of financial services: International perspectives*. Routledge.

Penrose, E. T. (1952, December). Biological analogies in theory of the organization. *The American Economic Review*, 42(5), 804–819.

Peverelli, R., & de Feniks, R. (2019, July). The four waves of insurtech. *The DIA Community*.

Pollari, I. (2021). Top Fintech Trends in H1i21. *KPMG*.

Ralston, P., & Blackhurst, J. (2020). Industry 4.0 and resilience in the supply chain: A driver of capability enhancement or capability loss? *International Journal of Production Research, 58*(16), 5006–5019.

Roth, R. R. (1983). The foundation of bionics. *Perspectives of biology and medicine, 26*(2)(Winter).

Sapriel, C. (2003). Effective crisis management: Tools and best practice for the new millennium. *Journal of communication management.*

Simon, H. A. (1997). *Models of bounded rationality. Empirically grounded economic reason* (Vol. 3). The MIT Press.

Simpson, A. (2017). *The innovation-friendly organization: How to cultivate new ideas and embrace the change they bring.* Springer.

Taddeo, M., & Floridi, L. (2018). How AI can be a force for good. *Science, 361*(6404), 751–752.

Tomsett, D. (2011, August). *What does 'the new normal' mean for business anyway?* Forbes Technology Council.

Turner, N., & Kutsch, E. (2015). Project resilience: Moving beyond traditional risk management. *PM World Journal, 4*(11).

Waters, D. (2011). *Supply chain risk management: Vulnerability and resilience in logistics.* Kogan Page Publishers.

Winter, S. G. (1964, Spring). Economic natural selection and theory of the organization. *Yale Economic Essays, 4,* 1.

Xu, Y. M., Yu, J. L., & Li, W. M. (2009, September). Evaluation of enterprise vitality and model of enterprise commercial age. In *2009 International Conference on Management Science and Engineering* (pp. 569–574). IEEE.

CHAPTER 3

Bionic Banking Transformation

Introduction

This chapter describes the concept of bionic banking transformation. It proposes an analysis of human-automation collaboration's deployment opportunities in the banking and insurance industries. Becoming bionic represents a solution for financial services providers to meet evolving and increasingly complex customers' needs. Financial institutions can use digital applications to provide quick and easy-to-use services, combined with attentive person interactions and emotional engagement when required. These organizations require significant investments, but they can become leading organizations since bionic operations deliver short-term results with reasonable arrangements. In some practical cases, it is possible to explore their congruence with the bionic banking theory. This chapter helps to better understand how bionic banking operates and precisely how they present the characteristic described above.

Bionic Transformation

Birth of Bionic Transformation

The bionic transformation process is a sequence of three digital changes. Each of them has a different impact on the organization.

© The Author(s), under exclusive license to Springer Nature Switzerland AG 2022
B. Nicoletti, *Beyond Fintech*, Palgrave Studies in Financial Services Technology, https://doi.org/10.1007/978-3-030-96217-3_3

- The initial phase is *digitization*. It consists of a shift from *analog to digital* practices. The impact of digital change is not relative to a whole process or system. It is limited to the automation of tasks and transmission of information. The adoption of paperless solutions is typical of this phase. Digital documents, digital payments, and electronic invoicing are examples of dematerialization. Digitization does not significantly impact the organization's value creation process. It helps in dematerialization, traceability, cost reductions, and reliability of transactions.
- The second phase is *digitalization*. This phase is relative to changes in operational processes and improvements in customer experience. The implementation of new digital solutions can achieve these benefits. P. C. Verhoef et al. (2019), in their multidisciplinary study about digital transformation, stated that: "through digitalization, organizations apply digital solutions to optimize existing business processes by allowing a more efficient coordination between processes, and/or by creating additional customer value through enhancing customer experiences." Financial institutions experience cost savings thanks to the digitalization and optimization of processes. Digitalization of the customer experience has changed the type of offering and how customers can access financial organizations. Platforms and digital accesses, such as social media, attract and influence customers' decisions by showing content tailored to individuals' preferences. Financial institutions have a growing interest in acquiring information about customers' behavior and processing this information in a customer-centered way.
- The third stage of digital change is the *bionic transformation* centered on the collaboration between humans and automation, such as robots and AI. It is the most intrusive stage. It directly affects and modifies the business model of the financial institution. Digital solutions and capabilities can provide a competitive advantage that allows enhancing value creation. The bionic transformation phase goes beyond dematerialization transition and the automation of the core banking processes. It involves a managerial and organizational change in mindset, strategy, culture, business model, and indirect aspects for automation and humans. The most significant impact of BT is business model innovation, which consists of reengineering current business components and introducing new ones, the launch of new products and services or the combination of old ones,

changes in financial institution's market position, and entering into new segments. This stage is complex and time-consuming. A business model innovation requires reconfiguring the assets, acquiring new competencies, and a structural reorganization of the financial organization. It involves defining a well-founded strategy and clear objectives to pursue beyond the simple implementation of new solutions.

From the 2000s, academicians and managers have focused on digital transformation. This model affected organizations and the whole society, which has experienced remarkable changes "toward digital." An example of this kind of change is the digital transformation of payments: from cash and paper-based financial instruments to digitized innovative payments processes, such as PayPal real-time monetary transactions. Pandemic put an accelerator to this transformation already undergoing.

This book considers a compelling case of transformation: named bionic transformation (BT). The analysis of BT is from a strategic and operational perspective. BT has an interdisciplinary nature since it applies to strategy management, information and communication technology systems, marketing, human resources and organizations, and operations management.

Defining Bionic Transformation

Before going into the details of bionic transformation characteristics, defining digital transformation (DT) can be helpful. To that extent, Table 3.1 provides an overview of the most significant conceptualizations present in literature. The set of definitions listed below describe DT as a phenomenon primarily related to organizations.

Based on these definitions, it is possible to structure a conceptual framework for the initial definition of bionic transformation as a phenomenon driven by external factors that impact several aspects of an organization and has specific purposes in terms of collaboration human-automation. By identifying similarities and differences among the definitions mentioned above, it is possible to add in-depth features to this broad concept of bionic transformation.

It is possible to examine the main characteristics of bionic transformation. BT is an evolutionary process that is, essentially, an ongoing transformation oriented toward the long-term. Another feature attributed

Table 3.1 Definitions of digital transformation

Source(s)	Definition
G. Westerman et al. (2011)	[...] the use of technology to radically improve the performance or reach of enterprises. [...] Executives in all industries use digital advances such as analytics, mobility, social media, and smart embedded devices—and improve their use of traditional technologies such as ERP—to change customer relationships, internal processes, and value propositions
PwC (2013)	DT describes the fundamental transformation of the entire business world by establishing innovative technologies based on the internet with a fundamental impact on society as a whole
M. Fitzgerald et al. (2014)	The use of new digital technologies (social media, mobile, analytics, or embedded devices) to enable significant business improvements (such as enhancing customer experience, streamlining operations, or creating new business models)
D. M. Mazzone (2014)	DT is the deliberate and ongoing digital evolution of a company, business model, idea process, or method, strategically and tactically
R. Bekkhus (2016)	Use of digital technologies to radically improve the company's performance
H. Demirkan et al. (2016)	DT is the profound and accelerating transformation of business activities, processes, competencies, and models to fully leverage the changes and opportunities brought by digital technologies and their impact across society in a strategic and prioritized way
T.Hess et al. (2016)	DT is concerned with the changes digital technologies can bring about in a company's business model, resulting in changed products or organizational structures or the automation of processes
R. Morakanyane et al. (2017)	An evolutionary process that leverages digital capabilities and technologies to enable business models, operational processes, and customer experiences to create value
G. Remane et al. (2017)	Fundamental alterations in existing and the creation of new business models [..] in response to the diffusion of digital technologies such as cloud computing, mobile Internet, social media, and big data

(continued)

Table 3.1 (continued)

Source(s)	Definition
P. C. Verhoef et al. (2019)	We define DT as a change in how an organization employs digital technologies to develop a new digital business model that helps create and appropriate more value for the organization

to this process regards the substantial effects that it has on the organization. BT implies a radical change. BT has disruptive consequences, which modify the fundamentals of an organization and take place at specific moments of the institution's life.

Since bionic transformation is a set of profound changes and is not an immediate transition performed inside the boundaries of an organization, this book considers and describes bionic transformation as an evolutionary process.

BT can include digital technologies. However, technology itself is not the sole driver of bionic transformation. BT arises as a consequence of market and social changes impacting the financial institution.

This conceptualization of BT allows determining the main areas of impact of its transformation. The organization's operational performance, customer experience, and business model innovation appear to be the most affected organizational aspects. It is impossible to ignore these three factors to achieve a successful bionic transformation of an organization.

BT is an organization-oriented process. This book does not analyze it from a social perspective. Based on this assessment, it is possible to finally define bionic transformation as an evolutionary and profound process, enabled by digital technologies and behavioral changes in the market and society, which aims to bring significant changes to the operational performance, the customer experience, and mainly to the business model of a banking organization to create value through the collaboration of humans and automation.

Drivers and Impacts of Bionic Transformation

Bionic transformation emerges as a result of the combination of several external factors.

- A market factor enabling the bionic transformation of organizations is the change experienced in competition. Globalization, innovation in technology, and centralization of regulatory authorities led to reducing entry barriers and generated global markets. Young native digital financial institutions and small fintech organizations dominate this new competitive landscape. A recent study aimed to demonstrate how 25 well-established pre-digital organizations were facing digital transformation challenges. The study reports that "born digital pioneers (such as Amazon, Facebook, and Google) have grown into influential giant bigtech organizations. Organizations long dominating their industries found their traditional value propositions under threat" (Sebastian et al., 2017). Digital natives' capabilities to innovate products and services created a new kind of supply, known as a *digital offering*. It determined a shift in the market composition, characterized by the demand for customized services over products.
- With excellent access to information and the possibility of being more connected, customers' behavior has significantly changed. On the one hand, customers have gained an active role in the production process since they have the opportunity to co-create value by customizing and tailor-making products: they have become "prosumers" (this word originated from the merge of the terms producer and customer). On the other hand, they have been more involved in after-sale activities to make organizations aware if they are satisfied with the purchase. Moreover, innovative solutions such as big data analytics and social networks allow organizations to update customer preferences constantly. The more customers are involved in creating value for services, the more it is essential to consider this bionic collaboration between automation and humans, the latter being customers, operators, or partners.
- Especially in services and banking, the customers' requests are for a personalized product or service. Automation only to a certain extent can achieve this customization in the products. The collaboration of humans and automation, mainly robots, can obtain this customization much more straightforward and significantly more effective and efficient.
- The spread of the Internet and Information and Communication Technology (ICT) led to digital technologies or, more precisely, SMACIT technologies (Sebastian et al., 2017). SMACIT is a

term that refers to innovative solutions, such as social, mobile, analytics, cloud computing, and the Internet of Things (IoT). Other vital technologies are blockchain, Augmented Intelligence (AI), robotic process automation, and data science. Organizations are still exploring implementing some emerging solutions effectively, efficiently, ethically, and economically, while others have started implementing new solutions. The successful solutions that allow organizations to maximize the utility of these technologies combine more than one of them. A successful combination requires that human and automation factors need integration to collaborate and interact in the best ways.

Stanford University, UC Berkeley, and MIT have established human-centered AI (HCAI) research institutes (Human-centered AI, 2019) to study what this book defines as bionic transformation. Their HCAI research strategies emphasize that the next frontier of automation (significantly Augmented Intelligence [AI]) is technological, humanistic, and ethical: AI enhances humans rather than replaces them. For example, researchers from Stanford University believe that AI research and development should follow three objectives: reflect the depth characterized by human intelligence technically, improve human capabilities rather than replace them, and focus on AI's impact on humans (Xu, 2019). Several leading high-tech organizations have advocated for AI solutions that are sustainable, responsible, ethical, secure, and inclusive by publishing guiding principles for AI technology development, processes, tools, and training (Xu, 2019). The first challenge is to move beyond simple interaction (Xu, 2019). With the addition of learning capabilities in AI-based machine intelligence, human-automation relationships have shifted from human–computer interaction to human-automation collaboration, integration, and human-automation teaming (Farooq & Grudin, 2016). The humans and automation are teammates and collaborative partners in this new setting. The active cooperation between the two cognitive agents with enhanced capability on the automation part (as it learns over time) brings added complexity to the HCAI design of automation solutions and considerable benefits.

The introduction of the current HAC methods was for non-intelligent solutions. Researchers suggest a series of enhanced HCAI methods specifically for AI solutions (Xu, 2019). HCAI professionals can also play a critical role in validating AI solutions. The traditional software verification method assumes that the system has no learning capability to change its behavior, which is predictable. The behaviors of intelligent systems develop over time. The verification evaluation of AI solutions needs collaboration between AI software engineers and HCAI professionals. Combining methods (e.g., software validation, user-involved User Experiences [UX] validation) may help achieve better results. Early UX evaluation of low-fidelity intelligent design prototypes requires alternatives such as Wizard of Oz (WOZ) design prototypes to simulate and validate augmented intelligence learning and intelligent behaviors (Murray, 2010).

Current AI-related standards focus primarily on ethical design issues, such as the guidelines published by IEEE (Vakkuri et al., 2020). There are no specific HCAI design standards for guiding AI solutions; each HCAI community is developing them.

More advanced is Human-Automation Team Interaction (HATI), which aims to build automation that is more than autonomous systems able to execute actions and interact with humans following the guidelines of the HAI domain. Automation (such as robotic) teammate is an active team member and not a simple tool for acting. Thus, the standpoint of teamwork for building human-automation teaming interaction applications is shared with the vision in which automation must work jointly with other resources rather than acting upon others (Hoffman & Breazeal, 2004).

Apart from these factors in services, especially in banking, the transformation must correctly overcome the dual risks of commoditization and diminishing trust (McIntyre et al., 2020). It is necessary to understand precisely how customers' banking requirements and preferences have changed and how sentiment among some customer groups has changed. There is the need to understand whether these changes in behavior are permanent and will last beyond a temporary phenomenon due to the pandemic environment that will hopefully revert when traditional everyday life resumes.

Banking can adapt to customers' new behaviors and preferences. The key to this will be introducing humanness through a "digital brand personality" and embedding personalized experiences in the customer journeys at relevant times (McIntyre et al., 2020). This customization ensures that interactions with automation are as natural and free flowing as possible and that an escape to a human operator is available. Chief marketing officers have a vital role to play. By infusing brand personality and humanness into all customer interactions, including direct marketing actions like calls, emails, direct mail, push notifications, and on-website digital placements, they can help balance the loss of genuine human interactions. In a world where customers use digital banking accesses much more frequently, creating an optimal CX requires financial institutions to balance initiatives that mimic humanness and put actual human operators in front of customers whenever essential. Video conference calls or visual computer sessions, where appropriate and frictionlessly integrating digital and telephone accesses, can create an optimal customer journey that blends the convenience of automation with the personality and empathy of humans. If financial institutions neglect this aspect and focus only on adjusting their operating model to support customers' increased use of digital accesses, it may create an ineffective digital offering.

Financial institutions unable to adapt to these external changes and fail to transform bionically could disappear. To complete this transition, institutions need to have specific resources and capabilities in terms of human operators and automation. The definition of these requirements is bionic capabilities. The most relevant among them are empathy, personalization, organization agility, data-driven, and networking capability.

Empathy is the ability to recognize and understand other peoples' emotions, respond appropriately emotionally, and influence others' feelings (Goleman, 1996). Specific skill examples include communication, relationship building, leadership, advocating and negotiating, work-life balance, social, teamwork, cultural diversity, and charisma (Caprino, 2012).

Personalization refers to providing individual services to customers as per their needs, requirements, and preferences. Personalization in banking tackles several distinct customers' needs such as trust, information, service, and expert advice (Mukherjee & Nath, 2003). A personalized experience delivers the correct individual experience at the right time. Personalization efforts should start and end with a deep understanding of the customer.

Organizational agility is an organizational ability to recognize unexpected changes in the environment and appropriately respond swiftly and efficiently by utilizing and reconfiguring internal resources, thus gaining a competitive advantage in the process (Žitkienė & Mačerinskienė, 2014).

Since the value of automation comes from the use of data, data must drive management. Many of the organizations' functions rely on data such as Customer Relationship Management (CRM), marketing, Human

Resources (HR), procurement, and even executives in the decision-making process. For these reasons, organizations must enhance their analytics skills. It is essential to consider the data reliability and governance issues. Organizations need to verify data source and usefulness when collecting information.

Digital technologies have led organizations to interact with an increasing number of stakeholders and consequently to establish networks. The networking phenomenon refers to using new solutions to exchange information and build relationships with other stakeholders. Four different perspectives: customers, operators, vendors, and partners can help in analyzing networking. Digital solutions allowed customers to become directly involved in all banking operations.

Danske Bank
Danske Bank is a Nordic financial group that originated in 1871 in Copenhagen. It provides banking services in Denmark, Finland, Norway, and Sweden. It has over 22,000 operators, and in 2020 it generated revenues for DKK 4.6 billion (about €618 million). It serves 3.3 million retail and commercial customers and 1,938 corporate and institutional customers through its two respective service lines: Personal & Business Customers and Large Corporates & Institutions.

Danske Bank has started a transformation process to become a "better bank" by 2023 (Danske Bank, 2020a). This transition aims to meet customers' expectations more efficiently and faster, stand out in a highly competitive environment, provide an improved digital experience, cut costs, and adopt an agile working way. These relevant changes are addressing the needs of customers primarily but also of operators and the whole society. Thanks to the human-automation collaboration, the first core value is delivering competitive financial solutions through the most substantial knowledge, skills, and technology (Danske Bank, 2020a).

The main activity already performed concerns reducing the offering portfolio for both the service lines and introducing new simplified products. Danske Bank's effort to deliver a customer-centric solution has led to introducing the so-called Open Banking Initiative (Danske Bank, 2020b).

Danske Bank's customer-centric approach involves using different communication accesses, called "Omnichannel Integration," which includes in-person consultancy, online chats and assistance, and the opportunity to book online meetings.

The transformation undertaken by the bank is also motivated by the need to pay more attention to compliance, risk, and control of performance and activities. For this reason, Danske Bank has sustained investment in augmented intelligence tools to fight financial fraud (Teradata, 2018). The analysis performed by the software allows identifying the highest number possible of true positives fraud cases avoiding false positives misguidance in support of the operators.

Humans' supervision is still necessary to better understand whether the bank is dealing with a financial fraud case or not. Therefore, it is possible to say that within Danske Bank, persons and robots collaborate to execute daily activities.

The aspects presented above demonstrate that Danske Bank has started a substantial evolution toward bionics. Indeed, it is possible to recognize the hybrid nature of bionic banking within Dansk Bank because of the coexistence of the workforce and automation for what concerns the delivery of financial services and in the channel used to build and strengthen relationships with its customers.

For what interests the personal side of the organization, Danske Bank operators can deliver innovative financial solutions thanks to the expertise they have gained combined with a good command of emerging technologies. Danske Bank provides operators continuous training at every staff level and ongoing feedback to grant an elevated level of competencies. Within this context, operators can take the initiative and embrace alternative practices such as co-creation and co-working, aiming to adapt continuously to changing market and customers' needs. These considerations highlight how Danske Bank focuses on the people dimension while adopting emerging automation solutions.

As stated in the theory of bionic banking, Danske Bank has a sharp vision aimed to be trusted by customers within the regional area of Northern Europe. The mission is a customer "promise" to provide them guidance, knowledge, and the tools they need to make their investments decisions.

Danske Bank's mission is a strategy developed to transition to "bionic" and intended to increase customer delight and operators' engagement, positively impact society, and achieve the highest result possible for shareholders (Danske Bank, 2020a).

It is interesting to analyze what makes a bionic enterprise so flourishing and different from the fintech organization of today. There are three drivers of a bionic transformation.

- Humans and automation carry out the transformation collaboratively and in an integrated way thanks to the bionic nature of operations. They differ from the standard processes where persons operate, and technology is an accessory tool.
- The modular architecture of the bionic systems creates an ecosystem of integrated components supporting interactions without incurring substantial transaction costs. The modular architecture leads to implementing an agile system with no constraints of capacity and accessibility.
- Bionic algorithms extract insights in real-time and automatically process information acquired from other applications learning from data. Humans use these as primary inputs for operational processes. In this sense, continuous learning through automation becomes a competitive benefit because of the acceleration in learning.

Decision-Making Process
A deep understanding of augmented intelligence and its integration in the organizational decision-making of financial institutions augment human capabilities and support more effective decisions. Augmented intelligence should be decision-making support rather than an autonomous decision-maker. Organizations adopt smoother and more collaborative designs to make the best of AI within their decision-making process. Augmented intelligence is an efficient tool to deal with complex situations, while human capabilities seem to be more relevant in cases of uncertainty and ambiguity. Augmented intelligence also raises new issues for organizations regarding their responsibility and acceptance by society as there is a gray area surrounding these technologies in front of ethics and laws.

Some scholars have considered the complementary relationship between automation (mainly AI and robots) and humans in decision-making (Dejoux & Léon, 2018; Jarrahi, 2018; Pomerol, 1997). AI cannot have advanced capabilities since some tasks cannot be decomposed as rules and put into codes and algorithms. Some jobs will remain in the human field as humans excel in collecting information from senses and perception, while AI can analyze them for pattern recognition (Brynjolfsson & McAfee, 2014).

One of the challenges of management relies on the organization's adaptability to handle change and transform itself. In collaboration with the MIT Sloan academicians and BCG, a report stated that managers could address these organizational challenges using soft skills and new ways of human–human interaction and cooperation and human-automation interaction and collaboration (Ransbotham et al., 2017).

AI can assume three roles in decision-making (Dejoux & Léon, 2018):

- Assistant,
- Forecaster,
- Decision-maker in alternative to the managers.

AI and humans in decision-making can overcome the challenges of uncertainty, complexity, and ambiguity resulting from the environment (Jarrahi, 2018). Y. Galily (2018) states that while AI merely replaces human tasks, it also enables humans to focus on other activities such as creativity. The assumption is that organizations should build a comprehensive strategy regarding their core competencies to succeed. They should organize themselves to build core competencies and make them grow (Prahalad & Hamel, 1990). Knowledge-based banking organizations manage to do it by putting information to productive use in their services at every level of their organization.

Soft skills are attributes that robots do not have or cannot imitate and constitute a competitive advantage for humans (Brynjolfsson & McAfee, 2014). As digital solutions have evolved, they integrate into tools and equipment used in the workplace. Humans collaborate with digital co-operators (Snow et al., 2017).

This setting helps to reach an efficient collaboration and decision-making between humans and automation (Snow et al., 2017). Shared situation awareness, possible through digital platforms and software, creates current, accessible, and valuable information for all the organization members, enabling them to make decisions under challenging situations (Snow et al., 2017).

A new division of labor emerges where AI takes care of analytical, repetitive tasks while humans use intuition, imagination, and senses in the decision-making process (Brynjolfsson & McAfee, 2014). The collaboration of self-organized and autonomous actors makes the decisions.

The first type of decision-making approach is intuitive. According to E. Dane et al. (2012), intuitive decision-making is "affectively-charged judgments that arise through rapid, nonconscious, and holistic associations" and it is "a form of knowing that manifests itself as an awareness of thoughts, feelings, or bodily sense connected to a deeper perception, understanding, and way of making sense of the world that may not be achieved easily or at all by other means" (Dane et al., 2012; Sadler-Smith & Shefy, 2004). Intuition is a cognitive approach that is opposed to rational, analytical, and logical thoughts (Dane et al., 2012; Sadler-Smith & Shefy, 2004). Intuition is a phenomenon that humans experience daily and use naturally (Sadler-Smith & Shefy, 2004). Intuition also includes expertise, implicit learning, sensitivity, creativity, and imagination (Sadler-Smith & Shefy, 2004; Jarrahi, 2018). Intuition is also related to a gut feeling sensation or instinct to understand key problematics (Sadler-Smith & Shefy, 2004). Therefore, banking professionals experiencing a gut feeling can identify quickly whether an innovative service is likely to make it or not, whether a financial investment has potentiality to turn into making money (Sadler-Smith & Shefy, 2004), and so on. This type of intuition is called superior or intuitive intelligence: "the human capacity to analyze alternatives with a deeper perception, transcending ordinary-level functioning based on simple rational thinking" (Jarrahi, 2018).

Intuition relies on expertise (Sadler-Smith & Shefy, 2004). Indeed, according to E. Sadler-Smith and Shefy (2004), domain experts are the individuals that can exploit at best intuition for decision-making. The concept of domain expert is an individual who has accumulated knowledge and expertise in a specific field thanks to experiences (Kahneman & Klein, 2009; Klein, 1998; Salas et al., 2010). As intuition relies on subjectivity, the decomposition of this process in tasks like a rational process is impossible. It is similar to tacit knowledge obtained through experiences and familiarity (Dane et al., 2012; Jarrahi, 2018; Klein, 2015). Intuitive decision-making links emotions, sense-making, and gut feeling (Dane et al., 2012; Jarrahi, 2018). There is a connection between intuition, perception, and subjectivity. Intuition builds upon experience and familiarity (Klein, 2015) and depends on expertise and feelings (Sadler-Smith & Shefy, 2004).

Rational decision-making is objective and impersonal; there is no personal judgment. Intelligent automation can potentially emulate humans' rational processes in decision-making (Jarrahi, 2018).

Dow Jones

Dow Jones brings together world-leading data, media, membership, and intelligence solutions to power organizations and professionals. Dow Jones

> uses artificial intelligence tools and has human expertise. Dow Jones calls the combination "authentic intelligence" (Marr, 2021).
>
> A Dow Jones team involves overseeing systems used to raise alerts when banks and other financial institutions might be at risk of doing business with people placed on international sanctions lists: a critical piece of compliance (Marr, 2021). An AI system unexpectedly cleared several transactions that an analyst expected would have been rejected on one occasion due to the names involved. A check of the data used to decide a list of sanctioned people suggested the automated application had removed them. At this stage, the analyst stepped in and manually verified the removal with the data provider, acting on personal instinct that something was wrong. The data provider has removed the names by mistake. It is improbable that machines alone would provide this level of oversight and avoid a potentially expensive and dangerous mistake.

Advancements of Bionic Transformation

The introduction of digital solutions, the external social changes resulting from bionic transformation, and the progress in business management systems led to further developments in the bionic enterprise management research field (Table 3.2).

With BT's advent, one of the focuses of the research in bionics is on the so-called bionic banking system (BBS). One of the impacts of bionic transformation concerned banking processes optimization. More precisely, the combination of digitalized information, new technological trends, and shifts in customers' demand originate the concept of Digital Banking (DB). DB is a "process which, with the support of solutions such as virtual reality, computer networks, rapid prototyping, and database, is based on customer demand to analyze, organize, and recombine the product, process, and resource information, implement the product design and function simulation and rapid prototyping, and then to perform rapid production to meet customer demand and quality standards" (Zhou et al., 2011). Digital banking does not represent the latest innovation in banking. As anticipated above, bionic banking systems are the most recent solutions intended to improve banking processes. According to BBS theory, banking systems' essential characteristics come from the collaboration of humans and automation. The single adoption

Table 3.2 Development of BBS

	First wave (1950s–1970s)	Second wave (1980s–1990s)	Third wave (2000s-2010s)	Fourth wave (2020s–)
Advances in bionic solutions	Early symbolism and connectionism school, production systems, knowledge inference. Simple expert systems	Statistical models in speech recognition and machine translation, artificial neural network in pattern recognition, expert systems	Breakthrough in applications of deep eLearning in speech recognition, patterns recognition, big data, high performance computers	Vast array of solutions starting to use advanced automation solutions, such as AI, chatbot, robo-advisors, and similar, AI-based augmented analytics. Need to increase sustainability of the solutions
Human needs	Not considered	Not considered	Initial solutions providing useful and real problems	From supportive to integrated human role
Focus	Technological solutions	Technological solutions	Integrated solutions, ethical design, technological enhancement, human factors design	Bionic solutions
Characteristics	Research center driven	Research center driven	Technological enhancements and application plus a human centered approach	Move more and more from research center to the industrial and service world

Source Modification by the Author or the table of comparison of different AI waves (Xu, 2019)

of technology does not determine their efficiency. BBS comprises several parts, for example, operators, which interact with automation and are autonomous in the decision-making process. The underlying biological properties of BBS regard each component's ability to adapt to external events and to collaboratively self-managing (Tharumarajah, 1996).

Further advancements in bionics guided by BT innovation are related to an institution's business model innovation. Studies showed that organizations are experiencing a transformation into bionic entities from the collaboration of persons and automation, for example, augmented intelligence applications in robotic process automation. This fusion originates the so-called bionic banking, where biological and technological systems collaborate to reach exponential growth. Bionic organizations are not present in large numbers in today's markets. They have exciting potential.

Conclusions

The primary purpose of this chapter is to develop a deeper understanding and more profound knowledge about the role of automation and humans' collaboration in the banking processes.

Some conclusions of this analysis are that currently, automation cannot replace humans in the decision-making process. Automation offers a faster and deeper analysis of specific topics than humans. It cannot integrate empathetic and ethical intelligence. Automation cannot solve a dilemma or solve a new problem out of its scope of expertise without having human inputs and training. Automation's role in the processes is an assistant and support to humans in analyzing and formulating alternatives. Humans still have a significant role in the banking transformation.

This chapter highlights that actor-oriented organizational design supports humans in the process of automation within bionic banking. This organizational design supports the keys concept of bionic banking and enables humans to collaborate effectively, efficiently, economically, and especially, ethically.

The analysis shows that automation:

- Can reduce uncertainty through its ability to make objective forecasts and repetitive operations while humans experience and its comprehensive approach are vital in the bionic transformation.
- Has superior abilities to analyze complex data and give sense to it. Their decisioning is limited to a specific field of expertise.
- Can clarify ambiguity as long as it should answer the right question. It lacks critical thinking, empathy, and contextualization. These are human characteristics able to enhance the processes.

There are new challenges for organizations and society related to the development of automation. There is a need to clarify automation's responsibility, both within organizations and from a legal point of view. This situation is closely related to ethics, as giving moral values to automation raises many issues. Through AI, RPA, and data science, bionics is a revolution that will deeply modify organizations and society.

REFERENCES

Bekkhus, R. (2016). Do KPIs used by CIOs decelerate digital business transformation? The case of ITIL. In *Digital Innovation, Technology, and Strategy Conference*.

Brynjolfsson, E., & McAfee, A. (2014). *The second machine age: Work, progress, and prosperity in a time of brilliant technologies*. WW Norton & Company.

Caprino, K. (2012, April). What you do not know will hurt you: The top 8 skills professionals need to master. *Forbes*.

Dane, E., Rockmann, K. W., & Pratt, M. G. (2012). When should I trust my gut? Linking domain expertise to intuitive decision-making effectiveness. *Organizational Behavior and Human Decision Processes, 119*, 187–194.

Danske Bank. (2020a, November). *Danske Bank wins international award for best open banking initiative* (Press Release).

Danske Bank. (2020b). *The essence of Danske Bank*.

Dejoux, C., & Léon, E. (2018). *Métamorphose des managers* (1st ed.). Pearson.

Demirkan, H., Spohrer, J. C., & Welser, J. J. (2016). Digital innovation and strategic transformation. *IT Professional, 18*(6), 14–18.

Farooq, U., & Grudin, J. (2016). Human-computer integration. *ACM Interactions, 23*(6), 27–32.

Fitzgerald, M., Kruschwitz, N., Bonnet, D., & Welch, M. (2014). Embracing digital technology: A new strategic imperative. *MIT Sloan Management Review, 55*(2), 1.

Galily, Y. (2018). Artificial intelligence and sports journalism: Is it a sweeping change? *Technology in Society*.

Goleman, D. (1996). *Emotional intelligence: Why it can matter more than IQ*. Bloomsbury Publishing.

Hess, T., Matt, C., Benlian, A., & Wiesböck, F. (2016). Options for formulating a digital transformation strategy. *MIS Quarterly Executive, 15*(2).

Hoffman, G., & Breazeal, C. (2004, September). Collaboration in human-robot teams. In *AIAA 1st Intelligent Systems Technical Conference Online Proceedings*, Conference Proceeding.

Human-Centered AI. (2019). Converge with global tech visionaries. *Insights, 26*, 42.

Jarrahi, M. H. (2018). Artificial intelligence and the future of work: Human—AI symbiosis in organizational decision making. *Business Horizons*.

Kahneman, D., & Klein, G. (2009). Conditions for intuitive expertise. *American Psychologist, 64*(6), 515–526.

Klein, G. (1998). A naturalistic decision-making perspective on studying intuitive decision making. *Journal of Applied Research in Memory and Cognition, 4*(2015), 164–171.

Klein, G. (2015). A naturalistic decision-making perspective on studying intuitive decision-making. *Journal of Applied Research in Memory and Cognition, 4*(3), 164–168.

Marr, B. (2021, October). *AI And data at Dow Jones: Why humans are the machine behind AI*. Linkedin.com.

Mazzone, D. M. (2014). *Digital or death: Digital transformation: The only choice for business to survive smash and conquer*. Smashbox Consulting Inc.

McIntyre, A., et al. (2020). *Making digital banking more human*. Global Banking Customer Study an Accenture Paper.

Morakanyane, R., Grace, A. A., & O'Reilly, P. (2017, June). Conceptualizing digital transformation in organizations: A systematic review of literature. In *Bled eConference* (p. 21).

Mukherjee, A., & Nath, P. (2003). A model of trust in online relationship banking. *International Journal of Bank Marketing*.

Murray, D. (2010). *Interaction design*. University of London International Programmes.

Pomerol, J. C. (1997). Artificial intelligence and human decision making. *European Journal of Operational Research, 99*(1997), 3–25.

Prahalad, C. K., & Hamel, G. (1990). The core competence of the corporation. *Harvard Business Review, 68*(3), 79–91.

PwC. (2013). *Digitale Transformation – der gro€ßte Wandel seit der Industriellen Revolution*. PricewaterhouseCoopers.

Ransbotham, S., Kiron, D., Gerbert, P., & Reeves, M. (2017). Reshaping business with artificial intelligence: Closing the gap between ambition and action. *MIT Sloan Management Review, 59*(1).

Remane, G., Hanelt, A., Wiesboeck, F., & Kolbe, L. (2017). *Digital maturity in traditional industries—An exploratory analysis*.

Sadler-Smith, E., & Shefy, E. (2004). The intuitive executive: Understanding and applying 'gut feel' in decision-making. *Academy of Management Perspectives, 18*(4), 76–91.

Salas, E., Rosen, M. A., & DiazGranados, D. (2010). Expertise-based intuition and decision-making in organizations. *Journal of Management, 36*(4), 941–973.

Sebastian, I., Ross, J., Beath, C., Mocker, M., Moloney, K., & Fonstad, N. (2017, September). How big old organizations navigate digital transformation. *MIS Quarterly Executive, 16*(3).

Snow, C. C., Fjeldstad, Ø. D., & Langer, A. M. (2017). Designing the digital organization. *Journal of Organization Design, 6,* 7.

Teradata. (2018). *Danske Bank fights fraud with deep learning and AI*. Teradata Corporation, 10, 18.

Tharumarajah, A. (1996). Comparison of the bionic, fractal, and holonic manufacturing system concepts. *International Journal of Computer Integrated Manufacturing, 9*(3), 217–226.

Vakkuri, V., Kemell, K. K., Kultanen, J., & Abrahamsson, P. (2020). The current state of industrial practice in artificial intelligence ethics. *IEEE Software, 37*(4), 50–57.

Verhoef, P. C., Broekhuizen, T., Bart, Y., Bhattacharya, A., Dong, J. Q., Fabian, N., & Haenlein, M. (2019). Digital transformation: A multidisciplinary reflection and research agenda. *Journal of Business Research*.

Westerman, G., Calméjane, C., Bonnet, D., Ferraris, P., & McAfee, A. (2011). Digital transformation: A roadmap for billion-dollar organizations. *MIT Center for Digital Business and Capgemini Consulting, 1,* 1–68.

Xu, W. (2019). Toward human-centered AI: A perspective from human-computer interaction. *Interactions, 26*(4), 42–46.

Žitkienė, R., & Mačerinskienė, I. (2014). *A master's thesis writing guide* (educational book). Mycolas Romeris University: Faculty of Economics and Finance management.

Zhou, Z., Xie, S. S., & Chen, D. (2011). *Fundamentals of digital manufacturing science*. Springer.

CHAPTER 4

Bionic Banking Business Model

INTRODUCTION

This chapter provides a direct answer to the book objectives. It considers the business model canvas, a visual tool helpful in defining how a bionic enterprise creates and delivers value, and briefly presents its structure and applicability to financial services. To understand this bionic banking entity's functioning in-depth, it is necessary to accurately examine and describe each building block that composes the business model canvas.

BUSINESS MODEL CANVAS (BMC)

Not all the financial institutions performing a bionic transformation succeed in evolving into an organization where persons and automation collaborate. Aside from low investments in automation and data, many organizations fail in this transformation process. One of the reasons is the lack of concern about the organizational structure. Bionic organizations can effectively achieve their transformation by going beyond the existing business standards and, in many cases, even disrupt their core processes. The main obstacle financial institutions face during this transition is understanding how to move away from their obsolete business configuration and innovating their business model.

The business model is the conceptualization of how an economic organization creates, transforms, and delivers value. A more detailed definition depicts the business model as "the description of how a business can create value through the services and products it proposes to its customers, its value architecture (including its resources and internal and external value network), and how it can capture the value to convert it into profit." (Lehmann-Ortega & Schoettl, 2005).

The business model concept comes from the "*Theory of the business*" developed by Peter Drucker in 1994. According to this author, each economic reality has assumptions at the basis of its functioning referred to the organizational behavior, the ultimate business purpose and the relative values, the customers it serves, its competitors, the processes and dynamics, and the organization's strengths and weaknesses. Drucker believed that the formulation of a business model could support the transformation of organizations. To accomplish a bionic transformation effectively, financial institutions need to define in advance the assumptions at the basis of their innovative business model (bionic business model).

The question that automatically arises in this situation is: "where to start?" Organizations should rely on a high-potential visual analytic tool like the Business Model Canvas (BMC) to address this need. Alexander Osterwalder developed this framework applying a design science approach to his studies in business model generation (Lehmann-Ortega & Schoettl, 2005). BMC is a template that can guide financial institutions in understanding their business configuration in a straightforward and structured way. Figure 4.1. shows a BMC as modified by the author of this book (Nicoletti, 2021a, 2021b).

The business model has ten conceptual parts that describe the relevant elements for the organization's management. They are building blocks identifiable as the twelve Ps:

- Philosophy.
- Proposition of value.
- Proximity with the customers.
- Place and distribution accesses of the services or products.
- Partition of the market.
- Processes.
- Platforms.
- Persons.
- Partners.

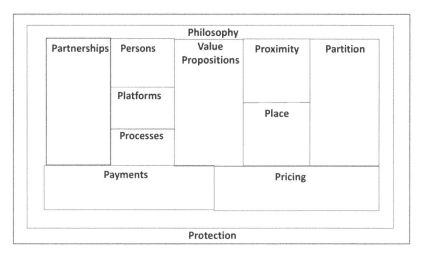

Fig. 4.1 Modified business model canvas

- Pricing and revenues.
- Payments for costs and investments.
- Protection.

It is possible to develop the business model peculiar to a bionic financial organization through a detailed analysis of each building block. The resulting bionic business model is an analytic guideline helpful in this disruptive transformation process. It clarifies the essential components necessary to become bionic; and a "way to do business" typical of innovative organizations where persons and automation are interdependent.

Before describing each building block, it is relevant to state that each component should directly or indirectly connect with the others. For example, by considering a bionic organization's value proposition, it is impossible to disregard the customer segment that value addresses and the distribution accesses delivering products or services. The relationship between critical resources, processes, platforms, and the investments necessary to implement them represents another linkage between building blocks.

The BMC refers to the potential future configuration of a bionic financial organization. The resources, processes, value propositions, and other vital determinants that characterize the enterprise before the transformation are insignificant. The resulting BMC has to resemble how a financial organization will look once completed the bionic transformation process.

An Extended HAI Framework

This section proposes an extended Human-Automation Integration (HAI) framework (Fig. 4.2) (Xu, 2019). The framework includes three main components:

- The ethically aligned design creates automation solutions that avoid discrimination, maintain fairness and justice, and do not replace humans.
- Technology that fully reflects human intelligence further enhances automation to reflect human intelligence's depth (more like human intelligence).

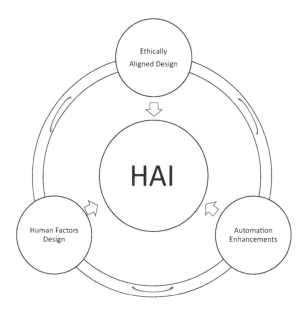

Fig. 4.2 Human automation integration framework (*Source* Elaboration of the Author from Xu [2019])

- Human factors design ensures that AI solutions are explainable, comprehensible, helpful, and usable.

This framework promotes a comprehensive approach, providing the financial institution with safe, efficient, healthy, and satisfying HAI solutions.

The HAI framework presents synergy across the three domains. For example, ethical automation design emphasizes the enhancement of human capabilities rather than their replacement. It requires HAI design to ensure that human operators can fast and effectively control an intelligent system in an emergency so that it is possible to avoid fatal accidents and assure resilience.

Figure 4.3 refers to the general components of the bionic model and describes the basis of platform organizational structure. This model synthesizes the operational models developed out of BCG framework (Hutchinson et al., 2019) and KPMG target operating model approaches (Barrelet, 2021).

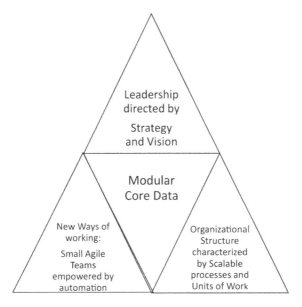

Fig. 4.3 Operational bionic model

Bionic Banking BMC

The study published in 2019 by the Boston Consulting Group (BCG) defines a bionic enterprise as an organization where innovative solutions, in particular AI, and human capabilities are interrelated to deliver superior customer experiences and relationships, robot-augmented operations, and to achieve higher rates of innovation in products, services, and business models (Aré et al., 2019). Starting from BCG's bionic theory, it has been possible to generate a more detailed conceptualization of the "formula to become bionic."

Figure 4.4 provides a visual representation of the enablers and outcomes that characterize a bionic enterprise.

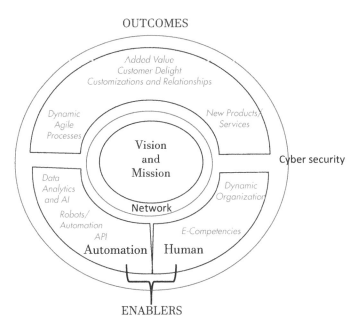

Fig. 4.4 Outcomes and enablers of a bionic enterprise

Philosophy

The central node of the bionic model concerns vision and mission. When running and transforming an organization, the vision describes the desired future position of the organization, while the mission defines the organization's objectives and its approach to reach those goals.

Vision

It is possible to analyze the vision statement of bionic banking from two different perspectives. On the one hand, it refers to the desire to become today's "financial institution of the future." On the other hand, the connection is with the ambition to become a "social enterprise," an organization that achieves its business objectives by respecting and supporting its operators' needs and the external environment. The vision statement has not to be self-celebratory of what a bionic organization already does. Instead, it has to define the socio-entrepreneurial contribution of a fintech institution based on its unique strengths.

Mission

For what concerns bionic banking, the mission consists of boosting the potential of persons and automation to deliver value to customers and the other members of the ecosystem wherein it operates. Once leaders have identified the mission, leaders should communicate and convert it into practical actions. The translation of the mission statement is a set of well-defined, clear objectives and achievements the fintech organization has to reach. In the case of a bionic transformation, the objectives related to fintech organization's mission are to:

- Build personalized customer relationships,
- Implement human-automation-driven processes,
- Provide innovative value offerings.

By accomplishing these three objectives, the fintech organization gains competitive advantages in the market.

- Digitally supported customer relationships allow tracking information about them and their preferences to meet their satisfaction

successfully. Customers' delight contributes to making fintech organizations earn a competitive advantage, increasing brand reputation and visibility.
- Automation-augmented operations optimize the core processes and lead to significant efficiency and economics, reducing operating costs and time.
- With a high rate of innovation in the products and services, the bionic organization can achieve a differentiated competitive advantage. Combining bionic activities and Research and Development (R&D) function experimentations, it is possible to innovate products and services quickly. In this way, the fintech organization gains the first-mover benefit.

In addition to acquiring competitive advantages, a fintech organization's goals during the bionic transition aim to create value. For example, creating a solid relationship between the customer and the organization generates an intangible but worthwhile value in customers' loyalty.

Concerning the approach that bionic banking implements to reach these goals, the strategy should integrate with the high-level vision and mission of the business. This approach means that a strategic alignment of the bionic transformation objectives is necessary with those that financial institutions had planned to achieve in a short time. A successful approach to this robust growth process should involve automation strategies. The change in a bionic direction involves organizations exploiting digital tools and solutions. Most cases support achieving a successful bionic transformation. The overall business strategy translates into clear and prioritized tasks. They do not need to be complete in a short period and by all the hierarchical levels of the organization. The management and the top executives should share their vision and motivate the lower levels to collaborate during this transition.

Enablers
The enablers are automation and humans. Their description and characteristics are in the next section.

Outcomes
One fundamental component of the "formula to become bionic" concerns the results that the bionic organization desires to achieve. They directly relate to the first factors examined above: the vision and mission.

This approach should put bionic banking in place to complete its mission. This action requires briefly discussing the objectives it wants to pursue.

- The orientation of bionic banking is toward customer delight, which goes beyond customers' satisfaction, satisfying more than the customer requests. Customer delight deals with anticipating the customers' needs and exceeding their expectations. It takes place when customers are positively surprised by the service so much that they feel emotions. Some of the actions must be customizations and relationships enhanced thanks to the agility of bionic banking. In addition to cutting-edge customer relationships, the "fintech organization of the future" should aim to optimize its business models + with the introduction of AI and robotic process automation tools supporting dynamic operations.
- Bionic banking interactions with its customers add value by using digital tools. Customer engagement and customer relationships have already experienced a change: introducing e-commerce and online and smartphone sales accesses. Practices such as customers' retention, after-sales assistance have become "user-friendly." A step forward in this direction is the use of data science, augmented intelligence, and RPA. These solutions, on one side, offer customers personalized products, services, and tailored marketing while, on the other, allows the financial institution to acquire precious information, such as the preferences and the inclination to churn.
- Another fundamental goal is that bionic banking should create innovative offerings with innovative products and services. To this end, organizations cannot exclusively rely on the potential of innovative solutions and data, but they need to leverage human creativity. People are an essential resource because they can innovate products and services by combining their intuitions and feelings with the findings resulting from data.

Only a moderate number of organizations have recognized the benefits of bionics because most businesses are afraid of the investments necessary to undergo this transformation. Many organizations are only now starting to approach bionic transformation. Notwithstanding these obstacles, an increasing number of bionic organizations are currently active. They are located mainly in Asia and operate in telecommunication, fintech, and technology industries (Anderson et al., 2020).

From the initial studies about these bionic organizations, three relevant elements emerged concerning the results they have achieved over the years going from 2015 to 2018: their annual investments for research and development/R&D function increased by 1.5%; the Earnings Before Interest Taxes Depreciation Amortization/EBITDA (also knowns as operating margin) grew by 1.8% each year; the enterprise value more than doubled (it increased by 2.4%) per year. These key performance indicators provide evidence of the potential and success of bionic organizations (Grebe et al., 2020).

Customer Value Proposition

The conceptualization of the bionic business model starts from analyzing the value proposition building block of the BMC. It regards the set of products and/or services the bionic organization introduces into the market to deliver value to its customers. The value proposition is not referred to as the "physical" description of the product/service nor explains how to use it. It deals with all the benefits in the customer experience in using the product or service, from the satisfaction of users' needs or the solution of a problem they are willing to resolve.

Respond to the following questions establish the value proposition that characterizes bionic banking (Nichols, 2020):

1. What is the value that banking delivers to its customer?
2. Which of the customer's problems is bionics helping to solve?
3. Which are the customer's needs that the value proposition addresses?
4. How to fill the gaps?

For ordinary organizations, the characteristics of an output that contribute to creating value are mainly related to novelty, performance, speed, design, price, accessibility, duration, and practicality. Bionic banking brings a stream of products and services to the market with a high rate of innovation, technology application, and sustainability.

The rapid introduction of advanced solutions and the increasing customers' requests for satisfying personalized human needs has led to the appearance of Innovative Value Propositions (IVP) (Chen, Z. et al.,

2020). The IVPs analysis plays a critical role in the successful planning and design of the smart product/service system (PSS).

There is a criticism concerning the sustainability of the operations created by these value propositions. Since the bionic financial organization has a significant automation and robotics implementation level, its processes involve high energy consumption, negatively affecting the environment. AI-driven robots, peculiar to bionic organizations, have been enhanced with intelligent software applications and algorithms capable of measuring, controlling, predicting, and optimizing utility consumption, such as electricity, which in the long-term lead to a reduction of these resources waste.

Customers Proximity

Another building block that composes the bionic business model concerns an organization's relationship with its customers. Defining what type of relationship, a fintech organization wants to build is essential because of its impact on the customers' perception of the institution. Bionic banking needs to understand the connection with customers and what it is based on if the organization wants to benefit from this relationship in a long-term horizon effectively.

Before analyzing the leading types of relationships bionic banking can set up with its customers, it is essential to describe the motivations that encourage a financial institution to prioritize customer proximity (Geib et al., 2005). The purpose of relational marketing activities regards the increase of sales. They work on strengthening the relationship with customers to convince them to continue buying. Customer proximity strategies also aim to acquire new customers. Marketing best practices in customer acquisition leverage social media, online communities, and platforms through which it is possible to reach a broader audience.

In some cases, customer proximity programs are necessary to avoid customer churn. Churn is losing customers who leave the fintech organization and prefer to buy substitute products from competitors. To minimize the churn rate, fintech organizations need to identify customer retention strategies.

Lastly, economic organizations improve the relationships with their customers to increase customer loyalty. Customers' loyalty is meaningful for organizations because it leads to repeated purchases, positive word-of-mouth among other prospects, and a high pricing tolerance. In this sense, customer loyalty represents a competitive advantage.

Regarding the type of relationships that bionic organizations generate with their customers, the analysis can focus on three high-potential best practices of the theory of relational marketing: online communities, co-creation, and personal assistance with chatbots.

- Online Communities refer to individuals who socially interact and share opinions, problems, judgments, experiences, and advice about a common interest topic. Online communities are built-in a "virtual space" on the Internet, especially on social media. A characteristic of online communities is establishing a network between members, which results in a shared sense of belonging to that system of connections (Trang et al., 2020).

  Online communities have great potential in generating customer proximity and building relationships based on trust, loyalty, and satisfaction. In relational marketing, these three factors are pivotal when establishing long-term relationships. The relationship builds on trust. It is related to the brand's reliability and the visibility of its actions. Successful examples in the financial world of virtual communities are crowdfunding and group insurance.

- Co-creation is a relationship that organizations establish with their customer through their direct or indirect involvement in the value creation process. In this practice, the role of customers moves from passive individuals who receive value from businesses to active players in the value proposition creation and production process. Social media, online networks, and platforms enable the value co-creation process because they allow continuous and immediate interactions between customers and organizations.

  Customers are usually indirectly involved in the ideation phase for the value proposition generation by sharing knowledge, posting ideas and/or criticism, and improving existing value propositions. Another contribution of customers may be related to the design of the product. Online applications and software provide interactive toll for creating innovative content or changes that simultaneously involve more than one user. This situation is an example of the so-called joint co-creation activity (Kamboj et al., 2018).

A recent procedure emerging from co-creation, which involves customers and organizations in social networks, is branding co-creation. Branding co-creation concerns customers' engagement in brand identity creation and definition of the fintech organization values (Hajli et al., 2017).

In all the cases presented, co-creation is a relationship between customers and an economic organization where customers have no more a passive role in the spirit of bionic. They contribute to value development with their resources that generally are professional practical capabilities, knowledge, personal opinions, and intellectual competencies.

Examples of co-creation in financial services are wealth management and unit-linked insurance policies.

- Personal assistance is the relationship between the fintech organization and one customer to provide information and product details in the pre-purchase stage or solve problems after the sale. These procedures were executed in person in the physical branch by a representative of the financial institution. Now more assistance is provided through online access. The emerging solution for personal customer service is the chatbot. Chatbots are AI-based computer software that communicates with customers through chat messages using natural human language. These software agents can interact with customers and have conversations with them by understanding their requests and consequently replying (Adam et al., 2020). Augmented intelligence algorithms generate chatbot's abilities to simulate and replicate human discussions.

MetLife

MetLife is a global provider of insurance, annuities, and operator benefit programs (Capgemini Financial Services Analysis, 2021). Founded in 1868, the company is one of the world's leading global life and health insurers. With headquarters in New York, MetLife serves more than 90 million policyholders across 60 countries.

MetLife executives sought an easy-to-use tool to help sales agents remotely engage with customers during the pandemic and continue to satisfy their needs. The goal was to use digital tools to recreate seamless,

> personalized Customer Experience (CX) interrupted by lockdowns and limited face-to-face opportunities (Hızıroğlu, 2021).
> As the pandemic sparked anxiety among policyholders who wanted to connect quickly with consultants, implementation speed was critical. Within weeks, MetLife set up an in-house team with multi-functional skills, including product development, sales, ICT, and legal. The multi-functional team used existing building blocks, embedded video, and the organization's cloud-based sales platform to develop an automation tool to enable agents and customers to engage virtually. The tool's video capabilities allowed customers and sales agents to seamlessly communicate and access multiple layers of information in a personal setting. Agents can invite advisory experts to conversations as needed, and customers can include friends or relatives. Leveraging the tool, MetLife agents could swiftly respond to customers within a safe, non-face-to-face environment.
> With a 90% adoption rate, the automation tool was a key enabler to the MetLife sales team during the lockdown. With a combination of human touch and digital elements, the tool offered outstanding customer experience, which led to increased customer delight, acquisition, and retention. Agents reduced paperwork and travel because the digital tool allowed anytime, anywhere customer engagement.

Place and Distribution Accesses

The importance of the omniaccess is increasing due to the presence and use of many accesses. The last century was about omnichannel—adding technologies to existing structures. The new century is about omniaccess—adding capabilities to a digital core. The difference is that omniaccess assumes that financial institutions are cloud-native, with digital at the core. The premise for omniaccess is that financial institutions are cloud-based with digital on top. This situation means customer information is unified across systems and allows fintech organizations to support their customers regardless of the access mode, contact method, offering fintech organizations a far superior customer experience. This new situation puts contact centers as a centerpiece of the fintech organizations' CX strategy going forward. This approach will be the key for competition in the twenty-first century, as digital at the core and data at the center are going to be the competitive factors that differentiate financial winners from losers.

More importantly, there is the need for a balance of digital and physical access with a consistent omniaccess strategy. Customers, and operators, should feel they get the same experience in real-time, all the time, on any access. This reason makes data rationalization and consolidation critical. To offer omniaccess, data cannot be fragmented and siloed. In omniaccess, data aligns to accesses rather than customers. Omniaccess, with a rationalized and consolidated data core offered via digital platforms to devices, is the critical competitive differentiator for the future. However, just as important is that omniaccess is offered for both physical and digital services. Customers do not want purely digital, and they do not want strictly physical. They want consistent customer service regardless of whether they are talking direct, human-to-human, or swiping on their app. The customer relationship winners will be the financial providers who understand this and excel in the customer interface for physical and digital omniaccess.

A fundamental component of the bionic financial organization model concerns how services, and more generally value, are delivered to customers. When choosing adequate distribution accesses, organizations evaluate their customers' characteristics and buying behaviors, the type of value proposition they are offering, and the size of the market in which they operate. The purpose of a fintech economic organization in making these assessments is to reach as many customers as possible.

Bionic banking should consider that technological innovations have changed the way customers approach products and services. For example, traditional direct purchasing accesses such as through salespeople and catalogs have become obsolete and inefficient. They require more time and effort concerning mobile accesses, which provide immediate information through a click. Omniaccess should also be assured for accesses through the branches. Banking transactions made in branches or agencies allow interaction with customer service operators and salespeople who can transmit trust and engage customers with personal contact. An additional benefit associated with in-branch transactions is that customers can directly try products and services to immediately perceive the value and quality of the services and perform a preliminary assessment of whether it meets their requirements.

Omniaccess is becoming even more critical with open banking. Open banking is a banking practice that provides third-party financial service providers open access to customer banking, transaction, and other financial information from financial institutions through the use of Application

Programming Interfaces (APIs) (Laplante & Kshetri, 2021). A significant competitive success of online banking is the high accessibility associated with media such as websites and smartphone applications. The accessibility should combine with ease-of-navigation, making buying online straightforward and intuitive for the customers less familiar with the technology.

A success factor of online banking is the amount of information that users can collect by comparing prices, the descriptions provided by the financial institutions, and the reviews about the financial services made by other customers. In this sense, it is possible to derive that online banking grants the so-called information symmetry (the opposite of information asymmetry) between customers and vendors since the Internet is a tool for acquiring valuable information. It supports rational decisions.

During the study of the most suitable distribution accesses for bionic banking, it is necessary to consider two of the assumptions in the formula to become bionic. These organizations have a hybrid nature, originated from the interdependence between virtual robots and persons, and a strong presence of innovative solutions.

Bionic distribution platforms merge traditional purchasing accesses' digital and analog success factors such as "brick and mortar" shops, e-commerce, online marketplaces, and wholesale stores. In this way, bionic accesses combine the convenience, accessibility, and information availability of e-commerce websites with the possibility to experiment with the product physically. This hybrid modality allows organizations to leverage the online and offline customer experience (Böger et al., 2019).

The characteristics of this innovative channel are mainly related to the opportunity to compare many products and services, access an online variety assortment, try the services in person if possible, and order and pay online.

> **Jingle**
> An example of a bionic distribution platform is Jingle, an Austrian startup that launched in 2018 an app that uses augmented intelligence to simplify the buying experience. (eCommerce News, 2018). A chatbot provides the app to communicate with customers who are searching for a specific product or service. It shows all the available alternatives, listing prices and details, and the location of the different local stores. Then, the customer has three different options: buying the product online with home delivery,

going to the physical store, reserving the good online, and reclaiming it later in the shop.

B8ta
A Californian startup has developed another bionic solution for the shopping experience in 2018, which is called B8ta. B8ta can be considered a "retail store designed for discovery" (Howland, 2018). It offers businesses the service to place and show products in the store by paying a periodical fee. It is similar to a physical showroom or a marketplace that is not oriented to sell. B8ta does not sell products. It just displays them. The characteristic of this solution is that each store has consultants available for advising customers and giving further details about the product. Since consultants do not have to attract customers and convince them to buy, customers are more inclined to ask for information. Another success factor of B8ta is the use of High Definition (HD) cameras to monitor customers' expressions, tablets wherein it is possible to search prices, product descriptions, and chatbots for assistance. Thanks to these tools, B8ta can collect data about customers' behaviors and preferences, which are then sent to producers to understand customers' attitudes better.

There are descriptions of practical applications in the boxes with multiple-accesses exploitation strategy and the combination of the digital with the personal side. Because of this, they are the most recent expression of bionics applied to the way products and services are sold and delivered.

Partition of the Market

The analysis of the building blocks of the bionic business model requires the identification of customer segments. The success of an organization comes from acquiring new customers and from maximizing the lifetime value of already existing customers. Global markets, dematerialization of services, and high demand for tailored solutions have increased customers' volatility. This situation implies, at least, that organizations need to understand customers' socio-demographic, geographic information, and purchasing preferences to suit their needs better, keep customers delighted and loyal. At a later stage, from the information collected, the organization can partition the market into segments, that is, groups of customers, so that organizations can derive a more personalized approach to each group.

Customer segmentation divides customers into segments. Each segment has customers similar to each other. In this way, it is possible to leverage their standard features and shared characteristics to manage relationships with them better.

Customer segmentation is essential to decide the mix of humans or automation based on the segment's characteristics. Clear and well-described segments of customers can provide a financial institution, in particular, the marketing and sale departments, with the necessary information to execute activities such as to better:

- Design targeted marketing campaigns (that is, campaigns focused on specific groups of customers).
- Design specific products to address the needs of determined groups of customers.
- Select more appropriate communication accesses for different segments.
- Identify ways to improve products or service opportunities.
- Set up customer relationships.
- Quantify pricing elasticity and price tolerance.
- Focus on the most profitable customers.
- Improve customer service and dedicated personal assistance.
- Upsell and cross-sell products and services.

To segment, customers it is possible to use statistical, business analytics, and business intelligence techniques conjointly. The statistical tool necessary to segment customers is cluster analysis. Clustering is an optimization problem that consists of grouping data observation so that the instances belonging to the same group (cluster) are as similar as possible. When compared to the cases of the other groups, are as dissimilar as possible. Specifically, cluster analysis is a data-driven analytical technique part of data science AI algorithms into the sub-field of unsupervised machine learning.

The research in customer segmentation has led to the so-called engagement-based segmentation that divides customers into groups based on behavioral characteristics of customers' social participation in online communities, communication accesses, and e-commerce accesses. Rather than using surveys and direct questionnaires to customers to collect data about their company involvement, analysts have defined several Key Behavioral Indicators (KBI) (Trivedi et al., 2018).

For example, this analysis makes it possible to identify the customers who interact and participate the most in online communities and social accesses managed by a fintech organization. These individuals seem to be the most loyal to the brand as well. Engagement-based customer segmentation can help generate in-depth insights into how customers engage and use media touchpoints accesses individually. Therefore, this situation facilitates businesses in the decision-making process and in formulating strategies to increase customer retention, increase sales, and launch marketing campaigns.

Processes

Another building block of the Business Model Canvas helpful in conceptualizing a bionic financial organization's business model concerns the processes and the critical activities to be performed. A process is a series of activities to achieve a specific objective that ultimately contributes to creating value. The unit of work of a process is the activity, also called a task.

According to their core business, organizations execute different types of processes and activities. However, there are some essential processes common to every economic organization, such as those that regard marketing, R&D, and accounting activities. This analysis focuses on the characteristics of a bionic fintech organization's processes and activities.

To sum up, the processes of a bionic organization can have a moderate level of automation achieved by implementing robotic process automation software. Because of this, bionic operations involve both personal resources and robots, which collaborate in this reality in the sense that the one does not replace the other, but they work in a complementary way.

In addition to this, the processes of bionic organizations have resilience and agility, representing a competitive advantage for operating in today's markets marked by a high level of uncertainty and volatility.

> **Aflac**
> A Fortune 500 company, US-based Aflac protects more than 50 million people through subsidiaries in Japan and the United States (Capgemini Financial Services Analysis, 2021). Aflac offers supplemental insurance designed to work alongside typical health coverage by giving policyholders a financial buffer to offset an unplanned hospital stay, illness, or accident.
>
> Aflac leaders sought a modern, omniaccess solution to improve response times, automate processes, and simplify service across popular service accesses to enhance contact center operations. Aflac's contact center received thousands of emails each week with requests pointing to seven separate inboxes requiring manual classification and work assignment. The email volume was continuing to surge due to a rapidly shifting global pandemic.
>
> The organization's One Digital Aflac vision encapsulates a mission to transform and reinvent how it connects with customers, agents, and policyholders. Focusing on customer-centricity, Aflac leveraged AI-powered technology combined with its Pega Customer Service application to improve overall email productivity, contain more inquires, and resolve customer issues faster.
>
> Automation dramatically accelerated response time by immediately classifying and assigning contact center emails to cases while directly responding to straightforward inquiries that do not require agent interaction.
>
> Since implementation, Aflac automatically processes and responds to more than 30% of incoming inquiries without the need for human intervention. Automation quickly simplified service across Aflac's contact center while accelerating resolution time for customers. Aflac process successfully in this way more than 3000 emails each week, nearly a third via Straight Through Processing (STP). The remaining 70% of emails are handled quickly, thanks to AI-generated suggestions for agents. The new system bridged the gap between technology and business teams, eliminating lengthy manual processes for agents.

Platforms

To build the bionic business model, it is necessary to consider the BMC building block about the critical platforms for the organization. A platform is a group of technologies used as a base upon which to develop

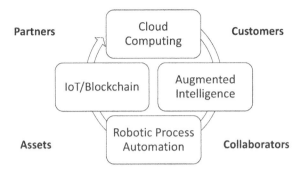

Fig. 4.5 Support from the platforms

other applications, processes, or technologies.[1] In this chapter, the term platform shows any information and communication system or automation support. In this sense, the support from the platforms has increased over time (Fig. 4.5).

An increasing number of financial institutions consider investing in automation as a priority, considering that the sector has lagged other industries in adopting digital technologies due to regulations, cultural resistances, and assets involved (Watson, 2017). Many traditional financial institutions upgrade their digital capabilities, improve customer engagement, and collect data to manage new and old risks. In some cases, financial institutions have increased spending on research and development to foster in-house innovation. In other cases, they have innovated thanks to external solutions and enterprises.

It is interesting to analyze the platforms relevant to bionic banking. This chapter examines the most pertinent of these platforms, one at a time to explore their uses in support of bionic banking (Lu, 2017). These platforms are classified, considering the model in Fig. 4.6.

The opportunity for financial institutions to use better platforms is significant. When appropriately used, these solutions can provide information and insights to support strategic decision-making, marketing, sale, and operational processes. They can help with the accurate tracking and reporting of revenues, costs, and risks. It is possible to automate many transactional tasks.

---

[1] adept-plm.com/glossary/platforms/. Accessed 16 October 2021.

	Automation	Output
Listen/Read	IoT/Sensors, Social & Open Data, Text & Images, Paper/Prints	Data processed by machines or humans
Memorize/Analyze	Blockchain, Big Data, Data Science, Data Analytics	Analysis, Reports
Lean/Predict	Machine Learning	Predictions
Understand/Reason/Recommend	Artificial Intelligence	Recommendations, and decisions
Interact/Train/Support.	Robotic Process Automation	Actions/Interactions

Fig. 4.6 Cognitive platforms

The digitization of banking processes has several benefits (Härting et al., 2019). The banking institutions can focus on their strategic tasks and better contribute to the organization's performance. There is an overall increase in organizational performance. Automation supports administrative tasks and complex decision-making processes. Automation is the basis for setting up new business models, services, and products. Digitizing banking processes comes with challenges from the current procedures and processes. Financial institutions must overcome these difficulties to fully use the improved characteristics of bionic banking as an asset (Bienhaus & Haddud, 2018).

The platforms are all operable in collaboration with humans (Akter et al., 2020). The most relevant ones regarding human–robot collaboration (HRC) are the following ones.

Augmented Intelligence
Augmented intelligence is a set of computing technologies that enable computers to have person-like intelligent capabilities. These capabilities can provide a rationale to make decisions based on the input information and context. This book refers to these technologies as Augmented Intelligence (AI) rather than artificial intelligence to stress that bionic banking relies on human-automation collaboration. The core competencies of AI in automation regard the ability to use a natural common language, recover data from databases, find patterns in data of all types, solve

and apply mathematical theories, and perform diagnosis and predictive analyses.

Some practical applications of AI are chatbot accesses that can mimic human language for dedicated customer service or the use of Machine Learning (ML) techniques to predict customers' churn.

Alerting and preventing fraud with AI is an early step for businesses moving to digital transformation and AI tools. Among its potential benefits, AI can (Jarrell, 2021):

- Put new and innovative technologies to work in creating better customer experiences.
- Detect suspicious behavior that resembles instances of fraud detected in the past.
- Identify potential fraud red-flag anomalies in large datasets that merit human research.
- Help stem the financial losses suffered by US companies to fraud each year.

Many scholars believe that AI has the potential to make organizations gain a competitive advantage. Only a few organizations have implemented AI systems because of the underlying data infrastructure and talents required. AI requires that the organization collect, store, and process vast amounts of data, massive data.

Other scholars have considered that a partnership between AI and humans could help overcome the limits and weaknesses of each other in decision-making (Brynjolfsson & McAfee, 2014; Dejoux & Léon, 2018; Jarrahi, 2018). In decision-making between humans and AI, Dejoux et al. explained that the first step consists of explaining the problem to AI. Then, AI analyzes a consistent amount of data present in the system thanks to algorithms (Dejoux & Léon, 2018). Starting from this analysis, AI proposes different patterns to humans. Two options emerge: AI chooses the pattern and automates the solution by itself, or humans choose one pattern according to their values and objectives (Dejoux & Léon, 2018). To sum up our part about the role of AI and humans in decision-making processes, there is a continuum describing the decision-making process and the related decision-maker in Fig. 4.7. Intuition and rationality are the furthest parts of the continuum. We have coupled those two indicators with the three types of combinations of decision-makers

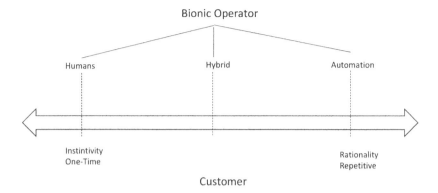

Fig. 4.7 A continuum of the bionic approach

that we have described, humans only, the relationship between humans and AI, and autonomous AI (Claudé & Combe, 2018).

An exciting development of Augmented Intelligence is the generative artificial intelligence (van der Zant et al., 2013). It expands the AI toolkit from classification, optimization, and prediction to the generation of high-value artifacts (for instance, words, images, designs, and code) Top Strategic Technology (Mullen et al., 2021). Generative AI is not yet a creative panacea, but it will enable financial institutions to accelerate the bionic transformation and further reallocate human resources to support higher-value creative jobs.

FCA

The Financial Conduct Authority (FCA) in the U.K. worked with Synthesized to generate an alternative dataset representative of the original, but that cannot be linked back to the original. This means it is not vulnerable to linkage attacks and is safe for. The result is a safe-to-share synthetic dataset that will allow participants of the Digital Sandbox Pilot to analyze fraudulent digital banking transactions and apply this knowledge to better detect fraudulent activity in their own environments. It also helped develop innovative solutions to detect and prevent fraud and scams exacerbated by the pandemic.

Machine Learning

Machine learning (ML) is an application of AI. It allows software applications to learn from experience without being explicitly programmed. It is helpful, for example, in predictive analysis (Choi et al., 2020). Machine learned applications are not programmed. They are trained, similarly to what happens in humans. This solution's basic principle is to build algorithms that can access data, find patterns, and use advanced statistical tools to predict the results and help make decisions in several areas.

Machine learning enables computer programs to automatically improve their performance at some tasks through experience (Pham & Afify, 2005). This solution connects with pattern recognition and statistical inference. Research on machine learning has focused on classification, developing a model from previously classified examples that correctly categorizes new cases from a similar population. Many banking problems fall under this category. Banking professionals need to assign a class label to an object, or a situation based on the specific values of a set of parameters so that the machine can learn. A typical example is credit scoring.

It is possible to train machine learning with data which allows an extensive statistical model to guess solutions to particular problems. This method requires substantial amounts of correct data and massive computing power to invert the matrices needed to "train" the computer model. With this new way of "programming" computers, virtual robots can perform and collaborate with humans in many new mental tasks, like visual recognition, handwriting recognition, or language translation.

Many of the new mental capacities gained by computers are helpful in office and service jobs. Many new service-sector tasks are more automatable now than previously, which is one reason machine learning is more than simply better ICT.

Financial institutions have begun exploring and using ML in many ways to serve their customers better and meet increasingly demanding regulatory requirements (Wall, 2018). Programs like intelligent business analytics show that machine learning can enable financial institutions to improve their decision-making power and improve efficiency (Injadat et al., 2021). The machine learning methods can also develop cybersecurity systems to keep the data storage and process secure for financial institutions.

The main areas in which ML can help in financial services are:

- Credit risk.

- Strategies for investing and order execution.
- Anti-money laundering.
- Know your customer.
- Cyber-security.

ML is coming to play an increasingly significant role in financial services. The global AI fintech **market** is predicted to reach $22.6B in 2025 (Columbus, 2020).

Cloud Computing
Cloud computing provides access to on-demand resources and ICT infrastructures such as computing power, databases, applications, software, and servers (Nicoletti, 2013). Cloud computing originated from information technology virtualization and standardization practices. The main characteristic of cloud services is the scalability, the broad network access, and the distribution of resources. Scalability provides the opportunity to reduce or increase the width of services and the computing power requested through a simple subscription with the cloud provider. It is possible to easily access the information and application stored in the cloud from every physical location and automation application using the customer cloud permission credentials. Moreover, the cloud provides a centralized environment in a distributed infrastructure since organizations can store their information on a unique system.

In bionic banking, cloud computing assures the possibility to connect humans and automation, especially robots, in their collaborative work.

Three main categories of cloud services according to the level of computing power and infrastructure required. They are Software-as-a-Service (SaaS), Platform-as-a-Service (PaaS), and Infrastructure-as-a-Service (IaaS).

- SaaS involves the use of a software application installed in the cloud. Charges are typically through a pay-as-you-go model or on-demand
- PaaS is a platform for developing software on the cloud without building and maintaining the infrastructure and environment that such development processes typically require.
- Infrastructure-as-a-service involves a method for delivering everything from operating systems to servers and data storage as part of an on-demand service.

The massive benefit of cloud technology is that it does not require onsite any underlying owned infrastructure such as servers or operating systems. The cloud provider owns and provides every resource and is also responsible for the maintenance and update of the system. Moreover, cloud technology enables a significant level of business agility since it is a scalable technology easy to integrate with the already existing digital tools.

Data Science
Data science concerns autonomous or semi-autonomous data management using sophisticated business intelligence techniques and tools (Sarker, 2021). Data science allows discovering insights, making predictions, or generating recommendations meaningful for creating business value and gaining competitive advantage. Data science helps process big data, high volume, velocity, and variety of data from different sources.

Advanced analytics combined with big data can extract value-added insights that ultimately support making decisions more efficient, accurate, and faster.

The prominence of data science within organizations has given rise to teams of data science operators collaborating on extracting insights from data instead of individual data scientists working alone. Data science teams are highly collaborative and work with various stakeholders and tools during the six common steps of a data science workflow (a reference-model data science workflow begins with creating a measurement plan, moves through technical stages to an eventual delivering stage of analysis or model or working system. Some organizations also check for bias and/or discrimination during technological development) (Zhang et al., 2020).

Data and Analytics (D&A) leaders in charge of D&A strategies need to become competent data-driven decision-makers. This situation means that they need to combine the right amount of data and analytics with knowledge (knowing how to do the job), soft skills (ability to do it), and the right mindset (wanting to do it).

D&A leaders often mention culture as the no. 1 critical activity to the D&A team's success. There is a need for data-driven persons to work together toward a shared set of goals and objectives. Establishing a data-driven culture is all about people skills.

Robotic Process Automation (RPA)
Robotic Process Automation (RPA) is a business and technology practice that seeks to automate "robotic" tasks. RPA is essentially based on virtual robots. IEEE defines RPA as "a preconfigured software instance that uses business rules and predefined activity choreography to complete the autonomous execution of a combination of processes, activities, transactions, and tasks in one or more unrelated software systems to deliver a result or service with human exception management" (Hofmann et al., 2020; Van der Aalst et al., 2018).

In 1994, the Fraunhofer Institute for Manufacturing Engineering and Automation (Fraunhofer IPA) phrased the following definition of virtual robots, which is still valid today "A service robot is a freely programmable mobile device carrying out services either partially or fully automatically. Services are activities that do not contribute to the direct industrial manufacture of goods, but the performance of services for humans and institutions" (Schraft et al., 2004).

An RPA initiative configures and manages virtual robots that act as synthetic ICT application users, automating highly repeatable, highly structured, high volume clerical tasks that involve the use of existing ICT applications (Ward-Dutton, 2018). RPA solutions provide a non-invasive alternative to coding automated task logic for simple processes in a new application or service. RPA solutions create and use specialized integration APIs or integrate the new code with existing systems by other means (hooking into underlying databases via triggers, hooking into application code directly, or simply screen-scraping from existing application front ends).

There are two common ways to deliver the core technology in RPA (Leno et al., 2021):

- In attended RPA, the robots that automate interactions with customers' desktop applications execute within each customer's desktop environment itself, working side-by-side with each customer. Robots are used as automated assistants, carrying out often repeated but standalone clerical tasks on the customer's behalf, with significantly faster speed and fewer errors. It is also referred to as robotic desktop automation (RDA) (Quanton, 2018). Attended automation is mainly for processes that cannot be automated end-to-end. Research indicates that this type of automation improves operators' work by focusing on the customer or task requiring decision-making instead of being tied up in manual and time-consuming tasks but requiring no human intervention for specific process steps (Nott, 2018). It is a collaboration of automation and humans: "Humans collaborating with robots can get more done, faster, and with fewer errors. Their robots can do the dull, tedious tasks so operators can focus on the work they love." Automating parts of the process allows the processes, operators, and therefore the organization to be more efficient.

- In unattended RPA robots also automate customers' desktop applications but execute on a separate server or virtual machine (or multiple servers), automating interactions with applications "behind the scenes" and carrying out their work when triggered by other software systems. Here, robots work in a lights-out mode, working without any direct input or direction from customers. Unattended automation refers to end-to-end process automation without any human intervention or prompts to launch a bot (Hızıroğlu, 2021). The bots are invoked on a schedule or on-demand and achieve straight-through processing (DMG Consulting, 2019). Unattended automation is possible for repetitive and stable transactions that consume time but do not require decision-making, such as bulk reporting (Hızıroğlu, 2021). Attended and unattended automation are not mutually exclusive. They can work in tandem, which is hybrid automation (Leibowitz, 2018).

Another classification of RPA software is based on their use within an organization and consists of:

- Rule-based, knowledge-based, and learning-based virtual robots can learn predefined rules. They can execute repeated activities in situations characterized by a low degree of variability.
- Knowledge-based RPA can acquire information and collect and transfer data.
- Learning-based software can correlate data. For this reason, they are considered "smarter." To provide virtual robots with data-driven intelligence, RPA combines with AI techniques, particularly machine learning abilities, to check for deviations and predict problems.

RPAs are not to fully substitute operators either to automate businesses completely. RPAs are a kind of trade-off solution. For what concerns the implementation of RPA, an organization needs to assess its "as-is" situation pertaining to available capacity and resources, operating processes organization, and strategic management objectives. In introducing virtual robots, it is fundamental to consider that RPA affects different business units and departments. For this reason, the automation process requires a redesign with the collaboration of several resources and profiles not only limited to ICT specialists.

Governance is an essential aspect of the use of RPA. It is necessary to pay special attention to the operations team (Hızıroğlu, 2021; Kedziora & Penttinen, 2021). The operations team is composed of controllers who focus on maintaining the production-stage robots (Kedziora & Penttinen, 2021). The support work entails monitoring the software, handling the associated scheduling, and performing simpler bug-fixing. Another important role of members of the operations team is providing after-care assistance associated with stakeholder management. This role is essential, as these members are the primary contact point for the banking units concerning day-to-day operations and must keep in touch with the individual units well. Appropriate, extensive RPA testing by the operations team ensures that the robots can detect errors, learn from mistakes, and improve output accuracy (Kedziora & Penttinen, 2021). Solid testing infrastructure in conjunction with solid RPA software support makes continuous monitoring more straightforward. Attention can be directed instead to detecting, correcting, and preventing any RPA irregularities that might arise after system changes (Kedziora & Penttinen, 2021). The operations team ensures high-quality robot code and high predictability levels, supporting and controlling the robot evolution process. These mechanisms can protect against the robots' failure and deterioration.

In addition, the interplay between RPA agents and humans is fascinating. When a case turns out to be exceptional, the RPA agent may hand over the case to a human. By observing the human handling complex cases, the RPA system can learn (Aalst et al., 2018).

RPA interacts with persons in three different types of activities:

- Routine tasks which are those repetitive activities such as calculations and conversions.

- Abstract tasks which are that involve professional and intelligent competencies such as problem-solving, decision-making, and communication skills.
- Manual tasks are mainly practical job activities that require adaptability, assessing the environmental conditions and implications.

RPA aims to optimize routine tasks while the performance on the remaining categories of activities is not better. As a result, automation can replace for what concerns the execution of technical and low-reasoning works. Persons are involved in activities that require intellectual abilities and can aspire to job positions such as managers, engineers, data scientists, analysts, and auditors. Persons are pivotal resources in processes that involve creativity, such as product design and imagination, or coordination, such as planning.

RPA and Banking
The combination of RPA and Augmented Intelligence (AI) is called CRPA (Cognitive Robotic Process Automation) or IPA (Intelligent Process Automation). It has led to the next generation of RPA bots (Villar & Khan, 2021). It can transform the banking industry by making the core financial operations exponentially more efficient and allowing financial institutions to tailor services to customers while at the same time improving safety and security. Intelligent automation is enabling financial institutions to redefine how they work. It has also raised challenges regarding protecting customer interests and the financial system's stability. Deutsche Bank successfully automated Adverse Media Screening (AMS), accelerating compliance, increasing negative media search coverage, and drastically reducing false positives.

Advanced RPA, with built-in Optical Character Recognition (OCR) and data analytics capabilities, can extract unstructured data from scanned or email documentation, analyze it and present it in a structured and fully digitized format to a virtual attendant. The virtual attendant can then alert a human operator about the new customer and inform the operator on how best to communicate with that customer going forward. The system also alerts operators to discrepancies between data on the forms and the customer's ID documentation, improving compliance.

Automation refers to the use of RPA in processes previously performed manually. Virtual robots are generally appreciated for their core capabilities in dealing with data, integrating systems, and enhancing processes.

RPA can transfer data, such as uploading files and encrypting files regarding their ability to process data. Virtual robots can analyze data and convert data from one format to another, such as optical character recognition activities.

Benefits of RPA
The effects of RPA implementation are several, generalizing Mendling et al. (2018):

- Standardization thanks to the ability of RPA to perform transactions in a very consistent way. RPA software can integrate different data structures, applications, and solutions of diverse natures. For example, robots interact within the organization's information and communication technology (ICT) ecosystem, with interfaces developed for persons and automation. RPA systems do not change the underlying information systems architecture since they are a "lightweight technology" (Mendling et al., 2018).
- Informational concerns the acquisition of analytical insights through monitoring and controlling executed by virtual robots.
- Transformational at a business process management level if necessary to reorganize and reengineer processes after implementing RPA. Concerning process enhancements, the main functionalities of virtual robots are controlling flows of operations and detecting events such as changes of data in files.

RPA adoption leads to productivity enhancement at an organizational level since it is believed that improvements in reliability, speed, or costs of a given task or process impact the overall business performance. The primary foundation for RPA's ability to increase productivity is Kremer (1993) developed the O-ring model. According to him, a failure in one of the phases of the operational process causes the entire production to fail.

RPA software provides great accuracy from an ethical perspective since, for example, these programs allow to make business operations fair and not influenced by corruption. In some other scenarios, RPA can predict future scenarios, such as plant and machinery malfunctioning, and their functionalities represent and benefit what concerns protecting operators from risky events.

The RPA market will continue to grow. More organizations will adopt RPA to get the benefits of automation and RPA as an effective solution to the cumbersome existing processes (Hızıroğlu, 2021). There will also be better integration of RPA with other systems and other advanced solutions that current RPA technology does not cover. Technology will transform the workforce: "As an efficient collaboration between digital workers and human talent becomes vital, digital workforce management and governance will become increasingly prevalent... We will see new crossover between the chief human resources officer and chief information officer roles" (Casey, 2019).

> **MetLife**
> MetLife Investment Management Customer Services Group (MIM) is a significant investment management firm operating in the UK financial services industry. Its customer services group (CSG) has invested in RPA. The implementation was full of best practices in RPA implementation and for the researcher to adopt a unique model that incorporates Benefits, Limitations, Challenges, and best Practice (BLCP) framework specific to CSG through a field survey, including a series of interviews and a case study.
>
> The empirical part of this qualitative research took three years. A researcher examined RPA implementation elements through a systematic literature review and semi-structured interviews involving critical members involved in RPA implementation within the investment management organization and RPA experts worldwide. In this study, the researcher was employed in an institutional investment management company's customer service group (MIM CSG). This group provided the researcher a platform to find out the potential uses of RPA in the CSG processes. The objective was to determine if RPA is a viable automation solution aligned with the digital transformation strategy of her employer.
>
> This research proved that RPA is the right automation tool for MIM CSG, fully aligned with the overall digital transformation journey of MIM. The BLCP framework is a versatile tool and can establish a comprehensive best practice framework in digital transformation journeys. The rough ROI evaluated at MetLife was a sizable 41%.

Persons

Automation is the easy part of a successful digital transformation. People are the difficult part of becoming bionic. Concerning the personal and intellectual resources essential for bionic banking, it is necessary to study them conjointly since intellectual resources are proper of persons.

An essential component is a human side in an organization based on the interdependence of automation and humans. The transformation should be from processes operated by humans and supported by automation to human-designed and supervised processes executed by automation. Human capabilities symbolize a crucial requirement to ideate, audit, innovate, and complement operations (Ghazy & Fedorova, 2021).

One of the main criticisms of bionic transition is that automation could create potential job losses in executing the business's core operations.

On the one hand, it is possible to agree with this comment. New automation solutions can be a source of disruption, as they can transform the customer experience and the core activities of a business and innovate the business model.

On the other hand, there is a shift in how these organizations use human capabilities. This situation is due to the introduction of new roles and positions in the critical functions of a banking organization. For example, none but humans have the intelligence and the competencies to decide where and how to use automation. Profiles such as machine learning engineers, data scientists, and project managers who own technical, design, and digital skills are increasingly necessary (Nicoletti). The leading solution financial institutions must implement for preventing mass replacement is retraining employed people by acquiring further professional expertise, e-competencies, and new working attitudes such as cooperation, responsiveness, and flexibility.

Research indicates that production and employment should include at least partially persons (Corvalàn, 2019; Susar & Aquaro, 2019). Even with the most pessimistic estimation, the human factor will play a large part in short- and medium-term employment. Considering the current technologies today, only a tiny part of the jobs, such as 5%, can be completely automated. Only half of the various activities in the current jobs can be automated (Manyika et al., 2017). New technologies usually replace specific tasks rather than eliminate jobs and often create new products, new markets, and new jobs and increase operators' productivity (Bruckner et al., 2017).

Participants in a research project agreed that challenges related to roles between operators and robotic or automated tools followed a master-servant model (Issantu, 2021). From respondents' stories, the master-servant model could be exploded into four possibilities: master-tool, master-collaborator, human follower, and robot commander-human servant. Of the four dominant roles perceived through the collected data, participants judged two favorably (robot as a tool or a collaborator), mitigated with one (human as a follower), and generally rejected the one with the robot as a commander.

Kopeć et al. (2018) claim that one of the most prominent possibilities in Industry 4.0 is the combination of RPA to the lean and digitize principles (Nicoletti, 2012). Their "human-centered" method proposal involved designing virtual robotics accompanied by interactive and collaborative AI solutions, including machine learning and neural networks. This model replaces repetitive and manual tasks with high-skilled jobs, increasing their meaningfulness and lowering costs, such as automatic tests, code deployment, and customer service (Kopeć et al., 2018).

Specific skills and competencies for digital transformation show a gap between available skills and required skills. Reskilling the existing workforce might be challenging (Schlegel & Kraus, 2021). Many new positions can be found in the consulting sector, which raises questions about the permanent versus temporary nature of the requirements and the difficulty of acquiring the required knowledge.

The implementation process of this bionic approach can consist of the following stages (Kopeć et al., 2018):

1. Analysis of automation penetration and potential within the organization.
2. Workshops with operators to identify opportunity areas.
3. Living Lab approach to process analysis with data-collection workstations.
4. Participatory design of specific virtual robots.
5. Supervised Training of AI-based solutions.
6. Operator empowerment training sessions.
7. Co-programming and co-maintenance of virtual robots in RPA and retraining and updating of AI.

It is also necessary to change the overall structure for the organizational dimension of a banking organization in the bionic transformation. In most cases, organizations are composed of well-structured business units that have defined tasks and objectives. Each unit has its executive function that collaborates at a higher level with the organization's management. In a bionic organization, different functions need to communicate to distribute data, use the same technologies and share human talents. The configuration that emerges inside these innovative organizations is a dynamic structure such as a network-centric entity composed of self-managing and organizing teams characterized by leaders, which could also be informal (Kopeć et al., 2018). This decentralization model facilitates the flow of information and makes the whole fintech organization more flexible and adaptive to external changes.

Automation may require better social reskilling. There is an automation of the modular, predictable, and routine. The human work is the opposite; it is dynamic, unpredictable, and more inherently human (De Smet et al., 2021). This work requires social and emotional skills, elevated human judgment, creativity, spontaneity, and innovation. It tends to be purpose-driven and anchored in human interactions. In other words, the most critical and value-adding work for people to perform in future will be dynamic, team-based, complex, and cross-functional (Kopeć et al., 2018).

The workforce of bionic banking must have good digital skills. In case of a lack of knowledge about digital tools, ICT, and OT, organizations need to train their workforce for collaborating with automation.

Some activities require both the human component and the software leading to the co-existence in the workplace. For example, the software executes machine learning analyses for sales forecasting because they involve sophisticated algorithms and a significant amount of computing power. The software needs to be "fed" with input data. In this case, humans are responsible for collecting and selecting the most meaningful and valuable information and inserting them into machine learning applications. Ultimately, personal judgment and interventions are pivotal to transform a machine learning engine's outcome into actual decisions. In this example, persons and robots cannot carry out the activity independently but rely on collaboration and interdependence.

The main criticism related to the adoption of automation concerns the so-called polarization of job positions. RPA implementation aimed to relieve persons from technical and repetitive tasks. On the one hand, leads to an increase in demand for high-wage and high-education jobs such as data business analysts. On the other hand, automation leads to the request for low-wages and low-education jobs such as data preparation or cleansing. In response to this objection, it is possible to state that it is necessary to carefully redesign operators' roles because of the changing organization and responsibilities within an organization. In these realities, people need to work jointly with automation, aware that automation is only a support tool and perceiving them as collaborators rather than threats. To this extent, the human–robot collaboration strategy should provide operators with training to acquire the digital skills necessary to work with virtual robots.

Operators can focus on high-value tasks involving human judgment automation (Fallis & Fuchs, 2019). For example, the virtual attendant may detect a process error or exception and prompt the operator to validate the relevant data in real-time. The role of people inevitably shifts, and changes as financial institutions go bionic. In a tech company, human expertise is not within specific activities silos. Financial institutions need to create a broader functional model such as that everyone thinks in terms of constant overall enhancement. In today's typical bank, day-to-day operations take up to 90%, with only the remaining 10% devoted to change and innovation. In future, the balance will become likely: 40% of operators run standardized processes, 20% manage the exceptions to standardized processes, and 40% are dedicated to change and continuous innovation (Erlebach et al., 2020).

On human-automation collaboration, a Deloitte study about global person capital trends (2020) suggests introducing Superteams. They are cross-functional workgroups composed of persons and AI-powered robots. Virtual AI-based assistants that understand natural language voice commands and complete tasks for the customer, such as sending emails or performing phone calls, can support operators. On more complex tasks, AI tools can be used, for example, by workgroups in checking for errors in the complex analysis performed by persons.

Miles Everson and John Sviokla (2018) stated that bionic organizations should invest more in the way persons and automation work together and the consequent "behavioral capital." The definition of behavioral capital is the information resulting from monitoring aggregate behavior of people and automation. They can be a source of improvement for the value of their respective activities.

It is possible to use a Virtual Reality (VR) headset to train the operators and familiarizing them with automation and its technologies

(Fåland et al., 2020). Operators can also familiarize themselves with digital libraries and apps to perform essential tasks on the field.

An online version of the training program introducing operators to new ways of working and relevant emerging technologies can be made available organization wide. Digital learning sessions about automation and new ways of working should be hosted regularly by the organizations, showing the relevance of this topic to senior management and the organization's objectives. They are motivating operators across the organization to adopt a digital mindset.

Soft skills for the persons help in decision-making. They are not enough. Humans also need knowledge based primarily on experience. Operators have learned how to be a decision-maker. They also need the right mindset (they want to do it). Organizations need to set principles (why to behave) and create habits (how to behave) to reinforce those principles. The combination of skills, knowledge, and mindset is competency. Establishing a data-driven culture is, essentially, about establishing competent decision-makers.

Bionic banking needs data. Providing operators only with more data and analytics tools is not always a successful strategy. It can lead to information overload. Information overload is not just a problem of too much information; it is also a common problem (Bawden & Robinson, 2020). The human system, the brain, often fails to process data in the right way. It is necessary to combine the correct data with competent decision-makers to establish a data-driven culture.

ANZ Bank

ANZ Bank is one of the growing number of organizations deploying digital assistants to deal with common customer queries (Paredes, 2018). Google AI, used by ANZ's new digital assistant Jamie, or IBM Watson, provides expertise in the natural language process digital humans' use, combining emotional intelligence and AI. ANZ developed Jamie using Soul Machines' Human Computing Engine (HCE). HCE is a virtual nervous system modeled on how the human brain and nervous system work. It supports Jamie to express humanly personality and character.

Jamie can answer 30 of the most frequently searched-for topics on the Help section. Around 90% of customers who have spoken to Jamie think it is suitable for ANZ to introduce the technology. Creative aspects of work tend to produce eustress (as opposed to distress). Eustress is a stress response resulting from positive emotions such as a sense of accomplishment or empowerment. AI takes the monotony out of work, as a consequence operators can employ latent skills by shifting focus to more creative, non-routine aspects.

Gartner predicts that through 2022, organizations that use augmented intelligence tools, such as digital assistants, as an essential element in their digital workplace will increase their Net Promoter Score by 20% (Bova, 2018). During that time, AI will support one in five operators engaged chiefly in non-routine tasks. All jobs will have both non-routine and routine work. Organizations should plan to augment and not completely replace traditional human-facing accesses for support functions to avoid harmful customer delight.

The Gartner report also cautions organizations to avoid eliminating humans on the work floor. Depending on the nature of the change, the AI model may be slow or unable to react to fundamental assumptions applied when trained (Paredes, 2018). There could be much damage before noticing that the human-automation collaboration is disconnected. Persons should own the final responsibility to handle anomalies and exceptions and anticipate their occurrence based on factors different from traditional models. The Gartner report recommends that application leaders responsible for the digital workplace scale business processes but rely on deep domain expertise to improve automation quality.

Partners

Fintech organizations operate in markets and industries wherein a large variety of actors such as vendors, customers, competitors, regulators, and investors, and now more and more robots, have the potential to impact how value is created and delivered. When developing the bionic business model, it is essential to evaluate how the organization interacts with external actors and with whom. It is also necessary to understand the reasons why bionic financial organizations operate with partners.

Many economic organizations establish relationships with other parties to overcome the lack of expertise, knowledge, or specific resources. For example, an investor can bring the financial resources necessary to be sustainable and grow into the organization.

Collaborating with partners is a way for the organization to become more flexible and eliminate some constraints. Customers involved in the product/service ideation process allow businesses to adapt to market demands and exploit new opportunities.

However, according to BGC's study entitled "The new logic of competition," the way business interacts with other parties is changing due to new market forces and economic trends (Kimura et al., 2019). The main factors that, according to the authors, are modifying the types of relationships organizations build are the following:

- More complex and dynamic competition.
- Blurring industries boundaries.
- Decrease in product and fintech organization lifetime.
- Technological progress and disruption.
- High economic and political uncertainty.
- Manage a more competitive scenario.

In this complex context, organizations can remain sustainable by building collaborative networks with stakeholders. As a result, new market architectures that extend the boundaries of an organization are emerging—ecosystems (Fenwick & Vermeulen, 2020). In generating ecosystems, economic organizations distribute their activities, assigning them to a large group of organizations-collaborators belonging to different industries and/or specialized in diverse core operations, to be sure to meet volatile market demand and rapidly adapt.

These architectures significantly increase business potential since they grant access to an exponential amount of data from different sources. They enable rapid experimentation for innovation, and they create connections to reach a broad range of partners and customers. Organizations that manage the ecosystem are called orchestrators. Not all organizations have the capabilities to become orchestrators. The success factors for creating networks concern the alignment between orchestrator and partners' culture, partners' complementarity concerning the resources provided, and the organization requirements and partners' commitment in the ecosystem based on trust and reliability toward the orchestrator. The organizations incapable of orchestrating can also be a relevant part of the ecosystem to gain visibility, accessibility to resources, and being less threatened by competition.

It is possible to conclude that the winning strategy for bionic organizations is to build or join ecosystems. This strategy involves giving up the traditional practices of business such as cost-leadership and economies of scale, determining the role to play, and being aware that value is created for the whole ecosystem and not only for one organization.

> **Zurich Insurance Group**
> More than three thousand multi-tied agents work with the Zurich Insurance Group to offer policies to Portugal's individuals and small-to-medium enterprise customers. The insurer created an omniaccess platform for agents (Capgemini Financial Services Analysis, 2021); the goal was to roll out a system that enabled integrated management of agent portfolios and swift response to agent needs. Zurich aimed to quickly get the new platform up and running to streamline the sales process and increase agent productivity.
>
> The platform included a comprehensive omniaccess agent experience, beginning with a dedicated online portal available on PCs, tablets, and smartphones that would be simple for agents to use while handling all other aspects of their business. Leveraging the agile method, the implementation team powered up the application called MyZurich within four months. MyZurich allows a person to quickly monitor and act on his/her risk management information, in all locations, in real-time.
>
> A principal function is the AI-driven smart-leads generation tool that enables agents to cross-sell proactively and contact potential customers at the right time with the right proposition.
>
> Agents can access MyZurich functions via the web, mobile phone, or tablet.
>
> - Biometric login.
> - Mobile notifications on the fly for referral processes.
> - First notification of loss.
> - Management dashboard, portfolio view.
> - Quote generator, policy issuance.
> - A 360-degree view of customers, policies, claims, and receipts.
> - 20 non-life quoting tools.
> - Mid-term policy adjustments.
> - Ability to edit customer data.
> - Receipt collection.
> - Electronic signature.
>
> Within the first two months of launch, 80% of the Zurich distribution team had used MyZurich. The engagement between Zurich Portugal and agents is fast, straightforward, and flexible. Agents using MyZurich

> generate around 4500 quotes each day and issue about 1000 policies. A dedicated MyZurich team will continue innovating customer-friendly solutions that can meet unexpected challenges with agility to keep Zurich Portugal on the leading edge of insurance distribution.

Pricing and Revenues

A fundamental component of a business model deals with the earnings and revenues an economic organization can collect from the value delivered to the customers. The set of various sources of revenues for a business is called revenue streams. They typically depend on the different activities performed by the organization. The sale of assets, products, services, subscription or use fees, advertising, renting, and leasing generated revenues.

An essential activity in revenues management concerns selecting new pricing models, especially in the case of credit. In particular, it leads to the shift from static pricing to the so-called dynamic pricing model. Static pricing consists in applying a margin to the unitary costs spent when offering services. Static prices are standardized and, consequently, equal for each customer. Dynamic pricing involves analyzing and studying market conditions, customer preferences concerning each segment, and competitors' offerings. Based on these factors, prices are constantly updated and calibrated according to customers willing to buy services and pay for them. Financial institutions with a large audience of customers, characterized by differing preferences, distribution accesses, and payment modalities, typically need a flexible price structure that repeatedly changes.

AI-based software is beneficial to analyze inputs about customers' transactions history and behaviors to generate dedicated price alternatives in advance. The dynamic pricing model is also related to two different pricing approaches: personalization and Customer Lifetime Value (CLV) maximization.

- Personalization. Fintech organizations that offer a customized value proposition such as personalized products or dedicated

customer experiences use specific pricing strategies. Personalization is setting a special price and is mainly about creating unique content and providing added value propositions. According to BCG research about new revenue management, travel and tourism service providers increased revenues from 6 to 10% using calibrated prices (Beckett et al., 2020). This situation is due to an increase in customers' satisfaction since the service successfully met their request. There was also an increase in the conversion rate from intent to buy to a completed transaction.
- CLV maximization strategy. Customer lifetime value is the total amount of money a customer is expected to spend on services during their fintech organization's lifetime (Kumar & Rajan, 2020; Earle et al., 2015). It is more profitable to satisfy existing customers and boost them to repeatedly purchase rather than acquire new customers who perform a one-time buy. Incentivizing frequent acquisition through targeted promotions and commercial offers or offering "packages" of products is a way to effectively contribute to the long-term relationship between customers and the organization.

The combination of advanced technology and a high amount of data available to bionic organizations is a success factor in implementing effective credit scoring and a dynamic pricing structure.

Payments and Investments

Costs, similarly, to revenues, vary from business to business since they are related to the core operations executed by each organization. The cost structure is the set of expenses an organization incurs. It is typically composed of fixed and variable costs. Fixed costs are costs sustained that do not vary over time, while variable costs generally fluctuate according to production output. Since this book aims to identify a standard business model disregarding the core business of each organization, it is not possible to list or quantify the costs typical of each organization. However, it is possible to distinguish economic organizations in broad terms based on the costs sustained. According to each business' approach to costs, an organization can be cost-driven or value-driven (Nicoletti, 2021a).

- Cost-driven. A cost-driven business focuses on costs minimization. In making decisions, these organizations take into account mainly costs and usually select the alternative that allows to reduce them. In doing so, they tend to maximize the profit margins. Delivering low-value value propositions at a reduced price generally characterizes these organizations. Their operations present a high level of automation since it allows them to be more efficient in production and cut workforce costs or even outsource some processes.
- Value-driven. Value-driven businesses are not inclined to control costs but focus on delivering the highest value possible to customers. These organizations usually provide customized value prepositions tailored based on the preferences of each customer. Because of this, they put great effort into the product ideation and design phase and offer dedicated customer services. Their efforts aim to create a superior customer experience, and the final output is generally an expensive service.

The two cost structures can have two harsh realities. Bionic organizations, for example, present some characteristics peculiar to a cost-driven organization, such as the adoption of automation and a value-driven structure for what concerns the attention devoted to customers' delight.

Nevertheless, because of the recurring issues that threaten business continuity, such as economic recession, market volatility, governmental crises, it has been generally agreed on the necessity for businesses to "do more with less." (Close, 2020). This context pushes economic realities to reduce the number of financial resources spent while simultaneously maximizing value. To do so, bionic organizations should review and focus their investment portfolios on opportunities that generate outcomes in the short term. These short-term projects aim to enhance the organization's digital capabilities that represent a source of cash flows. For example, a typical investment portfolio for a bionic organization comprises a small number of projects with strategic benefits opportunities, such as dynamic pricing systems or bionic distribution accesses implementation.

Concerning long-term-oriented projects already in progress during the transition toward bionic, it is critical to evaluate whether they remain in line with the vision and mission of the organization. If not, but the opportunity generates relevant value, it is necessary to accelerate their completion to obtain value in the shortest time possible and reduce investments costs. Contrarily, if the projects are not consistent with the new vision and mission statement and do not originate significant value, there are no reasons to continue them. As a result, bionic organizations need to prioritize investment projects based on the time horizon they deliver the expected return according to a strategic vision.

Protection

Cyber-Security

Cyber-security describes the collection of tools, policies, guidelines, risk management approaches, actions, training, best practices, assurance, and technologies to protect the availability, integrity, privacy, and confidentiality of assets and persons in the connected infrastructures. The cyber-security tools apply to government, private organizations, and citizens. These assets include connected computing devices, personnel, infrastructure, applications, services, telecommunications systems, and data in the cyber-environment (Vybornov et al., 2020).

Interpol confirmed that cyber-attacks during the pandemic emergency increased substantially. Since organizations and businesses shift to remote systems and networks with staff working from home, criminals are taking advantage of security vulnerabilities to steal data, generate profits, and cause malfunctioning (Interpol, 2020). Security vulnerabilities are related to the employment of innovative solutions that increase the need to share sensitive data through operators' interactions across a mobile workplace. This situation happens due to the continuous increasing levels of data collected and used that needs protection.

Cyber-attacks that exploit these vulnerabilities are attacks launched from one or more computers against other robots, devices, information systems, or networks performed mainly by terrorists, criminals, hacktivists, nation-state actors, and hobbyists. The goal of these attacks may be either to disable the target automation or system or where to get access to specific data.

The following types of cyber-attacks increased during the pandemic (Lohrmann, 2020):

- Malware stands for malicious software. It is a term used to refer to harmful or intrusive software downloaded from a computer, which can do anything from stealing data to encrypting files. A common type of malware is ransomware, which involves hackers who control a computer system and block access until the victim pays a ransom.

- Phishing emails are emails pretended to come from a trustworthy entity to convince victims to give up sensitive information, such as customer names, passwords, and credit card details. The term refers to fishing because of the similarity of using bait to catch a victim.
- A denial-of-service or Dos attack is a technique that bombards a target computer with unnecessary requests to overload the system and prevents legitimate parties from accessing it to cause disruptions to ordinal operations. If multiple robots perform the attack, there is distributed denial of service or DDoS attack.

A cyber-attack, impacting more than 30,000 USA organizations, regarded Microsoft Exchange Server. As a result of cyber espionage activities, hackers identified some vulnerabilities in Microsoft Exchange Server and accessed thousands of email servers of Microsoft customer organizations. The purpose of the attack was to steal sensitive data from email accounts (Novet, 2021).

To fight security incidents, organizations need to build an approach to plan and respond. It should include.

- Creation of principles, rules, and leading practices to prepare a team for incidents.
- Identification of whether an attack has taken place.
- Containment meaning short-term damage limitation by isolating compromised systems.
- Eradication to repair the isolated and damaged systems.
- Recovery is necessary to bring the systems back online.
- Lessons learned is a review of the incident required to understand what happened and suggest ways to prevent it in future.

This practice of stopping cyber-attacks is generally associated with cyber-security. Cyber-security strategies aim to minimize the likelihood of a cyber-attack and prepare for that eventuality. The impression is that the more security tools an organization implements, the more protected the system is. In some cases, the opposite is true: the more complex a system is, the more likely it is that a customer will try to overcome the security measures to make the entire security architecture useless. The most efficient way for organizations to protect themselves is by using a combination of trained people, processes such as incident response, and technology tools for antiviruses, intrusion detection systems, and firewalls that build a security architecture.

Fraud

Financial fraud has far-reaching consequences in the finance industry, government, corporate sectors, and ordinary customers (Fig. 4.8). Increasing dependence on innovative solutions such as cloud and mobile computing has compounded the problem. Traditional methods involving manual detection are time-consuming, expensive, and inaccurate, but they are also impractical in the age of big data. Not surprisingly, financial institutions have turned to bionic processes using statistical and computational methods together with high-level professionals.

Fraud risk management is the process of managing all fraud risks in the organization (Omair & Alturki, 2020). This process includes evaluating potential fraud risks associated with business processes to ensure business objectives (Cotton et al., 2016). Fraud risk management embraces fraud detection and prevention, which are necessary for an effective strategy to

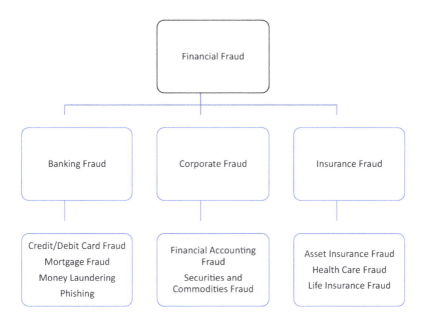

Fig. 4.8 Types of financial frauds

combat fraud (Baesens et al., 2015). Fraud detection aims to discover and recognize any fraudulent activities. Fraud prevention aims to avoid or reduce fraud. Both are independent and should be aligned and considered jointly (Baesens et al., 2015). The fraud triangle theory (DiNapoli, 2008) offers a universal model for describing and understanding key fraud characteristics (Clinard & Cressey, 1954).

The fraud triangle theory states that fraud is more likely when three factors are present (Huang et al., 2017):

- Pressure or incentives. To conduct fraud, the perpetrator must have an incentive or pressure to commit fraud (an operator might have a financial or another type of obligation).
- Opportunity. The perpetrator can commit fraud by taking advantage of weak internal control systems, inadequate security of organization assets, or unclear policies relative to an acceptable behavior.
- Attitude or rationalization. The perpetrator rationalizes the fraudulent behavior (an operator argues he/she has not received what he/she deserves).

Fraud can be of three types (Lutz, 2015):

- Fraudulent reporting concerns deliberate misstatements or omissions of amounts or disclosures (for example, adjustment of accounting records).
- Safeguarding of assets includes protecting entities' assets (e.g., property, cash) from theft.
- Corruption covers bribery and other illegal acts.

Fraud detection is an essential part of the modern finance industry. A literature review studied research into intelligent approaches to fraud detection, both statistical and computational (West & Bhattacharya, 2016). Though their performance differed, each technique could reasonably detect various forms of financial fraud. In particular, computational methods, such as neural networks and support vector machines, to learn and adapt to new tools are highly effective to fraudsters' evolving tactics.

Compliance

The GDPR gives customers the right to know when organizations are making automated decisions of any importance about them (Lui & Lamb, 2018). The GDPR also provides the right to challenge automated decisions. Nevertheless, the right to challenge will not apply once there is any human intervention in the decision-making process. It only applies to decisions that are automated wholly or partially throughout the entire process (Articles 2 and 22). Chatbots and robo-advisors will need human advisers to assist with more complex, sensitive matters. Therefore, it is unlikely that robo-advice in financial services will be completely automated, certainly soon. The right to challenge decisions under the GDPR is unlikely to provide much help to customers.

CISOs and their cyber-security teams have the ethical responsibility to closely supervise their AI algorithms' behavior, tailoring the specific type of algorithm to the nature of its tasks (Badhwar, 2021). To ensure that AI systems uphold the interests and well-being of the business and technology enterprise they serve, cyber-security teams must make informed choices, using unassisted (or unsupervised) AI algorithms for state-of-the-art cyber-security defense and using human-assisted (or human-supervised) algorithmic systems to control what a company's AI does.

Conclusions

This chapter presents an in-depth analysis of each of the building blocks of the business model canvas. Each building block constitutes a vital component of the bionic business model built along with this book. The co-existence of persons and technology is a recurring element in the resulting business model, and it reflects the "philosophy" upon which base the theory of the bionic organization.

It is possible to describe the main determinants briefly to clarify the overall view of the bionic business model. Innovation characterizes the value delivered by a bionic financial organization. It is possible to distinguish into five different innovative value propositions according to the need they satisfy:

- Optimizing the use of the products or services,
- Facilitating activities performed by customers,
- Providing feedbacks,

- Optimizing the interactions with the environment,
- Sharing unused resources.

Apart from the innovative nature and value generation, all of these propositions pursue a secondary objective. These value propositions are potential sources of social value, meaning organizations address sustainability issues by delivering these items or through the operations executed to create that value. To understand their customers and meet their requests, the organizations establish relationships with them and strengthen the existing ones. The best practices used by bionic organizations in interacting with their customers are online communities, co-creation platforms, and chatbots for personal assistance. All the information about customers, collected through different communication accesses, are used by fintech organization to divide the market into segments of individuals that share the same features. In this way, the organization can address each segment's needs and increase the overall customer delight. Bionic organizations can employ advanced machine learning techniques to perform cluster analysis for segmenting customers.

Furthermore, one of the critical pillars of the collaboration of humans and automation is in the distribution accesses bionic organizations use to reach their customers. The symbolic expression of human–robot interdependence is in the way operating processes are executed. The critical processes of a bionic organization are characterized by a moderate level of automation, represented by RPA, and the complementary intervention of persons. Since RPA does not fully automate the business, this solution is optimal to create a bionic reality wherein there is no predominance of automation over humans or vice versa. The resources necessary to develop this new type of organization concern both automation and human capabilities. It is possible to state that augmented intelligence is the technological tool with the highest potential and widespread applications concerning bionic. A bionic organization cannot disregard the adoption of augmented intelligence, cloud computing, and data science. While for what interests the personal dimension, the bionic banking operators have to be familiar with these emerging tools to work with them effectively.

The organization has to deal with many different partners for what concerns the external environment in which a bionic business operates. The winning strategy for interacting with all the stakeholders and gaining a competitive advantage is to build ecosystems. They are networks composed of a high number of parties with different but complementary interests. Ecosystems represent a flexible and resilient solution to cope with the uncertainty of industries and global markets.

A successful business model takes into account revenues and costs generated by the organization. On the one hand, bionic organizations can predict customers' willingness to pay for the value delivered. They adopt a dynamic pricing method according to which prices vary periodically based on external and internal factors. On the other hand, the cost structure of bionic banking is a combination of a value-driven and a cost-driven system because it operates based on the "mantra": deliver more value by optimizing costs.

The combination of automation and humans provides resilience and flexibility. It is also essential to protect it from the bionic organization's security and safety point of view.

Considering this chapter, the final Business Model Canvas for bionic fintech organizations appears rather innovative and challenging in the market (Fig. 4.9).

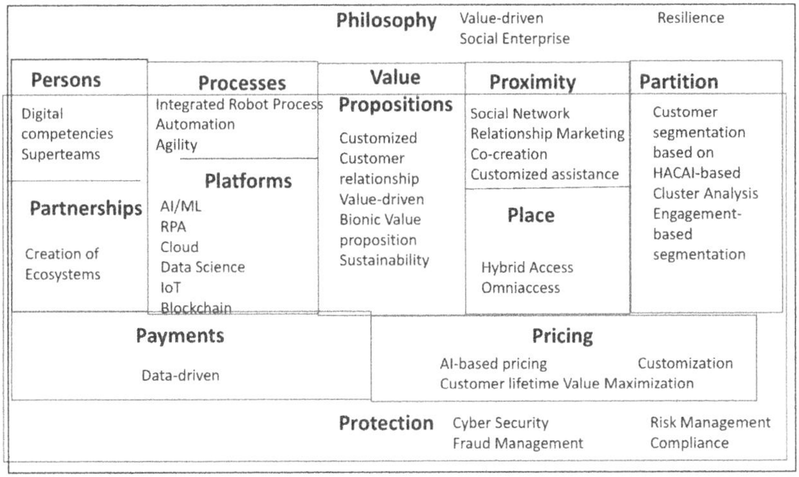

Persons	Processes	Philosophy	Value Propositions	Proximity	Partition
		Value-driven Social Enterprise			Resilience
Digital competencies Superteams	Integrated Robot Process Automation Agility		Customized Customer relationship Value-driven Bionic Value proposition Sustainability	Social Network Relationship Marketing Co-creation Customized assistance	Customer segmentation based on HACAI-based Cluster Analysis Engagement-based segmentation
Partnerships	Platforms			Place	
Creation of Ecosystems	AI/ML RPA Cloud Data Science IoT Blockchain			Hybrid Access Omniaccess	
Payments			Pricing		
Data-driven			AI-based pricing Customization Customer lifetime Value Maximization		
		Protection	Cyber Security Fraud Management		Risk Management Compliance

Fig. 4.9 Bionic business model canvas

REFERENCES

Adam, M., Wessel, M., & Benlian, A. (2020). AI-based chatbots in customer service and their effects on user compliance. *Electronic Markets*, 1–19.

Akter, S., Michael, K., Uddin, M. R., McCarthy, G., & Rahman, M. (2020). Transforming business using digital innovations: The application of AI, blockchain, cloud and data analytics. *Annals of Operations Research*, 1–33.

Anderson, W., Franke, M. R., Grebe, M., Leyh, M., & Rüessmann, M. (2020). *How bionic organizations translate digital maturity into performance*. Boston Consulting Group-BCG. Featured Insights.

Aré, L., Bailey, A., Hutchinson, R., & Rose, J. (2019). *The bionic company*. Boston Consulting Group-BCG. Featured Insights.

Badhwar, R. (2021). AI code of ethics for cybersecurity. In *The CISO's next Frontier* (pp. 41–44). Springer.

Baesens, B., Van Vlasselaer, V., & Verbeke, W. (2015). *Fraud analytics using descriptive, predictive, and social network techniques: A guide to data science for fraud detection*. Wiley.

Barrelet, C. (2021). Eyes on the horizon. *Home, kpmg*.

Bawden, D., & Robinson, L. (2020). Information overload: An overview. In *Oxford encyclopedia of political decision making*. Oxford University Press.

Beckett, M., Elder, J., Ferri, G., et al. (2020). *Bionic revenue management in travel and tourism*. Boston Consulting Group-BCG. Featured Insights.

Bienhaus, F., & Haddud, A. (2018). Procurement 4.0: Factors influencing the digitization of procurement and supply chains. *Business Process Management Journal*, 24(4), 965–984.

Böger, M., Wecht, C., & Stalder, C. (2019). Hybrid business platforms-marketplaces of the future. *Marketing Review St. Gallen*, 2, 38–44.

Bova, T. (2018). *Growth IQ: Get smarter about the choices that will make or break your business*. Penguin.

Bruckner, M., LaFleur, M., & Pitterle, I. (2017). *Frontier issues: The impact of the technological revolution on labour markets and income distribution*. Department of Economic & Social Affairs, UN.

Brynjolfsson, E., & McAfee, A. (2014). *The second machine age: Work, progress, and prosperity in a time of brilliant technologies*. W. W. Norton.

Capgemini Financial Services Analysis. (2021). *World Insurance Report 2021 executive interviews*.

Casey, K. (2019). *Robotic process automation (RPA) in 2020: 5 trends to watch*. Enterprisersproject.com.

Chen, Z., Lu, M., Ming, X., Zhang, X., & Zhou, T. (2020). Explore and evaluate innovative value propositions for smart product service system: A novel graphics-based rough-fuzzy DEMATEL method. *Journal of Cleaner Production*, 243, 118672.

Choi, R. Y., Coyner, A. S., Kalpathy-Cramer, J., Chiang, M. F., & Campbell, J. P. (2020). Introduction to machine learning, neural networks, and deep learning. *Translational Vision Science & Solution, 9*(2), 14–14.

Claudé, M., & Combe, D. (2018). *The roles of artificial intelligence and humans in decision making: Towards augmented humans? A focus on knowledge-intensive firms.*

Clinard, M. B., & Cressey, D. R. (1954). Other people's money: A study in the social psychology of embezzlement. *American Sociological Review, 19*(3).

Close, K., Grebe, M., Schuuring, M., Rehberg, B., & Leybold, M. (2020). *Is your technology ready for the new digital reality?* Boston Consulting Group-BCG. Featured Insights, Boston.

Columbus, L. (2020). *The state of AI adoption in financial services.* Forbes.

Corvalán, J. G. (2019, April). Keynote: PROMETEA. Artificial intelligence to transform public organizations. In *2019 Sixth International Conference on eDemocracy & eGovernment (ICEDEG)* (p. 15). IEEE.

Cotton, D. L., Johnigan, S., & Givarz, L. (2016). *Fraud Risk Management Guide*. COSO, Committee of Sponsoring Organizations of the Treadway Commission.

De Smet, A. Mysore, M., Reich, A., & Sternfels, B. (2021, July). *Return as a muscle: How lessons from COVID-19 can shape a robust operating model for hybrid and beyond.* McKinsey Paper.

Dejoux, C., & Léon, E. (2018). *Métamorphose des managers* (1st ed.). Pearson.

Deloitte. (2020). *Beyond COVID-19: New opportunities for fintech companies.* Deloitte Center for Financial Services.

DiNapoli, T. P. (2008). *Red flags for fraud* (S. J. Hancox, Ed.). Office of the State Controller.

DMG Consulting. (2019). *DMG Consulting—I've heard there's some confusion about an order the Federal Communications Commission (FCC) released concerning automatic dialers calling cell phones. What's the issue?* DMG Consulting LLC, West Orange, NJ.

Earle, R. H., Rosso, M. A., & Alexander, K. E. (2015). User preferences of software documentation genres. In *Proceedings of the 33rd Annual International Conference on the Design of Communication,* 46. ACM.

Ecommerce News. (2018, November). *Austrian app Jingle wants to boost local shopping.* Ecommerce News Europe.

Erlebach, J., Pauly, M., Du Croo De Jongh, L., & Strauß, M. (2020, November). *The sun is setting on traditional banking* (BCG Paper).

Everson, M., & Sviokla, J. (2018, Autumn). The bionic company. *Strategy+Business, 92* (Autumn).

Fåland, J. O., Stausland, K., Eide, L., Kulseth, S. S., & Hamre, V. G. (2020). *Johan Sverdrup 2025.* Equinor, Summer Internship, Stavanger, Norway.

Fallis, J., & Fuchs, O. (2019). *Transforming banking with smart automation*. Nice and Bain & Company.

Fenwick, M., & Vermeulen, E. P. (2020, March). Banking and regulatory responses to FinTech revisited-building the sustainable financial service 'ecosystems' of tomorrow. *Singapore Journal of Legal Studies, 165*–189.

Geib, M., Reichold, A., Kolbe, L., & Brenner, W. (2005, January). Architecture for customer relationship management approaches in financial services. In *Proceedings of the 38th Annual Hawaii International Conference on System Sciences* (p. 240b). IEEE.

Ghazy, K., & Fedorova, A. (2021). Industry 4.0 and human resource management in the hotel business. *Human Progress, 7*(2), 1–1.

Grebe, M., Rüßmann, M., Leyh, M., Roman Franke, M., &, Anderson, W. (2020, November). *How bionic companies translate digital maturity into performance*. BCG Related Expertise..

Hajli, N., Shanmugam, M., Papagiannidis, S., Zahay, D., & Richard, M. O. (2017). Branding co-creation with members of online brand communities. *Journal of Business Research, 70*, 136–144.

Härting, R. C., Reichstein, C., & Sochacki, R. (2019). Potential benefits of digital business models and its processes in the financial and insurance industry. In *Intelligent decision technologies 2019* (pp. 205–216). Springer Nature.

Hofmann, P., Samp, C., & Urbach, N. (2020). Robotic process automation. *Electronic Markets, 30*(1), 99–106.

Howland, D. (2018, June). *What b8ta has figured out about retail*. Retail Dive.

Huang, S. Y., Lin, C. C., Chiu, A. A., & Yen, D. C. (2017). Fraud detection using fraud triangle risk factors. *Information Systems Frontiers, 19*(6), 1343–1356.

Hutchinson, R., Aré, L., Rose, J., & Bailey, A. (2019). *The bionic company*. Published November 7.

Hızıroğlu, Z. H. (2021). *An empirical study on robotic process automation implementation: A case study on MetLife Investment Management Client Services Group* (Doctoral dissertation). University of Wales Trinity Saint David, Lampeter, UK.

Injadat, M., Moubayed, A., Nassif, A. B., & Shami, A. (2021). Machine learning towards intelligent systems: Applications, challenges, and opportunities. *Artificial Intelligence Review*, 1–50.

Interpol. (2020, August). *INTERPOL report shows alarming rate of cyberattacks during the pandemic* (Interpol Report).

Issantu, I. T. (2021). *User acceptance of logistics 4.0 and robotic warehouse solutions (RWS)* (Doctoral dissertation). Capella University, Minneapolis, MN.

Jarrahi, M. H. (2018). Artificial intelligence and the future of work: Human—AI symbiosis in organizational decision making. *Business Horizons*.

Jarrell, M. (2021). Artificial intelligence at square—Two use-cases. *Emerj*.

Kamboj, S., Sarmah, B., Gupta, S., & Dwivedi, Y. (2018). Examining branding co-creation in brand communities on social media: Applying the paradigm of Stimulus-Organism-Response. *International Journal of Information Management, 39*, 169–185.

Kedziora, D., & Penttinen, E. (2021). Governance models for robotic process automation: The case of Nordea Bank. *Journal of Information Technology Teaching Cases, 11*(1), 20–29.

Kimura, R., Reeves, M., & Whitaker, K. (2019). The new logic of competition. *Boston Consulting Group, 3*, 19.

Kopeć, W., Skibiński, M., Biele, C., Skorupska, K., Tkaczyk, D., Jaskulska, A., & Marasek, K. (2018). Hybrid approach to automation, RPA and machine learning: A method for the human-centered design of software robots. *arXiv preprint* arXiv:1811.02213.

Kremer, M. (1993). The O-ring theory of economic development. *The Quarterly Journal of Economics, 108*(3), 551–575.

Kumar, V., & Rajan, B. (2020). Customer lifetime value: What, how, and why. In *The Routledge companion to strategic marketing* (pp. 422–448). Routledge.

Laplante, P., & Kshetri, N. (2021). Open banking: Definition and description. *Computer, 54*(10), 122–128.

Lehmann-Ortega, L., & Schoettl, J. M. (2005). *From buzzword to managerial tool: The role of business models in strategic innovation* (pp. 1–14). CLADEA, Santiago de Chile, Chile.

Leibowitz, S. (2018). *What's the difference between "attended" and "unattended" RPA bots?* Cloud Computing News.

Leno, V., Polyvyanyy, A., Dumas, M., La Rosa, M., & Maggi, F. (2021). Robotic process mining: Vision and challenges. *Business & Information Systems Engineering, 63*(3), 301–314.

Lohrmann, D. (2020, December). *2020: The year the pandemic crisis brought a cyber pandemic.* Government Technology..

Lu, Y. (2017). Industry 5.0: A survey on technologies, applications and open research issues. *Journal of Industrial Information Integration, 6*, 1–10.

Lui, A., & Lamb, G. W. (2018). Artificial intelligence and augmented intelligence collaboration: Regaining trust and confidence in the financial sector. *Information & Communications Technology Law, 27*(3), 267–283.

Lutz, J. (2015). Committee of sponsoring organizations of the treadway commission: Internal control' integrated framework mit besonderer berücksichtigung der änderungen in der neuauflage 2013 - 2014.—14 Seiten Verzeichnisse, 84 Seiten Inhalt. Wien, Hochschule Mittweida - *University of Applied Sciences, Institut für Technologie- und Wissenstransfer, Masterarbeit*.

Manyika, J., Chui, M., Miremadi, M., Bughin, J., & George, K. (2017). *A future that works: AI, automation, employment, and productivity. McKinsey Global Institute Research, Tech. Rep, 60,* 1–135.

Mendling, J., Decker, G., Hull, R., Reijers, H. A., & Weber, I. (2018). How does machine learning, robotic process automation, and blockchains affect the human factor in business process management? *Communications of the Association for Information Systems, 43*(1), 19.

Mullen, A., et al. (2021, October). *Top strategic technology trends for 2022: Generative AI* (Gartner Paper)

Nichols, C. (2020, February). *Why banks need to develop their own customer-facing technology.* Linkedin.

Nicoletti, B. (2012). *Lean and digitize: An integrated approach to process improvement.* Gower Publishing. ISBN-10: 1409441946.

Nicoletti, B. (2013). *Cloud computing & financial services.* Palgrave Macmillan (also translated in Chinese).

Nicoletti, B. (2021a). *Banking 5.0.* Springer.

Nicoletti, B. (2021b). Introduction. In Lechman, E., & Marszk, A. (Eds.), *The digital disruption of financial services. International perspectives.* Routledge

Nott, B. (2018). *RPA use cases—Attended robots automation. UiPath.*

Novet, J. (2021, March). *Microsoft's big email hack: What happened, who did it, and why it matters.* CNBC.

Omair, B., & Alturki, A. (2020). A systematic literature review of fraud detection metrics in business processes. *IEEE Access, 8,* 26893–26903.

Paredes, D. (2018, July). *ANZ bank latest company to employ 'digital human'.* CIO.

Pham, D. T., & Afify, A. A. (2005). Machine-learning techniques and their applications in manufacturing. *Proceedings of the Institution of Mechanical Engineers, Part b: Journal of Engineering Manufacture, 219*(5), 395–412.

Quanton. (2018). *Robotic process automation: Preparation and early-stage planning.* Quanton, Auckland, New Zealand.

Sarker, I. H. (2021). *Data science and analytics: An overview from data-driven smart computing, decision-making and applications perspective.*

Schlegel, D., & Kraus, P. (2021). Skills and competencies for digital transformation—A critical analysis in the context of robotic process automation. *International Journal of Organizational Analysis.*

Schraft, R. D., Hägele, M., & Wegener, K. (2004). *Service-roboter-visionen.* Hanser Verlag.

Susar, D., & Aquaro, V. (2019, April). Artificial intelligence: Opportunities and challenges for the public sector. In *Proceedings of the 12th International Conference on Theory and Practice of Electronic Governance* (pp. 418–426).

Trang, N. T. K., Giang, N. M., Thuong, N. T., Trung, N. B. V., & Anh, N. K. (2020, July). Factors influence customers 'satisfaction toward online brand community: A case study of national economics university's online brand communities. In *Proceedings of the 12th NEU-KKU International Conference Socio-Economic and Environmental Issues in Development*.

Trivedi, N., Asamoah, D. A., & Doran, D. (2018). Keep the conversations going: engagement-based customer segmentation on online social service platforms. *Information Systems Frontiers, 20*(2).

van der Aalst, W., Bichler, M., & Heinzl, A. (2018). Robotic process automation. *Business & Information Systems Engineering, 60*(4). https://doi.org/10.1007/s12599-018-0542-4

van der Zant, T., Kouw, M., & Schomaker, L. (2013). Generative artificial intelligence. *Philosophy and Theory of Artificial Intelligence* (pp. 107–120). Springer.

Villar, A. S., & Khan, N. (2021). Robotic process automation in banking industry: A case study on Deutsche Bank. *Journal of Banking and Financial Technology*, 1–16.

Vybornov, A., Miloslavskaya, N., & Tolstoy, A. (2020, September). Designing competency models for cybersecurity professionals for the banking sector. In *IFIP World Conference on Information Security Education* (pp. 81–95). Springer.

Wall, L. D. (2018). Some financial regulatory implications of artificial intelligence. *Journal of Economics and Business, 100*, 55–63.

Ward-Dutton, N. (2018). *From RPA to DPA: A strategic approach to automation* (Pegasystems paper).

Watson, W. T. (2017). *New horizon: How diverse growth strategies can advance digitisation in the insurance industry* (Willis Towers Watson's Report).

West, J., & Bhattacharya, M. (2016). Intelligent financial fraud detection: A comprehensive review. *Computers & Security, 57*, 47–66.

Xu, W. (2019). Toward human-centered AI: A perspective from human-computer interaction. *Interactions, 26*(4), 42–46.

Zhang, A. X., Muller, M., & Wang, D. (2020). How do data science workers collaborate? Roles, workflows, and tools. *Proceedings of the ACM on Human-Computer Interaction, 4*(CSCW1), 1–23.

CHAPTER 5

Bionic Banking Life Cycle

INTRODUCTION

This chapter clarifies the structure of the bionic transformation. In particular, this chapter presents the essential characteristics of bionic banking and the outcomes that such types of organizations strive for.

This chapter presents the bionic banking life cycle based on the earliest results of existing bionic experiences. At the same time, this chapter provides awareness about the meaning of "being bionic" and the main factors that distinguish bionic banking, where humans and automation collaborate in traditional financial institutions and fintech organizations.

Since banking is a service, human customers are part of many services. Bionic transformation becomes even more critical where automation cooperation with humans become multi-faceted: customer, human service operators, and automation.

The chapter also describes a model to support innovation in bionic banking projects.

BIONIC BANKING ACROSS THE CUSTOMER LIFE CYCLE

Suppose financial institutions begin by prioritizing the use cases where automation, such as Augmented Intelligence (AI), models can add the most value. In that case, they can automate more than 20 decisions in diverse customer journeys (Agarwal et al., 2021). For example, leading financial institutions rely increasingly on automation and analytics capabilities within the lending life cycle to add value in five main areas: customer acquisition, credit decisioning, monitoring and collections, deepening relationships, and intelligent servicing (Fig. 5.1).

Recent studies have attempted to understand the impact of automation, and especially AI, on services. The service industry uses more and more AI. It is becoming an essential part of contemporary innovation (Huang & Rust, 2018) to handle various service tasks. A. W. Yip and Bocken (2018) highlighted that most financial institutions acknowledge the importance of digitizing their services. Reducing human interactions can make financial institutions more efficient in-service speed, cost, and sustainability (Li & Du, 2017).

Automation may be able to perform complex tasks that might not be able to be handled by humans. Financial institutions should generate commitment and trust between the financial institution and its customers to create long-term relationships (Madan et al., 2015). Virtual assistants based on AI ensure that bionic banking handle customer queries quickly. This possibility enhances the customers' experience and service quality estimation (Chu et al., 2012; Cui et al., 2017) assert that providing high-quality services can achieve customer delight. There is a need for financial

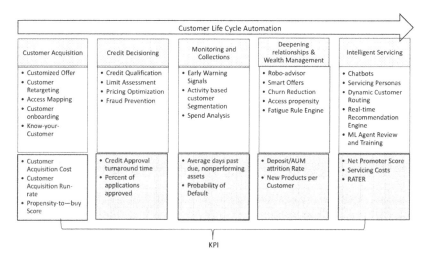

Fig. 5.1 Customer life cycle automation

institutions to prioritize their customers to guarantee high satisfaction levels and thereby retain their customer base (Chen, S. H., 2013).

There are several non-financial benefits associated with automation and its related solutions. According to C. M. Kuo et al. (2017), AI, service automation, and avatars might improve the perception of service quality through interactive and attractive ways of engaging and communicating with customers. Automation can please customers since it introduces more interactive methods of service delivery. Chatbots and avatars may be programmed to communicate in several languages, eliminating language barriers if staff can only speak in a single language (Ivanov & Webster, 2017). AI, service automation, and avatars can generate value for customers by making the delivery of services entertaining and funny (Chtourou & Souiden, 2010). AI and related solutions can also save operators time because they will not handle repetitive and tedious tasks. Service quality can also improve because AI systems never lose their temper and remain calm even when a customer becomes abusive, aggressive, or angry (Dignum, 2017).

Human beings are social people. There will always be customers willing to pay a premium for human interaction. Maybe in future, things will be different. It is not possible to replace human intuition, ethics, or the mind in the short term.

Automation affects the contribution provided by humans. A study on the effects of implementing RPA in an organization brought some interesting insights. The in-depth data collected before RPA and after RPA shows how automation removed the nuisance of repetitive tasks from operators (Parker & Appel, 2021). The teams' productivity increased, and they reported higher levels of engagement and flexibility to help customers. As operators need to spend less time capturing data and doing specific tasks, they can spend more time with customers, improve their level of service, and engage in more innovative behavior. This new situation generates an opportunity for financial institutions to rethink their business models and create value.

It is essential a detailed design of the collaboration human-automation. In some cases, before implementing RPA, the manual entry task served as an essential preparation process, allowing operators to gain insights into the customer while capturing their information (Parker & Appel, 2021). Post-implementation, operators had to achieve the same insights from the substantially shorter validation process (about one minute). Before implementation, the time operators spent with a profile before engaging with a customer was less around five minutes.

Customer Acquisition

T. Henry et al. (2018) underlined that onboarding, documentation processes, and performance tracking are areas where digitizing improves customer experience and reduces costs. They emphasized the importance of bionic solutions. Chatbots can help in this respect. A chatbot is a computer program, algorithm, or augmented intelligence that communicates with a person or another participant. The aim is usually to make customers feel that they are talking with a living person. Neff and Nagy define a chatbot as a type of program which engages customers in a conversation: "chatbots respond to customers' messages by selecting the appropriate expression from preprogrammed schemas, or in the case of emerging bots, through use of adaptive machine learning algorithms" (Neff & Nagy, 2016).

Chatbots are AI programs that simulate human conversations interactively, using pre-set sentences (Škavić, 2019). They can assist services (customer care) or marketing, such as social networks and instant messaging. More complex than speech-to-text programs, chatbots communicate with people using text (text chatbot) and voice (voicebot) (Nicoletti, 2021). Voicebots can hold a verbal conversation, understanding language, and providing answers.

Chatbots can reduce the administrative burden of onboarding new customers and turn those interactions into loyalty and upselling opportunities.

> **Rabobank**
> Rabobank is a large Dutch bank and is among the 30 largest financial institutions globally.[1] Rabobank and its subsidiaries have approximately 59,000 operators worldwide and serve 7.5 million. In 2018, the bank had a revenue of 12,020 billion euros. Rabobank is an early adopter of RPA, starting with a Proof of Concept (PoC) in the summer of 2016 and moving beyond a PoC in 2017 (Noppen, 2019). In terms of RPA adoption and automated processes, it is ahead of other financial institutions. As of early 2019, Rabobank has approximately 150 operational bots.

Credit Decisioning

Financial institutions are using AI solutions to make decisions about the provision of loans. Through artificial neural networks, AI systems can analyze the data of a borrower to make decisions about who should receive a loan rather than relying on background checks and credit scores alone (Eletter et al., 2010; West & Allen, 2018). The use of AI solutions in loan analysis helps to minimize human emotional bias that can affect a loan application process. AI to determine individuals who qualify for loans can produce more reliable information than credit scores (West & Allen, 2018). Therefore, AI can minimize the cost of processing loans and personal judgment, so improving customer service quality S. F. Eletter et al. (2010) further note that AI systems help financial institutions evaluate personal credit to minimize the risk of defaulters.

Financial institutions using AI have designed streamlined lending journeys. This implementation uses extensive automation and near-real-time analysis of customer data. It generates prompt credit decisions for retailers, Small and Medium-sized Enterprises (SMEs), and corporate customers (Agarwal et al., 2021). They search through many structured and unstructured data collected from conventional sources (such as bank transaction history, credit reports, and tax returns) and innovative ones (including location data, telecom usage data, utility bills, and more). Access to these non-traditional data sources depends on open banking and other data sharing guidelines and the availability of officially approved Application Programming Interfaces (API) and data aggregators in the specific market. Further, while accessing and leveraging customer personal data, financial institutions must secure data and protect customer privacy by local regulations (for example, the General Data Protection Regulation in the EU and the California Customer Privacy Act in the USA).

By using powerful AI models to analyze these broad and diverse data sets in near real-time, financial institutions can qualify new customers for credit services, determine loan limits and pricing, and reduce the risk of fraud (Agarwal et al., 2021):

---

[1] www.rabobank.com/en/home/index.html?languageDoesNotExists=it. Accessed 20 July 2021.

- Credit qualification: Leading financial institutions and fintech lenders have developed complex models to analyze structured and unstructured data, examine hundreds of data points collected from social media, browse history, telecommunications usage data, and more. The automation enables financial institutions to forecast the likelihood of default for individuals in a large and potentially profitable segment of unbanked and underbanked customers.
- Limit assessment: Leading financial institutions are also using AI models to automate determining the maximum amount a customer may borrow. By using databases with both conventional and new data sources, financial institutions can generate a pretty accurate forecast of a customer's capacity to pay.
- Pricing: Financial institutions generally offer highly standardized rates on credit, with sales representatives and relationship managers having some possibility to modify the rates within certain limits. Financial institutions with the support of AI can offer competitive rates while keeping their risk costs low.
- Fraud management: The competition for credit relationships becomes concentrated in digital accesses. The automated processing of credit applications and the use of data science and ML models allow to expedite credit approval and disbursement of funds. Om this way, the financial institution is in a good position to acquire new customers and increase market share opening at the same time new opportunities for combating fraud.

Credit decisioning with the support of AI can build the business while lowering costs with faster loan approval and disbursement of funds, fewer requests for documentation, and customized credit offers.

Another example of this type is increasing a customer's credit card limit, quickly responding to the customer's request. Thanks to the rapid advance and availability of collaborative virtual attendant technology, customer service staff can actively manage credit-limit requests over the phone, supported by automation. Automation helps them correct information more quickly and solicit additional information from the customer more efficiently and accurately answer customers.

Financial institutions and investment banking are increasing their investment in AI to leverage the benefits of this collaboration human-automation. For example, investment in financial AI in the USA from 2013 to 2014 increased to almost $12.2 billion (West & Allen, 2018).

Monitoring and Collection

The right combination of RPA, supporting solutions, and human interaction can also play an essential role in blocking lost or stolen credit cards (Fallis & Fuchs, 2019). End-to-end robotic automation allows customers to directly block their cards using interactive voice response (IVR). Thanks to AI, the system can authenticate the customer by his/her unique voiceprint. It can further identify all billing applications associated with the card and alert a human operator to step in when there is an issue to address. The customer ultimately benefits from the swift and highly personalized service experience since the virtual attendant robot can support the human operator.

Another interesting area is fraud alert investigations. Thanks to the integration of RPA with a case management system, human fraud investigators can focus on alerts. At the same time, the virtual attendant completes the time-intensive task of populating relevant data fields in the system.

Machine Learning (ML) can develop strategies for investing and executing orders (Huang et al., 2019). Traditional electronic trading programs follow specific rules in certain market conditions. New scenarios require reprogramming, with the need for some downtime. On the other hand, ML is dynamic: it can adapt to changing market conditions (Collie, 2021). AI tracks stocks, exchange rate values, and country economy. It can predict and inform about future threats (Christodoulou et al., 2021). ML requires human-automation collaboration. Humans should be able to overrule ML's investment decisions when necessary. On this respect, it is important for ML to provide an explanation of its recommendations to a human operator. This visibility is important for an AI platform.

These machine learning tools not only can manage extensive databases and order the sequence of decisions. They often show better prediction accuracy than the traditional predictions methods. For this reason, JP Morgan uses ML to execute trades for its customers in equity markets (Wall, 2018).

> **Square**
> Square is a financial services company that aims to "build common business tools in unconventional ways so more people can start, run, and grow their

businesses." Founded in 2009, Square reports total net revenue of $9.5 billion for 2020 (Jarrell, 2021).

Square provides payment processing systems and applications for small business owners. Square prioritizes risk management services for its customers to help protect them from fraudulent payment activity. The exposure is enormous. According to the PwC's 2020 Global Economic Crime and Fraud Survey's US findings, US companies suffered a total of $6.5 billion in losses due to fraud over the 24 months surveyed. They reported that "the rate of fraud and economic crime remains at a record-high in the US, experienced by 56% of US companies in [the] survey—significantly higher than the global aggregate of 47%."[2]

Standard fraud monitoring is available to business owners that use Square to process payments, Square offers a paid software solution, based on AI, for its customers interested in additional "insight and functionality to prevent unnecessary loss," called Risk Manager. Risk Manager provides sellers with insights into online payment fraud patterns and set up custom alerts and rules to alert on potential red flags.

Square uses machine learning algorithms to monitor transactions and create risk evaluations that sellers can review in their transactions dashboard- and preventing fraud with AI and preventing fraud with AI. These tools build machine learning models based on thousands of signals from the payment's ecosystem.

When the evaluation of the transaction is with high risk, the transaction is not automatically declined because it is more important to convey the risk level to the business owner and support them in making an informed decision based on some additional knowledge of their customers.

Another service called Square Secure provides business owners with email notifications for transactions that appear suspicious. This service provides live monitoring of a business' transactions while also identifying, reviewing, and reporting any transactions suspected to be fraudulent.

In the bionic spirit, Square leaves the final decision on a transaction to their customers, which have a better feeling of the market.

---

[2] www.pwc.com/gx/en/services/forensics/economic-crime-survey.html.

> **Valhalla Bank**
> The Swedish Valhalla bank improves daily finances for more than 300,000 private individuals, entrepreneurs, affiliations, and organizations. The bank endeavors to offer financial administrations that individuals genuinely need and that affect society. Their administrations are proposed to stabilize the increasingly complicated service offerings to help contributions arising on the market (Karahanli & Touma, 2021).
>
> Valhalla bank proactively seeks both explicit and latent needs of different customer segments. Any customer interaction data can become the source of optimizing call scheduling, script customization, or customer experience evaluation. Customers expect flexibility to choose between human interaction and self-service automation. When digital tools provide advanced functionality with maturity, sensitive topics can be dealt with digital tools to establish trust and security. Even though automation is perceived as cold with a lack of empathy, customers are ready to experiment with it as they are not comfortable nor satisfied with the current interactions. Regardless of the state of the digital journey of a financial institution, customers should be well-informed about technologies while banks prioritize ethical controls to provide transparent relationships in which any type of customer can feel valued.

Deepening Relationships: Wealth Management

Robo-Advisor is a financial service based on two components: investment advice and automatization through robots. The term robo-advice may include various levels of automatization. Algorithms typically provide the onboarding and risk profiling, the investment process can either be wholly rule-based or driven by a human advisor. Robo-advisors use a combination of human-automation, such as the robot, AI machine learning, natural language processing, data mining, and planning tools. These techniques enable the use of customer data for personalized advice and the addition of other services, like tax-loss harvesting, cash flow management, college savings, and automated investment- and retirement advice. Robo-advisors manage €53.5 billion worth of assets worldwide, expected to grow to over €6.2 trillion in 2027 (Haenen, 2017).

There is still an unaddressed potential for bionic robo-advisors. Where virtual banking led to the first revolution in banking, an increase in bionic robo-advisors leads to a second revolution. By automating routine services and providing online round-the-clock service with bionic robo-advisors, financial institutions can significantly reduce inbound calls while simultaneously boosting customer delight by delivering real-time personalization. Digitalization and online access increase and virtual banking become a channel on its own. Excellent customer service will be the crucial differentiator. These emerging methods offer a chance to get closer to the customer and boost sales (Haenen, 2017). Financial institutions must develop comprehensive Virtual Banking Assistant solutions because of ease of use, rapid accessibility, and full-time availability.

An ideal recommendation system proposes the best product to customers based on their interests or budget and explains its decision. Chen, C. C. et al. (2021) discuss a similar scenario with data from an e-commerce platform. Their system considers both personalized recommendations and explanations, which are also crucial in the financial domain. For example, the salesperson recommends a fund to the customer and explains why the recommended fund is suitable for the customer. In this case, the reason may be the salesperson's opinion.

There will always be a 'human in the loop (Government Office for Science, 2015). Humans still play an essential role because robo-advisers cannot provide human judgment or real-time sensitivity. To a large extent, robo-advisers can care about financial matters even if they cannot care about persons. Humans will and should control robots to deliver reliable and trustworthy financial services. There is a need for an AI collaboration style to overcome challenges such as bias, discrimination, privacy, and the use of big data analytics (Hung et al., 2020).

Based on the extensive literature on robotics in services, academics agree that humans should monitor robots because they can better manage cases of unplanned events. Bionic robo-advisors are robo-advisory solutions that incorporate a human relationship layer on top of their automated processes. Utilizing this relationship layer, financial institutions can leverage significant opportunities to benefit customers by increasing transactions and sales, customer value of the interaction, customer loyalty, and customer delight. Imagine a proactive robo-advisor covering all banking services with real-time personalization and human-like conversational support for customers based on their intent. Such a bionic robo-advisor has three benefits concerning the traditional way of traditional financial advisors.

- The utilization of bionic robo-advice promotes a new kind of holistic financial advice, going beyond traditional human advice. Using bionic robo-advice adds value to financial service providers because of human-automation collaboration in decision making, increasing diversification, and risk management capabilities. The additional value combines real-time, easily accessible, and more reliable financial advice by robots with the personalized touch of human advisors to spend more attention on specific customer problems.
- From a customer's point of view, bionic robo-advisors can lead to increased flexibility, better monitoring of the service process, time savings, and the avoidance of interactions with frontline service operators. Using bionic robo-advisors, customers determine their journey instead of being forced to a predefined one, exert more control over the financial advisory process, and determine how much personal advice they desire. Eventually, bionic robo-advisors should take over all financial advisory services by changing the customer journey and remodeling the role of human advisor into a supervisory and intervention role.
- Bionic robo-advice goes beyond benefits that are a result of improved automation. The psychological part is also essential. Scholars have shown that customers tend to express a more positive attitude toward a financial institution if they choose between two service accesses instead of being forced to one (Hu & Tracogna, 2020). Accenture confirms these insights showing that organizations that provide an automated platform with access to a human advisor score higher on customer loyalty and customer delight among investors than organizations that provide just human advisors (Syed et al., 2020). Therefore, the recommendation is for financial institutions to use customer preferences in design and development to customize their robo-advisory offerings. Up to 70% of Generation X and Millennials prefer bionic robo-advisors over human advisors (Nikiforova, 2017).

T. Cocca (2016) describes that finding new ways of utilizing digital opportunities becomes increasingly essential. The age gap in the preparedness to use digital solutions is diminishing since older customers find digital solutions appealing. It is possible to classify customers into four segments:

- Digital deniers (customers of a personal advisor, do not use virtual banking accesses),
- Bionic customer (customers of a personal advisor and virtual banking accesses),
- Mainly digital (with no human advisors, financial institutions manage more than half of the wealth).
- Fully digital (no need of advisors, financial institution manages online all of the wealth managed).

Correspondingly, it is possible to classify robo-advisors into three types (Fig. 5.2).

According to a survey measuring perceptions of wealth management customers in Austria, Germany, and Switzerland, the bionic customers present 79.9%, digital deniers 13.6%, and digital customers 6.5% of the group (Cocca, 2016). Among the findings was that bionic customers appear to use online services mainly for collecting information and conducting transactions, with only 25.9% using online accesses to seek advice at the moment. However, 45.4% of the bionic customers could imagine not dealing with an advisor, and instead of interacting with the online financial institution, 38.4% could imagine using virtual consulting from a third party.

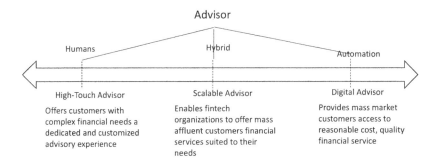

Fig. 5.2 Types of robo-advisors

Ping An Insurance
Ping An is a Chinese group in Shenzhen in 1988 that evolved from being an insurtech to a world-leading group in financial services. It serves 516 million internet customers and 200 million retail customers, for-profit, return on equity, and market capitalization. In 2020, Ping An ranked 7th in the Forbes Global 2000 list and 21st in the Fortune Global 500 list (Ping An Group, 2020).

The organization has invested in digital capabilities and innovative solutions such as AI and blockchain. It can offer innovative products and services that extract additional value from advanced solutions. Its operations are data driven. This approach allows the organization to make decisions in real-time and to anticipate trends. Ping An has used its resources for technological patents acquisition to achieve this objective and has hired new profiles such as data scientists and business technology experts.

Concerning Ping An Insurance value propositions, the service line for insurance is in two sectors: Life & Health and Property & Casualty. Ping An applies AI technology in its daily activities. For example, the group's Life & Health insurance line has fully automated the recruitment process and uses robotic applications to hire new agents. AI tools currently support its operators in executing their working activities, consistently approaching the "augmented agent model." A practical application of AI is operators' intelligent assistant "Ask Bob," a software solution able to provide agents a sale-enabling tool to increase productivity,

Ping An also has the right tools to provide a convenient and engaging customer experience. Ping An has adopted an approach called "Channel + Product." The definition of this approach is channel reform. Ping An Life utilizes innovative technology to support its various accesses, helping over a million agents efficiently develop their business pipelines and conveniently manage their teams, thus achieving per-agent productivity and revenue growth (Ping An Group, 2020).

The primary touchpoint with customers is the group's website, where it is possible to find a clear description of the service offered and tailored promotions. If the customer needs additional information, s/he can start a conversation with a chatbot AI-based software and immediately receives the necessary information. If the chatbot cannot satisfy the customer's requests, the conversation switches to a direct phone line with customer service. Additionally, if the customer needs to talk directly to an agent, the Ping An website can search for the closest agent based on customer location and agent availability. Once the customer has identified an agent,

> the more convenient communication channel is through WeChat mobile application.
> Although Ping An has widely adopted advanced solutions, particularly AI, the fintech organization employs a person-oriented approach in its operations. Concerning its workforce, Ping An has considered operators' welfare and offers them the opportunity to improve their skills with continuous training, especially innovative solutions implementation. These training initiatives called "training by expertise" are tailor-made according to each agent's level of competencies and relative gaps. In this way, operators' contribution is for what they can do best and strengthen what they cannot. Consequently, Ping An reaches a higher level of operators' satisfaction.
> Ping An Insurance has started a bionic transformation. Indeed, based on the bionic transformation approach, Ping An displays critical elements of a bionic organization wherein it is paid great attention to the persons, both concerning customers, and operators, while adopting an elevated level of automation.

Intelligent Servicing

In the banking sector, chatbots talk to customers and, among other services, provide information about their account balances, facilitate their bill payments, suggest ways to save resources, and help activate cards. At the same time, they assist the financial institutions in collecting feedback from customers. Examples of such chatbots are America's Erika, HDFC's EVA, and Bank of Australia's Ceba (Adamopoulou & Moussiades, 2020).

The integration of machine learning with the virtual assistant interface produces innovative results for customers. This integration works in many enterprises' contact centers or customer service departments (Fluss, 2017). Financial and non-financial benefits influence the adoption of human-automation collaboration. Labor cost saving is the primary financial benefit of adopting AI virtual assistants and related solutions. Self-service applications, chatbots, and service avatars can work 24/7, longer than the regular 40 hours per week for human operators (Ivanov & Webster, 2017). Chatbots can also serve many customers concurrently, which would be very difficult for human operators. Automated solutions are more efficient in performing tasks than human operators considering all these factors (Ivanov & Webster, 2017). West and Allen (2018) observed that intelligent chatbots or virtual chatbots have become widespread in the service industry and increasingly replace human customer service (Fluss, 2017). Virtual chatbots make self-service possible reducing the need for operators, which can complement the automation.

Chatbots can enable financial institutions to identify customers' problems and provide the most appropriate solutions. NatWest Bank in the UK built a digital human assistant named Cora (PYMNTS, 2018). This text-based chatbot is designed to answer customers' questions on the bank's online help pages. It can answer 200 basic banking queries and handling 100,000 chats per month. A new Cora enables a two-way verbal conversation with customers through a computer screen, mobile phone, or tablet (Samuels, 2019). According to Maskey (2018), analysts have estimated that financial institutions adopting AI will save over US$ 1 trillion by 2030 by improving their service quality leading to improved customer delight. Cost-saving is a significant benefit that financial institutions are likely to enjoy due to adopting AI. ANZ Bank is one such institution that uses digital assistants, such as chatbots, to handle common customer queries (Paredes, 2018).

Chatbots today are processed to handle relatively straightforward inquiries, which make up the majority of the volume. The chatbot can reply with questions, and the bot's answers stored in a knowledge base can pull out answers using an API. However, the chatbot has difficulty in answering complex questions making essential human collaboration.

Deutsche Bank
Around 90% of the issues banking customers call help desks could be resolved on a self-service basis using a real-time dashboard. Personal interaction and a designed customer journey are critical. A customer can be instigated to use a self-service route, possibly with telephone assistance, while learning a procedure, such as applying for a new account, for the first time. Alternatively, a consultant can drive them to get where they need to be. The Deutsche Bank Transaction Banking business operates a bionic approach with click-to-chat options (the sense of a person at the other end is critical) that can then progress to a call or possibly a site visit, depending on the problem (Deutsche Bank, 2018).

This possibility is finding its way into the corporates space and presents vast opportunities. Deutsche Bank launched the chatbot Debbie quickly, securely, and accurately (Rausch, 2021).

There is also an array of solutions that automate basic banking or treasury processes. Chatbots, for example, are being leveraged as a first point of contact for basic service requests, such as payment statuses. They free up staff to deal with the more complex, value-add processes (Edwards, 2020).

Bank of America
Banking is one of the best use cases for chatbots right now. They can make a difference at every stage of a customer's life cycle. As a market leader in the USA, Bank of America began a chatbot, called Erica, to send notifications to customers, provide balance data, suggest how to save money, provide credit report updates, pay bills, and help customers with simple transactions. Since the introduction, Erica's abilities have expanded to help customers make intelligent decisions (Lee & Shin, 2020).

Erica can help with branch addresses, IFSC codes, loan, and interest valuation reports. It can help on more than 200 banking transactions such as activating cards, monitoring account balance, making payments, or making use of cash suggestions.

Many customers ask unnecessary inquiries. These bots interface into most customer touchpoints like social media profiles, websites, app, and other platforms. They ask customers to specify their problems and either provide direct solutions or redirect them to the right person.

One of the reasons why customers appear to trust chatbots is because of the inherent absence of self-interest. There are several reasons why a combination of humans and automation in a chatbot is a winning recipe. Humans are still preferred to advise customers about complex financial products such as equity derivatives (Lui & Lamb, 2018) or when customers wish to complain or discuss a complicated matter or situation (Hosea, 2016). A common criticism of chatbots and robots is that they cannot empathize (Reid, 2017). They cannot display real emotions such as happiness, sadness, anger, or sense the customer's emotional state. Conversation is a skill. From a technical perspective, conversation management is a very high level of automation. Chatbots need to understand the context of a conversation and refer back to previous sentences. One can infer different contexts of a term. For example, the words credit card can refer to the personal credit card in one conversation but the company credit card in another conversation (Shevat, 2017). Conversation management is still at the very beginning of its development. A similar situation is for sentiment analysis. Sentiment analysis could enable chatbots to predict a customer's emotional status in a conversation.

Chatbots will learn over time and improve (Calvert, 2017). Chatbots are, in some functions, limited. Complex pieces of advice are outside the current expertise of robo-advisers and chatbots. Tax planning involving multiple jurisdictions is still the domain of human advisers. There is a real danger of chatbots providing wrong answers to customers with the financial institution's responsibility. Humans need to work with chatbots. The degree of visibility of informing customers about the use of chatbots is still unclear.

When a customer asks a question, the chatbot searches the libraries. If the answer is there, the chatbot will deliver it. If not, the chatbot should refer the customer to a human assistant (Lui & Lamb, 2018). The debate is no longer about humans *versus* automation. The issue is about integrating both so that customers receive a seamless service.

Bionic banking can also add proactivity to the customer proximity center. An organization such as a financial institution uses the data synthesized using AI to understand customers from different financial aspects. The organization can use the data to predict customer needs and offer appropriate services, making the customers' lives easier.

Banca Generali Private

Banca Generali Private is a financial institution that originated in 2000 and is part of the Generali Group. It counts over 2,000 private bankers and wealth advisors and serves its customers through 46 branches and 138 offices spread across Italy. The net bank income for the year 2020 has reached more than 270 million euro.[3]

Banca Generali Private has a well-defined vision and mission. Its future perspective concerns the will to become the leading private bank in Italy with solid leadership in the wealth management market. Its commitment is oriented to build trust in its customers by offering excellent services that also respect sustainability.

Banca Generali can be considered a bionic transformer because of the recurring presence of the personal dimension and automation in all its activities. For what interests the personal side of the financial institution, Banca Generali is part of a financial group that for more than one century has entirely relied on its operators: insurance agents, bankers, and financial advisors. Banca Generali transmits the distinctive touch to its customers by leveraging three central values: collaboration, empathy, and team spirit. The financial institution extracts value from its workforce by investing in its ongoing learning and professional growth.

The main application of the bionic paradigm of person-automation collaboration within Banca Generali Private is *Ro4Ad* which stands for robo-for-advisors, launched in 2019 and created in partnership with UBS Partners, a B2B financial institution that offers platform solutions (Fintastico Team, 2019). Robo-for-advisor is a bionic solution that merges personal and technological competencies in portfolio management. The origin of *Ro4Ad* is related to the spread of fully digital robo-advisors in fintech organizations. Robo-advisor is a solution built on a digital platform or website that provides algorithms for financial asset management and portfolio control. Customers have the opportunity to receive advisory services 24*7 by accessing a website through an internet connection without any interaction with a physical agent. Algorithms rely on augmented intelligence and work in this way: robo-advisor collects information about the market's financial situation and financial securities. It processes and analyzes this databased on the objective and portfolio preferences expressed by the customer. Robo-advisor's main goal achieved by robo-advisor is to containment of financial losses and risky investments (Travia, 2021).

The primary constraint that investors have experienced with robo-advisor is that these virtual advisors can manage a limited set of assets and do not offer service completeness as customarily done by physical agents. For this reason, Banca Generali private has chosen to create a robo-for-advisor and not a robo-advisor- The former is conceived as a supporting tool only for financial agents or bankers and not for direct access by customers. In this way, customers have the opportunity to receive on the one hand the same accurate and reliable advice as the one delivered by algorithms. On the other hand, they have the possibility to interact with a person that can understand their needs and transmit empathy. It is possible to talk about *Ro4Ad* as a hybrid solution that is neither entirely automatic nor physical. Banca Generali Private *Ro4Ad* performs three main activities (Bluerating, 2019):

- It monitors the risk associated with the customer's portfolio.
- It compares expected and actual results.
- It provides insights for trading optimization.

Customers' main benefits from *Ro4Ad* adoption are that financial agents can grant a high degree of personalization of the service delivered and real-time advisor for financial decisions.

Bionic Insurer

Innovative business models, such as the ones of the insurtech organizations, challenge traditional insurers. Traditional insurers need to develop digital capabilities and balance their operations' automation and human side to keep pace. According to BCG research on insurance operations, it is impossible to disregard three elements: an improved customer experience, a new approach to interactions and distribution, and the implementation of AI-driven services (Dirnberger et al., 2020):

- The customer experience of bionic insurers needs to grant streamlined steps and procedures by eliminating unnecessary processes. This elimination need generates from customers' expectations, which frequently change and are mainly related to the request for simple and intuitive interactions and to have "options." Options mean opportunities to decide the modalities of service delivery and interactions. This approach implies insurers' flexibility and the ability to "switch on and off" settings and clauses according to individual needs. Another innovation in insurance service offerings is the personalization of value propositions, such as the channel chosen to interact with insurers for support in case of damage or incident. Insurers can build a unique customer experience explicitly dedicated to each person through dynamic service personalization.
- The concept of "augmented agents" is based on the new approach to interactions and distribution of bionic insurance providers. Augmented agents are insurers who perform their tasks and operations in person with automation tools. This distribution model

[3] Banca Generali. Private. (n.d.). *In brief.* bancagenerali.com/en/about-us/in-brief.

is a "digitally enhanced face-to-face model." It is fundamental to ensure a person's touchpoint since, in many cases, the emotional and emphatical dimension is still necessary (Freese et al., 2020). AI algorithms allow agents to analyze data collected and automatically get valuable information. The salesforce is characterized by having digital capabilities and the necessary skills to exploit AI tools. However, bionic insurers cannot be defined as pure salespeople since they advise customers and proactively support them.

- The use of automation (such as AI) in-service delivery brings efficiency and productivity by reducing repetitive tasks and saving time and costs. Based on the successful implementation of automation services, there are data science systems and digital ecosystems. Data science systems enable the capture in real-time of data, store and automatically process them. A digital ecosystem allows integrating different applications and automation software on digital platforms to ensure a continuous flow of information.

Colonial Life
Colonial Life protects when the unexpected happens through employer-sponsored voluntary benefits (Capgemini Financial Services Analysis, 2021). Colonial Life's product portfolio includes disability, accident, life, critical illness, hospital confinement, and cancer insurance. Operating across the United States, the company works with more than 90,000 business and organizational customers to cover more than 3.7 million policyholders and families.

Pandemic lockdowns hit Colonial Life's dominant distribution accesses, independent agents, and brokers, hard. As the organization's customers (employers) shut offices and travel stopped, 12,000 sales agents used on face-to-face meetings needed a better way to conduct business remotely.

Colonial Life sought to rapidly support its salesforce with automation to complement its reputation for high-touch, personalized experiences. The goals were to stay true to its one-to-one business model, protect Colonial Life sales and broker partners from income losses, and support policyholders who needed them even more than in the past.

Colonial Life ramped up capabilities for an existing digital tool, Agent Assist, to maintain business continuity for its sales force. Agent Assist transitioned from a cold-lead generation tool to a CRM capabilities solution that supported warm leads and higher conversion rates. Agent Assist sent educational digital postcards to customers before benefits enrollment. Online benefits counselors and meeting schedulers helped to maintain regular customer contact.

Investment in automation such as Agent Assist helped Colonial Life survive the pandemic storm. Enabling automation to fill in for physical posters and sign-up sheets that policyholders traditionally saw at the office helped maintain strong workplace engagement. As a result, customer retention rose about 500 basis points as pandemic-weary policyholders knew they could count on digital support accesses. Automation adoption from Colonial Life stakeholders, agents/brokers, employers, and policyholders, increased across the board. More than 60% of Colonial Life's employer customers now use the insurer's customer portal regularly. Sales recruiting efforts increased by over 10%, due mainly to the organization's technical support and automation. Online claims submissions grew to more than 80% for policyholders compared with previous traditional mail, email, and fax.

Conclusions

Several organizations display characteristics of the bionic organizations, albeit not fully considered and especially optimized:

- They have a sharp vision and mission to become leading organizations in their specific market segment.
- Inside these realities, it is possible to recognize the hybridization between automation, particularly AI-based tools, and the human component represented by an approach focused on customers' and operators' needs.

Factual evidence of the bionic business model also in insurance is in the value propositions they deliver. It is very innovative and characterized by an appropriate level of personalization and the distribution accesses they adopt, combining human and automation expertise.

Some financial institutions have started a bionic transformation and have achieved remarkable results. Still, their evolution is not complete. This chapter presents the anatomy of the fintech organization of the future. Within these organizations, automation and humans coexist, and both are at the core of their functioning. Organizations need to reach a balanced trade-off between humans, who are flexible and unique, and automation that is exactly replicable but not so flexible and cannot rapidly respond to unexpected events and circumstances.

This chapter describes the fundamental parts of this bionic entity that correspond to the business vision and mission, automation, and human side. The objective is to achieve specific outcomes: improving customer relationships, achieving customers' delight, implementing automation-augmented human operations, and reaching higher rates of innovation in products and services.

This chapter underlines that there is still no widespread awareness about the potential of bionic transformation. Some of the issues that organizations face in their evolution processes are related to their inaptitude toward change. The majority of these barriers are static operating processes, unqualified human resources, insufficient sources of data, lack of the proper digital tools, and poor automation design not considering collaboration with humans.

The leading cause of the difficulties faced by organizations inclined to undergo the bionic transformation concerns the lack of a well-defined business model characteristic of bionic enterprises. This book aims to solve this problem and support in building a successful business model to represent a guideline for financial institutions pursuing bionic transformation.

REFERENCES

Adamopoulou, E., & Moussiades, L. (2020). Chatbots: History, technology, and applications. *Machine Learning with Applications, 2,* 100006.

Agarwal, A., Singhal, C., & Thomas, R. (2021, March). *AI-powered decision making for the bank of the future.* McKinsey & Company.

Bluerating. (2019, July). *Banca Generali, ora il consulente ha un'arma in più.* Bluerating.com.

Calvert, P. (2017). Robots, the quiet workers, are you ready to take over? *Public Law Quarterly, 36*(2).

Capgemini Financial Services Analysis. (2021). *World Insurance Report 2021 executive interviews.*

Chen, C. C., Huang, H. H., & Chen, H. H. (2021). *From opinion mining to financial argument mining.* Springer Nature.

Chen, S. H. (2013). Devising appropriate service strategies for customers of different value: An integrated assessment model for the banking industry. *The International Journal of Human Resource Management, 24*(21), 3939–3956.

Christodoulou, P., Zinonos, Z., Carayannis, E. G., Chatzichristofis, S. A., & Christodoulou, K. (2021). *Known unknowns in an era of technological and viral disruptions—Implications for theory, policy, and practice.* et/11728/11735 Hephaestus Repository, Neapolis University, Paphos, Cyprus.

Chtourou, M. S., & Souiden, N. (2010). Rethinking the TAM model: Time to consider fun. *Journal of Consumer Marketing, 27*(4), 336–344.

Chu, P. Y., Lee, G. Y., & Chao, Y. (2012). Service quality, customer satisfaction, customer trust, and loyalty in an e-banking context. *Social Behavior and Personality, 40*(8), 1271–1283.

Cocca, T. (2016). Potential and limitations of virtual advice in wealth management. *Journal of Financial Transformation, 44*(1), 45–57.

Collie, F. (2021). *How banks are harnessing artificial intelligence.* IE Investment Executive.

Cui, L., Huang, S., Wei, F., Tan, C., Duan, C., & Zhou, M. (2017, July). Super-agent: A customer service chatbot for e-commerce websites. In *Proceedings of ACL 2017, System Demonstrations* (pp. 97–102).

Deutsche Bank. (2018). *How can mortgage lenders reap the benefits of the paperless revolution?* corporates.db.com.

Dignum, V. (2017). Responsible artificial intelligence: Designing AI for human values. *International Telecommunication Union Journal, 1*(1), 1–8.

Dirnberger, E., Freese, C., Hu, M., & Urban, M. (2020). *What lies beyond digital for insurance operations?* Boston Consulting Group-BCG. Featured Insights, Boston. 12, 20.

Edwards. N. (2020, February). *The digital side of deutsche bank that you have not heard about.* Forbes.

Eletter, S. F., Yaseen, S. G., & Elrefae, G. A. (2010). Neuro-based artificial intelligence model for loan decisions. *American Journal of Economics and Business Administration, 2*(1), 27.

Fallis, J., & Fuchs, O. (2019). *Transforming banking with smart automation.* Nice and Bain & Company.

Fintastico Team. (2019, June). *Banca Generali sempre più fintech con Ro4Ad.* Fintastico.

Fluss, D. (2017). *The AI revolution in customer service.* DestinationCRM.

Freese, C., Gard, J., Taglioni, G., et al. (2020). *The building blocks of bionic distribution in insurance.* Boston Consulting Group-BCG. Featured Insights, Boston. 7, 20.

Government Office for Science. (2015). *Artificial intelligence: Opportunities and implications for the future of decision making.* Government Office for Science.

Haenen, A. M. (2017). *Robo-advisors for financial services: The effect of proactivity and human intervention on customer evaluation* (Master thesis). Eindhoven University of Technology, Eindhoven, Netherlands.

Henry, T., Wampfeler, J., & Clarke, M. (2018). The hybrid advice model. *Automation*, 178.

Hosea, M. (2016, May). How brands are using artificial intelligence to enhance customer experience. *Marketing Week*.

Hu, T. I., & Tracogna, A. (2020). Multichannel customer journeys and their determinants: Evidence from motor insurance. *Journal of Retailing and Consumer Services*, 54, 102022.

Huang, B., Huan, Y., Xu, L. D., Zheng, L., & Zou, Z. (2019). Automated trading systems statistical and machine learning methods and hardware implementation: A survey. *Enterprise Information Systems*, 13(1), 132–144.

Huang, M. H., & Rust, R. T. (2018). Artificial intelligence in service. *Journal of Service Research*, 21(2), 155–172.

Hung, J. L., He, W., & Shen, J. (2020). Big data analytics for supply chain relationship in banking. *Industrial Marketing Management*, 86, 144–153.

Ivanov, S. H., & Webster, C. (2017, October 19–21). Adoption of robots, artificial intelligence and service automation by travel, tourism and hospitality companies-a cost-benefit analysis. Artificial Intelligence and Service Automation by Travel, Tourism and Hospitality Companies-A Cost-Benefit Analysis. *International Scientific Conference "Contemporary tourism-traditions and innovations"*. Sofia University, Bulgaria.

Jarrell, M. (2021). Artificial intelligence at square—Two use-cases. *Emerj*.

Karahanli, N. G., & Touma, J. (2021). *Digitalization of the customer experience in banking use of AI and SSTs in complex/sensitive tasks: Pre-collection* (thesis). KTH Royal Institute of Technology, Stockholm, Sweden.

Kuo, C. M., Chen, L. C., & Tseng, C. Y. (2017). Investigating an innovative service with hospitality robots. *International Journal of Contemporary Hospitality Management*, 29(5), 1305–1321.

Lee, I., & Shin, Y. J. (2020). Machine learning for enterprises: Applications, algorithm selection, and challenges. *Business Horizons*, 63(2), 157–170.

Li, D., & Du, Y. (2017). *Artificial intelligence with uncertainty*. CRC Press.

Lui, A., & Lamb, G. W. (2018). Artificial intelligence and augmented intelligence collaboration: Regaining trust and confidence in the financial sector. *Information & Communications Technology Law*, 27(3), 267–283.

Madan, R., Agrawal, R., & Matta, G. M. (2015). Relationship marketing strategies in the banking sector: A review. *International Journal of BRIC Business Research (IJBBR)*, 4, 1–10.

Maskey, S. (2018). *How artificial intelligence is helping financial institutions*. Forbes Technology Council.

Neff, G., & Nagy, P. (2016). Talking to bots: Symbiotic agency and the case of Tay. *International Journal of Communication*.

Nicoletti, B. (2021). *Banking 5.0*. Springer.

Nikiforova, T. (2017). The place of robo-advisors in the UK independent financial advice market. Substitute or complement? *Substitute or Complement*.

Noppen, P. V. (2019). *The qualitative impact of robotic process automation* (Master's thesis). Utrecht University, Utrecht, Netherlands.

Paredes, D. (2018, July). *ANZ bank latest company to employ 'digital human'*. CIO.

Parker, H., & Appel, S. E. (2021). On the path to artificial intelligence: The effects of a robotics solution. In a Financial Services Firm. *The South African Journal of Industrial Engineering, 32*(2), 37–47.

Ping An Group. (2020, March). *Ping An life: Livestreaming channel + product reform blueprint to over one million agents across China*. Ping An.

PYMNTS. (2018). *Is AI's next evolution to digital humans?* PYMNTS.com.

Rausch, J. (2021, February). *Personalization in financial services: An imperative to stay relevant*. pkglobal.com.

Reid, M. (2017). Rethinking the fourth amendment in the age of super-computers, artificial intelligence, and robots. *West Virginia Law Review, 100*.

Samuels, M. (2019, July). Digital transformation: How one bank is using AI, big data and chatbots to create new services. *ZDNet*.

Shevat, A. (2017). *Designing bots: Creating conversational experiences*. O'Reilly Media Inc.

Škavić, F. (2019). *The implementation of artificial intelligence and its future potential* (Doctoral dissertation). University of Zagreb, Faculty of Economics and Business, Department of Informatics.

Syed, R., Suriadi, S., Adams, M., Bandara, W., Leemans, S. J., Ouyang, C., & Reijers, H. A. (2020). Robotic process automation: Contemporary themes and challenges. *Computers in Industry, 115*, 103162.

Travia, G. (2021, March). *Robo Advisor: Cosa sono, come funzionano e la lista dei migliori*. Finaria.

Wall, L. D. (2018). Some financial regulatory implications of artificial intelligence. *Journal of Economics and Business, 100*, 55–63.

West, D. M., & Allen, J. R. (2018, April). *How artificial intelligence is transforming the world* (Report).

Yip, A. W., & Bocken, N. M. (2018). Sustainable business model archetypes for the banking industry. *Journal of Cleaner Production, 174*, 150–169.

CHAPTER 6

Bionic Banking Project

INTRODUCTION

New solutions are rapidly redefining what financial institutions can do. What seemed fanciful as recently as a few years ago is now achievable and quickly becoming standard. Better collaboration human-automation, Robotic Process Automation (RPA), Augmented Intelligence (AI), virtual operator attendants, and other forms of intelligent automation have advanced fast.

These capabilities can have a broad set of potential benefits. Data science tools can discover trends and behaviors that enable financial institutions to improve customer loyalty, proactively find upselling and cross-selling opportunities, and identify broken processes.

The challenge for financial institutions is embracing and integrating automation and humans in intelligent automation to add value for the customers and the organization. Nearly all financial institutions have automation pilots of some sort. Few have reached the status of driving value at scale.

Bain and Nice have worked with retail financial institutions of all sizes to embed intelligent automation capabilities, supporting the banking workforce with new automation that boosts productivity and improves service delivery (Fallis & Fuchs, 2019). Their approach produces strong results in the near term while positioning customers to thrive in the medium and long-term future.

Financial institutions operate in an increasingly complex competitive, regulatory, and technological environment, with vast amounts of sensitive personal information at the heart of their operations. The consequence is that they face many critical considerations in deploying new automation.

There is optimism for how next-generation intelligent automation tools can transform banking processes in this rapidly evolving world. Existing human-automation solutions have already been implemented successfully in several financial processes.

Lean management and transformation are two driving forces of business success. Some aspects of lean management may negatively affect an organization's success with specific transformations with fundamentally different concepts. This chapter develops a process to minimize such impacts. It combines lean six sigma principles and tools with bionic transformation. In addition, the chapter discusses different examples where this method was successful.

HUMAN-AUTOMATION COLLABORATION (HAC) PROJECT

The micro-level and behavioral evidence suggest that using automation solutions in isolation may be fashionable and seen as progressive. Still, it is a real challenge for organizations to see a return on investment (Jacobides, 2021). This message comes, for example, through from all consulting reports on AI. For example, BCG Henderson Institute and MIT conducted a study (Ransbotham et al., 2020) showing that although more than 50% of organizations are deploying AI, only 11% report significant benefits from its implementations. These findings suggest that organizations still have to innovate to benefit from automation solutions. For example, even within organizations that invested in building foundational capabilities, such as AI infrastructure, talent, and strategy, only 21% achieved significant financial benefits. BCG recommends "organizational learning with AI," that is, implementing AI at scale while explicitly focusing on human-automation collaboration. This solution allows realizing significant financial benefits of up to 73%. These figures illustrate organizations' challenges, given the inherent complexity of automation and the effort and time required to redesign the organization around it (Ransbotham et al., 2020; Tambe et al., 2019).

To succeed is essential to follow the entire life cycle of human-automation collaboration along the main stages: of the bionic transformation.

Human-Automation Collaboration Models

Financial institutions should create an organization that works "bionically," with augmented intelligence and humans supporting and enhancing customer relationships. Bionic banking organizations leverage their data and analytics capabilities to serve a wide range of customer needs that can extend beyond traditional banking products and services. They will benefit from a bionic approach's insight, speed, and power only if their organization is agile enough to keep up with their environmental challenges.

Financial institutions still have advantages. Customers trust them. They have unique knowledge about their account holders and what they are doing with their money. Automation cannot cover all aspects of advice, and customers still prefer human help for complex or sensitive transactions.

What gave financial institutions a benefit in the past constitutes now issues: reliance on the inertia of long-standing customer relationships, the perception of "experience," the emphasis on stability rather than agility, and the expensive physical presence of branch networks (Wessel, 2021). The danger is that potential competitors, like the bigtech organizations (Nicoletti, 2021), figure out how to overcome the remaining compliance barriers.

These capabilities have a wide set of potential benefits. For example, data science tools can reveal trends and behaviors that enable financial institutions to improve customer loyalty, proactively spot upselling and cross-selling opportunities, and identify broken processes. New automation solutions can connect humans and automation, automating repetitive and tedious tasks so that operators can focus on improved customer services and more efficiently manage back-office operations. A more advanced form of automation technology, virtual attendant robots can enhance operator performance by offering real-time process guidance.

Automation and humans can interact in five ways (the five Cs):

- Coexistence occurs when human operators and automation are in the same environment but generally do not interact directly.
- Concurrence is when the human operators and automation work in the same workspace but at different times.

- Cooperation occurs is when the human operators and automation work in the same workspace simultaneously, though each focuses on separate tasks.
- Collaboration is when the human operators and automation execute a task together. The action of the one has immediate consequences on the other, thanks to specific physical or virtual connectors.
- Companionship (or Teaming) is when the human operator and automation decide dynamically roles and responsibilities.

Human-Automation Collaboration (HAC) is exciting for improved operational flexibility and efficiency toward mass personalization. Current HAC development mainly undertakes either human-centered or automation-centered manner reactively. Operations are conducted by following pre-defined instructions, without an efficient integration of automation and human cognitions. The following pages present a framework used for manufacturing but applied in this book to bionic banking and virtual robots (Li et al., 2021) and generalized from Human–Robot Collaboration (HRC) to Human-Automation Collaboration (HAC).

By implementing advanced banking solutions, artificial intelligence, robot processing automation, and big data analytics toward a generation of bionic banking, financial institutions are striving to achieve:

- High efficiency and flexibility of on-demand banking for mass personalization (Zheng et al., 2019).
- High accuracy and reliability for delivering complex services (Li et al., 2020).
- Effective domain expertise supporting physical or virtual branch transactions (Liu et al., 2020).

To tackle these challenges, human-automation collaboration (HAC) is a relevant implementation strategy, combining high accuracy, strength, and repeatability of automation with high flexibility and adaptability of humans to realize optimal overall effectiveness and productivity (Wang et al., 2020; Wang & Wang, 2021).

The evaluation of the evolution route of human-automation relationships depends on two criteria:

- Role of humans and automation in the collaborative work and

- Level of automation.

In an optimal HAC solution, human reaches an intuitive manner, while the automation achieves an adaptive manner, by dynamically adjusting their respective roles. There are various levels of HAC paradigms derived from the 5C architecture model of a cyber-physical system (Lee et al., 2015; Yao et al., 2018):

- Coordination represents humans and automation jointly working for a common goal.
- Conception denotes the perceptual capabilities of automation.
- Cyber stands for the adaptive control of automation.
- Cognition represents the cognitive understanding of activities/tasks.
- Configuration stands for the whole automation level, where humans and automation co-work in a self-organized manner.

Proactive Human-Automation Collaboration

Several paradigms/concepts have been brought up to date.

Symbiotic HRC has emerged, aiming to combine the best skills of robots and humans, which "possesses the skills and ability of perception, processing, reasoning, decision making, adaptive execution, mutual support and self-learning through real-time multimodal communication for context-aware human–robot collaboration" (Wang & Wang, 2021).

Proactive HRC is introduced and defined as "a self-organizing, bi-directional collaboration between human operators and robots in banking activities, where they can proactively work for a common goal in every execution loop over time" (Iarovyi et al., 2015). Following this definition, proactive HRC takes full advantage of each agent's capabilities and is essentially a follow-up phase of Symbiotic HAC with a high-level automation level. Automation allows a long-term bi-directional collaboration between humans and automation in banking activities.

Proactive HAC can be defined as an advanced form of symbiotic HRC with high-level cognitive teamwork skills to be achieved one step at a time (Li et al., 2021):

- Inter-collaboration cognition, establishing bi-directional empathy in the execution loop based on a holistic understanding of humans and automation solutions.
- Temporal cooperation prediction, estimating human-automation interaction of hierarchical sub-tasks/activities over time for proactive planning.
- Self-organizing teamwork, converging knowledge of distributed HAC systems for self-organization learning and task allocation.

Inter-Collaboration Cognition
It is possible to consider human-automation collaboration from two aspects: organizational structure and governance activities (Erten, 2021). The division of labor and operator abilities is under organizational structure, and decision-making and administration are under governance.

One of the ways to analyze the effect of new solutions in the workplace is to distinguish between professional jobs and tasks activities. Each job contains various tasks that require different cognitive abilities and levels. It is possible to classify the tasks in two dimensions: manual-cognitive and routine-non-routine (Erten, 2021). The base of routine tasks is on well-understood procedures. Clear rules and algorithms define them.

On the contrary, non-routine tasks require flexibility, creativity, complex problem-solving, and human interaction in the short and medium term. Augmented Intelligence (AI) can perform manual or cognitive routine tasks and support operators in non-routine tasks. AI allows humans who primarily perform normal duties and activities in organizations to improve themselves and take up jobs that require creativity, innovation, and social and interpersonal skills. Such collaboration in terms of the division of labor enables the optimization of the labor force and more efficient use of resources by directing persons to more value-added jobs (Bruckner et al., 2017; Corvalán, 2019; Eggers et al., 2017; Makridakis, 2017; Manyika et al., 2017; Young et al., 2019).

Another approach distinguishes between intuitive and analytical decision-making. Jarrahi (2018) approached the human-machines relationship through uncertainty, complexity, and doubleness, which are the main problems of decision-making activities. In this context, it is possible to distinguish decision-making in analytical and intuitive.

- Analytical approaches for decision-making come from deep knowledge.
- Intuitive approaches address the problem with a holistic and discrete perspective.

While the problem-solving ability of automation is analytical, that of humans is intuitive. These two types can be used as parallel decision-making systems to think through various possibilities more effectively. One way to embody the synergistic relationship between automation and humans is to combine the speed of automation with humans' superior, intuitive judgment, and insight in collecting and analyzing information. Automation can help manage complexity with their analytical skills. Humans' intuition helps with the ambiguity and doubleness of decision-making. M. H. Jarrahi (2018) conceptualized the combination of human-AI as "symbiosis". This combination is called human-automation collaboration in this book.

The human-automation symbiosis is possible in discretionary administrative power as a particular type of decision-making. Automation can be a governance tool in the field of administrative discretion. It is possible to use AI to make rational decisions regarding uncertain tasks regarding efficiency, productivity, equity, accountability, manageability, and feasibility. This discretionary administrative power, called artificial discretion, may need to be included as a governance component that increases and supports human appreciation in administrative tasks with too little or too much information. Depending on competitive values, the result may cause various possibilities or more than one reasonable solution (Barth & Arnold, 1999; Young et al., 2019).

Inter-collaboration cognition has the objective of human-automation collaboration in executing banking activities with bi-directional assistance derived from cognitive empathy. The holistic context awareness of the HAC scenario provides access to semantic knowledge, understanding, and reasoning for the bi-directional empathy. The inter-collaboration cognition supports bi-directional engagement proactively, with humans' roles and automation dynamically changing as required.

Temporal Collaboration
HAC in banking can be a time-sensitive task whose function modules consist of active collision avoidance (Realyvásquez-Vargas et al., 2019), decision-making, and customer journey planning (Kanazawa et al., 2019),

and so on. Therefore, scholars and banking practitioners aim to forecast the human operator's future activity beyond the existing adaptive control of robots, eliminating the limitation of uncertainty associated with human operators during the collaboration (Zhang, Liu et al., 2020). The next level is how-to-cooperate among the hierarchical sub-tasks/activities as the co-work progresses in time. The temporal cooperation of a human and automation in HAC consists of their temporal interaction and the hierarchical relation in the progression of the sub-tasks/activities (Morais et al., 2021). The discovery of current human intention and future interaction with the coexisting neighbors distills foreseeable semantic knowledge for efficient cooperation in HAC. The access to the predictability of the future semantic knowledge between these entities can facilitate time-sensitive collaboration intelligence for decision-making and customer journey planning, such as proactive assistance either from a human to a robot or from a robot to a human. The operator assistant system helps the human better understand his sub-task in collaboration and prevent operating errors (De Pace et al., 2020). To some extent, temporal cooperation prediction also provides the proper cooperation relation in future sub-tasks (Li et al., 2021).

Self-Organizing Teamwork
Self-organizing teamwork aims to resolve divergences of leader/follower roles between automation and humans by converging prior knowledge of co-works from decentralized HAC systems. Robots and human participators can understand which banking tasks/activities they are more qualified for in terms of their capabilities and change their roles on the fly according to specific situations.

The self-organizing network determines human and automation's roles in collaboration. It allocates the corresponding resources and sub-tasks to each participant. Outputs of the self-organizing network are the most crucial inputs of automation action planning and operator assistant systems. Self-organizing networks can be considered as the central brain of proactive HAC.

Habito
A fintech organization, Habito, combines mortgage advice through "digital mortgage advisers" with human advisers (Lui & Lamb, 2018). Habito

> can provide fast, personalized advice. They claim that their digital mortgage advisers can quickly overview a customer's mortgage in just five minutes. Human advisers then provide more detailed guidance on the application procedure (Temkin, 2017).

CRITICAL SUCCESS FACTORS OF BIONIC BANKING

CSFs are the areas in which satisfactory results can ensure success for a bionic banking initiative (Bullen & Rockhart, 1981). There are several Critical Success Factors (CSF) for bionic banking. Since these areas are critical, the management should closely monitor CSFs to determine whether events are progressing well and, if necessary, take remediation actions (Bullen & Rockhart, 1981).

The success of the transformation is no longer due to automation alone. "Digital natives," organizations born in the digital age and primarily operate online such as Amazon, Netflix, and Google, have demonstrated that human-automation collaboration is essential (Reeves, 2020). The human dimension is a decisive determining factor. By relying upon the potential of both automation and humans, digital businesses are on the way toward a significant consequent evolution: the bionic transformation of the entire organization.

Critical Success Factors for Bionic Banking

Bionic banking includes a set of solutions enabling humans and processes integrated with automation. These solutions change products, processes, business models, organizations, and systems significantly (Schmidt et al., 2015). They should also aim to increase sustainability.

The critical support factors for bionic banking are several. This book lists them for mnemonics reasons with words starting with "C": Collaboration, Complementarity, Cognition, Confidence, Contribution, Competence, Customization, Creatural (humanness), and Clarity (visibility).

The model classifies the bionic banking factors in hard and soft from the point of view of measurements. Measures can be either "soft," meaning subjective and qualitative, or "hard," meaning objective and quantitative. All these factors require strict management tools (or Command to continue with words starting with C). In turn, specific solutions support them.

Soft

- Collaboration refers to the need to have all the applications, robots, and operators working together.
- Complementarity refers to the fact that there might be additionality in automation and work done by humans.
- Confidence or trust must be the cornerstone of bionic banking solutions. The basis of trust is a stringent security policy. Cyber-attacks would be dangerous for a bionic system based on persons and non-human agents, highly integrated factors, and fragile units.
- Creatural refers to the humanness of the job.
- Competence in the case of bionic banking refers to e-competencies (Smit, 2016).

Hard

- Customization aims to satisfy as many needs as possible of each customer, in contrast to conventional tools, which try to reach as many customers as possible while meeting a limited number of customer needs (Coelho & Henseler, 2012).
- Cognition means intelligent use of data. All information systems, sensors, and numerical controls (all thanks to the integration connection tools) generate vast numbers of data, referred to as big data. It is important to analyze data which are at the base of decisions.
- Contribution to the organizations' financial results is essential in bionic banking as in many other business activities (Van Leeuwen & Klomp, 2006).
- Clarity (or explainability) means creating a suite of HAC solutions that enables humans to understand, appropriately trust, and effectively manage the emerging generation of artificially intelligent partners (Gunning, 2017).

The following pages examine each of the nine "C" in bionic banking.

Collaboration
Collaboration in the case of bionic banking has a more generalized meaning, including human-automation collaboration. This collaboration is a fundamental challenge for bionic banking. Automation can play a crucial role in performing organizational tasks more efficiently and empowering operators through symbiotic interactions with persons. Operators must take part in the design, analysis, and interpretation of automation-generated results dynamically.

Bionic systems face high technological requirements. Relationships are also meaningful in the physical world, where success depends on customization, consulting, or enablement. For a bionic system to reach critical mass, its designer must deeply understand and shape the real-world behaviors of the people and the automation (Reeves, 2020). This approach requires building strong relationships with multiple actors and often developing specific capabilities. Creating value in bionic banking requires not only transactions but also effective change management.

Traditional ICT applications have provided some support for exchanging information with the customers and the intermediaries (Kollmann, 2011). Solution advances in a bionic banking initiative significantly increase the potential to integrate with the customer. The critical change is the transition from an "exchange of information" to a "free flow of information" in the value network among the products, services, and related organizations (Schlick et al., 2014). It is necessary to coordinate this exchange effectively (Van Weele, 2010). A free movement implies a higher degree of exchangeability of the data, a higher degree of automation in transferring information, and integrated use of the data in the approach to data science (Lee et al., 2014). Application Programming Interfaces (API) significantly contributes to the collaboration,

The depth of integration (among financial institutions and customers) and the entire banking process' automation potential in bionic banking is much greater than in traditional banking services. The latter is limited to helping to complete the tasks using a computer application based on personalized information and documents exchange. The automation process, a higher degree of integration, and AI characterize bionic banking. The base of bionic banking is on digitization and advanced automation within the organizations and functions of the ecosystem. It is not limited to new and improved solutions inside the specific institution. The collaboration is within the ecosystem.

Next to the degree of integration, relationships with partners will differ in bionic banking, such as new services complementary to the banking services (Essig, 2006). Collaboration is the main factor for the survival of the banking environment. Eventually, organizations that will not be part of a collaborative ecosystem will tend to disappear.

Complementarity

As a consequence of technological change, human-automation relationships become increasingly complex and are not limited to a simple substitution of human labor by automation. Instead, there should be co-working in the sense of collaborative activity between humans and automation in providing services where both inputs are complementary. Co-working automation enhances the productivity of human labor. Automation still mainly takes place in a self-contained mode. Humans can learn, speak, think, and interact with the environment to perform actions and study. The most creative and vital ability of human beings is to learn new things. The human brain has the ability for self-adaptation and knowledge inference, which goes beyond experience (Zheng et al., 2017). Human intelligence is creative, complex, and dynamic (Guilford, 1967; Sternberg, 1984). The creativity of human beings means brings that human intelligence is skillful in abstract thinking, reasoning, and innovation, creating new knowledge and making associations. Humans are more adept at learning, reasoning, collaborating, and other advanced intelligence activities, thanks to the dynamic nature of human knowledge evolution and learning ability (Zheng et al., 2017).

Bionic systems will primarily involve existing niches with existing capabilities and existing competitors. Therefore, bionic systems must balance between creating entirely new capabilities and taking advantage of or actively reshaping existing ones (Reeves, 2020). They must be able both to create something new and to rejuvenate something old.

In considering an analogy with human intelligence, automation has the features of normalization, repeatability, and logicality. Normalization refers to the fact that automation can deal with structured information. Repeatability refers to the mechanical nature of automation. Repetitive work does not degrade the efficiency or accuracy of the solutions because of the powerful computing ability and characteristics of automation. Logicality means that automation (such as AI) deals with symbolized problems. This characteristic means that automation is better at processing some discrete tasks instead of discovering or breaking the rules by itself (Poole et al., 1997). AI and human intelligence each have distinct advantages, and they are highly complementary (Zheng et al., 2017).

Confidence
Highly integrated networks are vulnerable to systemic risks such as total computer applications collapse or hacking or internet viruses which can fully invade integrated systems.

Intelligent banking shares real-time information among all stakeholders in the ecosystem. They make banking processes excellent and transparent, but they must be secure. Security will require an entirely diverse set of capabilities and competencies to cope with cyber-attacks (Zhu et al., 2011). To find these talents requires finding new sources with the help of partners.in banking, such as partnership programs with universities and research centers. It helps explore new accesses such as social networks, social media, and similar.

Competence
Competence is the ability to do something well (Eraut, 1998). In bionic banking, the interest is for the so-called e-competencies (Romani, 2009). Human e-competences describe knowledge, competencies, and other abilities to use automation tools to perform a function respecting a standard in professional and/or personal settings (Fernández-Sanz et al., 2017).

Bionic systems need to develop to reach critical mass but, at the same time, must have a deep focus on particular problems and deploy the relevant domain expertise to address them. Their business model creates more value by solving specific problems rather than populating a large open niche (Reeves, 2020). This approach is the way in which they will be able to satisfy customer needs fully.

Only if the banking professionals have digital competencies, an organization can fully receive help from the opportunities offered by bionic banking. Core skills include good traditional skills like collaboration, effective communicating, initiative, persistence, trustworthiness, creativity, and diligence, which will become more central to career success (Oosthuizen, 2021). Operators' ability to keep learning to be current and upskill their abilities is even more important than the specific things they learn. Operators need to harness the skill to reinvent themselves over and over, thereby staying relevant. It is a conscious choice to keep learning.

Customization
High-tech ventures are likely to be more successful if they implement product and services customization strategies to target existing customers rather than addressing only new markets (Kakati, 2003). Customization of products and services supports customers' delight and getting more of them (Halstrick, 2020). Personal and individual treatment of the customer can be favorable if they perceive a unique and personal treatment. The effect is a compelling customer journey (Halstrick, 2020).

Cognition
Analysis of the data and their intelligent use are critical success factors for organizations that want to exploit the potential of bionic banking. Data analytics are an essential enabler for bionic banking (Koch, 2014). Intelligent solutions and related algorithms allow the combination, processing, and analysis of large volumes of data from many heterogeneous sources. Using all this big data in machine learning models, the organization can improve the knowledge of its customers, partners, and markets, forecast market trends, and remediate processes and products' shortcomings. Data science can help managers make better and more informed decisions. Big data analytics can automatically make operational decisions about banking in a growing number of cases, such as interests on loans or pricing decisions (Nicoletti, 2014a).

Data science is essential in bionic banking (Chiang et al., 2018). Data analytics, data mining, analysis, and big data distribution are critical supports for data science. They have the 9Vs characteristics: (Veracity, Variety, Velocity, Volume, Validity, Variability, Volatility, Visualization, and Value) needed to process the bionic banking data for adding value to the organization (Owais & Hussein, 2016) (Table 6.1).

The data analytics tools can support the organization and its partners in improving the design, marketing, sales, operations, and support. Predictive analysis of where and when to expect the next event, relevant from the financial institution's perspective, offers perfect services.

Contribution
Contribution, in bionic banking, refers to the financial, innovation, and sustainability additions. The productivity benefits resulting from traditional ICT application initiatives are a reduction in transaction and process costs. Bionic banking supports financial institutions to turn paper documents into digital ICT applications. Even more critical, a bionic

Table 6.1 Characteristics of big data

Life cycle	Collecting data		Integrity of data		Processing data		Visualize data	Worth of data
Name	Variety	Veracity	Variability	Validity	Volatility	Volume	Velocity	Visualization	Value
Characteristics	The types of data: • Structured • Semi-structured • Unstructured	The degree to which data can be trusted	The ways in which the big data can be used and formatted	The data is correct and accurate for the intended use	The retention policy is implemented Once retention period expires, data are destroyed or stored	The amount of data derived from myriad sources	The speed at which data can be generated	The making of all that huge amount of data comprehensible and easy to read, understand and report	The business value of the data collected

Source Own elaboration

transformation moves from a labor-intensive activity into automated workflows and sustainable ICT processes. Traditionally, ICT applications focused on process efficiency. The goals of bionic banking are increasing productivity, flexibility, and performance to meet today's customers' high customization needs (Kagermann, 2014).

Bionic banking also supports critical activities like managing relationships with partners, such as insurance organizations in the bancassurance. The driving factors of bionic banking contribution are improving sales, operations, and new services design. Bionic banking enables the development of faster design, sale, and operational processes (Schuh et al., 2014). The organization can activate new product-service functions and improve the banking margins (Schuh et al., 2014).

Clarity

The role of emotive responses in communicative behavior between automation and humans is relevant (Breazeal, 2001). Appropriately done, effective communication should be natural and intuitive for people to understand. This situation implies that the bionics emotive behavior should be life-like.

Transparency and visibility are essential to assuring an effective human-automation collaboration (Ezer et al., 2019).

Creatural (Humanness)

Some banking customers base their decisions on how they feel rather than on what they know. For operators to be effective in the workplace, they should engage their customers' hearts, minds, and souls (Oosthuizen, 2021). Ultimately, it is their humanness that defines and distinguishes them, Automation should support them in reaching these targets.

Significant Challenges

All these critical factors pose a substantial challenge and a potential change in financial institutions' work. They need an integral and complete bionic transformation of the organization and competencies, both of which should change synergistically (Geissbauer et al., 2016; Nicoletti, 2019). Organizations need to create new job profiles for example to support the need for AI experts, contract experts on intellectual property, or data scientists to analyze relevant data, their management, and their use.

A characteristic of bionic banking is the increasing digitization and networking of products, processes, business models, and value-adding activities. It requires significant investments. Bionic banking also involves integration with other organizations' information systems in the ecosystem (Nicoletti, 2019). All partners must have access to the relevant data and process them to support decision-making. Linked data offers a solution in this respect (Data 2014). Linked data is a method that allows to aggregate and collect data from distributed sources. For accessing the data on the web (Tomassetti et al., 2011), the data must be published under the condition of "open" use for a specific customer category. This publishing allows the organizations to browse and navigate the data by any media through deep linking and aggregate them (Azim et al., 2016). Linked data is now a mature solution with exciting potential. It requires large numbers of data related together. Linked data can supply powerful support to the relationship into the banking activities (Bizer et al., 2011; Nicoletti, 2019).

INNOVATION METHODS

Many methods can support the redesign of the processes described in this book. These methods are helpful to design and evaluate solutions based on human-automation collaboration. They can come from the tools used in lean principles, six sigma, agile management, and digitization. This book will not consider the latter ones since many publications cover them.

One of the best tools for process design is Quality Function Deployment QFD), commonly called the House of Quality (Chan & Wu, 2002). It identifies the potential customer value of the innovation based on customer (be then internal or external) needs and an innovation quality characteristic. The analysis through QFD can determine when innovation is valuable, so there is no waste of resources for innovation that may not be beneficial.

Another helpful tool is the Theory of Inventive Problem Solving (TRIZ). It is possible to define the requirements for innovation by introducing the TRIZ problem-solving approach in finding innovative solutions to technical problems, especially in product and service development processes. TRIZ helps in defining the solutions necessary to improve these processes. TRIZ is beneficial toward lean practice because it efficiently utilizes resources in the system to eliminate wastes.

Yamashima et al. describe another method, named the Innovative Product Development Process (IPDP) (Yamashina et al., 2002). It systematically integrates QFD with TRIZ and enables technical innovation for new products' practical and systematic creation of technological innovations. In IPDP, the target products' functions and mechanisms are deployed in parallel into hierarchical structures. The tool that most requires technical innovation is specified from analyzing customers' needs by calculating an index with suitable weights. The definition of the technical problems to be solved considers the relationship between the specified mechanism and corresponding functions or quality characteristics. The application of TRIZ helps in developing technical innovation.

There are exciting developments in ergonomics design approaches to deliver digital solutions and achieve a unified experience from interaction and business process design perspectives. The new method analyzes the opportunities new solutions may bring to enhance current ergonomics design approaches from integration and intelligence design perspectives. In this direction, an interesting approach is to address the challenges in today's ergonomics practices in delivering digital solutions with an Interaction, Process, Integration, and Intelligence (IPII) design approach (Xu et al., 2019).

Innovation Processes

Innovation can be in products or processes (Tushman & Nadler, 1980). Innovation can also be relative to an organization or business models (Nicoletti, 2014b). Breuer (2013) reports some successful examples of lean innovation in venturing (Ries & Euchner, 2013). Innovation can be incremental or radical (Ettlie et al., 1984), modular or architectural (Henderson & Clark, 1990). At the heart of innovation is the ability to connect the strategy and tactics associated with developing a system of innovation from a macro perspective with the mechanics of effectively transitioning ideas into business models.

Freeman and Perez (1988) define innovation as introducing new and improved ways of doing an activity. In an economic sense, innovation is successful with the first commercial transaction involving new or improved services, products, processes, or business model organizations. Innovation is restricted to intentional attempts to bring benefits from the transformation. Transformation might bring economic benefits, personal growth, increased satisfaction, group coherence, better organizational communication, productivity, and financial measures. The bionic transformation often includes technological changes such as new products, production processes, advanced technology, automation, and new information and communication technologies ICT).

Many methods help for acquiring a better understanding of the innovation process. These methods range from simple "pipeline" or "black box" models to complex models. Some of them focus on customer product innovation' others are concerned with industrial innovation. Although several methods help describe the innovation process, no model appears to be capable of being used as a generalized model of innovation (Koskinen et al., 2002).

Design Thinking

Design thinking (DT) is a method to introduce and implement bionic banking processes. It uses a customer-centric approach that helps discover nuanced, even implicit, customer needs at the start of the innovation process. It considers feasibility, including the available solutions and viability (Gruber et al., 2015).

Design thinking is different from traditional business thinking since (Brown & Martin, 2015):

- Shifts the focus in the direction of the customer. An empathy exercise achieves trying better to understand customer needs and behaviors from their perspective. It is important not to rely on what the customer says but on what he/she thinks, says, and does.
- Creates a stimulating atmosphere that promotes innovative ideas and encourages the participation and experimentation of the entire team.

- Requires a team with different profiles and diverse ways of thinking. The method promotes collaboration and the generation of innovative ideas, thus reducing the risk of relying on a unique idea.

Implementing design thinking is not enough to set up an innovation lab and apply design thinking within an organization. It is crucial to make it part of the day-to-day culture and processes (Liebau, 2016).

Design Thinking Method
The design thinking process has five stages (Siota et al., 2017):

- Empathize requires understanding the end-customers problems and needs.
- Define involves reviewing all the information collected to define the problem to be solved and start setting goals.
- Ideate requires thinking new ways to solve the organization core's issues. It involves generating ideas to produce innovative solutions.
- Prototype is essential to producing cost-effective and simple prototypes that generate feedback from potential customers or developers (Kelley, 2001). It is possible to prototype just about anything: a new product or service, a process, even an organization or a business model. What counts is moving the ball forward, achieving some parts of the goal of the new solution.
- Test aims to get feedback from the end customers. This stage is related to the Empathize stage since the aim is to verify the understanding of what the customer or prospect thinks about the product and why he/she feels that (Nash, 2015).

In a bionic banking project, adding the "Deploy" stage moving to implementation is necessary. It refers to deploying the solution in the real environment, making the essential tuning, and finding the lessons learned.

Umpqua
Umpqua Holdings Corporation, d.b.a. Umpqua Bank, is a financial holding company based in downtown Portland, Oregon, United States. The financial institution principal operating segments are personal banking and lending, business banking and lending, and wealth management. The

bank serves consumers and businesses in the community. As of 2015, Umpqua Bank had $24 billion in assets and $18 billion in deposits and was among the largest 60 banks in the nation.[1]

When the Umpqua bank acquired Sterling Financial Corporation, doubling its size, and creating the West Coast's largest community bank overnight, the CEO Ray Davis decided to reinvest in design thinking across the organization (Brown, 2015). Umpqua created and set up an exhibition at its headquarters in Portland, Oregon, focused on designing human-centered experiences, products, and technological tools. From executives to associates, teams large and small walked through the exhibit. Davis invited them to sign their names at the end only if they believed in the approach. Organization evangelists handed out Moleskines with tips on "how to be better-makers," An internal tool (built on IDEO's OI Engine) helps teams master design thinking through open-platform challenges.

Lean and Bionic Transformation

The lean and bionic transformation process represents the systematic interpretation of lean thinking principles regarding the different types of innovation and development, considering the possibilities of human-automation collaboration.

Human-automation collaboration is essential for any organization. It is becoming increasingly critical as the demands of the global economy increase. Organizations need to be agile, current, and smart to face the challenges of the changing global economy (Wilson & Doz, 2011; Oza & Abrahamsson, 2009). It is critical to define clearly its transformation process.

Based on observations in the Toyota Production System, D. Mehri (2006) illustrated some of the adverse effects of the lean design process on product innovation. In particular, he underlined that the original Lean Thinking method, rather than allowing open innovation, requires engineers to follow strict flows of design. Due to such a product design approach, heavily based on benchmarking and standardization, internal

---

[1] Securities and Exchange Commission Form 10-k. Commission File number 001-34624.

innovations become difficult. The lean and bionic transformation method allows overcoming these issues.

This section focuses on automation-human collaboration design, describes its phases, and shows how to use and benefit from the combination of Lean Six Sigma with the bionic transformation toward a powerful lean and bionic transformation for improving processes. The method aims to add value to the customers and the organization, improve effectiveness, eliminate waste, minimize operating costs, and reduce time-to-market by redesigning the business model's processes and automation in light of the human-automation collaboration. This approach is increasingly necessary for global success and is essential for the successful lean and bionic application to innovation processes.

Research Method
Essential for lean and bionic transformation is the definition of the value-adding of the innovation. Therefore, the starting point of lean and bionic transformation is a systematic method to define and handle target values and requirements regarding the innovation as an enabler for a lean development process: the value system. The value system represents a framework for mapping holistic, hierarchical, dynamic, and transparent processes (Schuh et al., 2008).

The value system defines, structures, and prioritizes values specifically for one specific innovation project. All relevant stakeholders in the innovation processes, like external and internal customers, define the values, considering the organization's strategy and culture. These aspects represent the basis for a value-oriented alignment of innovation projects and processes. According to Gudem et al. (2013), maximizing customer value is a core principle in innovation, but the value definitions depend on logical reasoning rather than real-life observations. Based on empirical insights concerning different stakeholders' customer value perceptions, these authors suggest a redefinition of the functional product value calculation in Lean Product Development (LPD). Their method integrates emotional customer value into the traditional model, which minimizes operating costs and reduces time-to-market.

Value system practices focus on the market orientation of products and services. Products and services rely on the value network to contribute to customer value (Nicoletti, 2021). Globalization, competition, and the high cost of production influence the value system imperatives. Organizations involved in the value system need innovation. Automation can support improvements in transformation performance in many organizations. There should be efforts to use automation as a tool to innovate processes, products, and services to establish improved management practices to harness better returns on investment and customer delight.

Lean and Bionic Transformation
Several macro-phases compose the lean and bionic transformation. Transformation to be successful must adopt a process that this chapter describes as the 7D's (Define, Discover, Design, Develop, Deconstruct, Deploy, and Diffuse). It is essential to apply this method and its tools in a strong partnership between the sectors of the organization involved, quality and support organizations (such as ICT, Finance, or Operations) (Nicoletti, 2012). Stakeholders from all parties need to align in setting up and staffing the transformation project team. More importantly, the organizations must treat the initial application of the lean and bionic transformation method as the beginning of a continuous cycle that generates improvements and lead to a change in the culture of the organizations toward lean thinking (Womack & Jones, 2003) and bionic transformation. A "problem" or "challenge" should not trigger process improvement efforts. It should be a substantial part of the organizational culture.

It is essential to blend process improvements and bionic solutions. Based on research and experience, one can profitably use the lean and bionic transformation method. The lean and bionic transformation method has seven macro and 29 micro phases (Fig. 6.1).

Financial institutions should focus on the following priorities and actions to assess the increasing list of solutions that support a digital process redesign. (At the end of each macro phase, the project needs checks, called tollgates, by the Bionic Transformation Steering Committee.)

Define

Lean and bionic transformation design needs to consider and organize collaboration, task allocation and organization, security, and programming on the same design scope (Pizzagalli et al., 2021). A User-Centered Design (UCD) approach seems to be a valuable solution for this challenge. End customers within a UCD (ISO 9241-210, 2010) must be

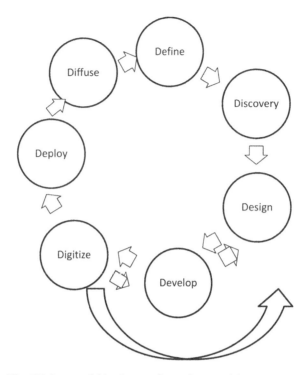

Fig. 6.1 The 7D lean and bionic transformation model

active in an iterative design process involving planning, testing, commissioning, and system assessment. The design process should allocate and define tasks between customers, operators, and automation and include multidisciplinary resources and skills in determining the requirements and the assessment phase. Examples of open and multidisciplinary approaches for designing complex, intelligent systems are available in the literature (Sell et al., 2018).

Requirement analysis is necessary to analyze all involved stakeholders' needs in the context of use, including personal and organizational needs and objectives (Takeda et al., 1993). This analysis is possible through qualitative descriptions and customer models, ergonomic research methods, or quantitative data collection and analysis.

This approach aims at a comprehensive design solution for human-automation collaboration by efficiently allocating security, collaboration modes, interfaces, managerial and task-oriented issues, and requirements in an iterative design and evaluation process revolving around the users and their context. This method matches the needs and solutions of human-automation systems with the UCD design cycle and specifications (Fig. 6.2).

Real-time simulations and interaction solutions can assist in evaluating customers, environmental and organizational aspects by providing insights into the system's state in all its components.

> **Barclays**
> Barclays' Head of Content Transformation, Raza Salim, stated that branches and human interaction will still be important in dealing with specific sensitive tasks (Lui & Lamb, 2018). One example is the transfer of large sums of money. Customers are more likely to prefer a human operator involved in that transaction to be accountable if something were to go wrong. Another example is that Barclays would not want AI to be applied when a customer contacts the bank following the family member's death to organize the deceased's finances. Barclays's view is that AI should

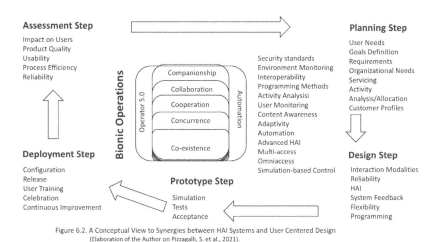

Fig. 6.2 A Conceptual view to synergies between HAI Systems and user centered design (Elaboration of the Author on Pizzagalli et al., 2021)

> give way to a human rather than an automated chatbot in these sensitive situations (Lui & Lamb, 2018).

Determining the best way to integrate intelligent automation solutions such as RPA or AI and humans in a way that effectively promotes customer loyalty, operational success, and operator satisfaction is a balancing act. A mature solution will address the distribution and combination of attended and unattended RPAs (Fallis & Fuchs, 2019).

The first steps of a lean and bionic transformation project are:

Macro Phase 1: "Define." In this stage, there is a definition of the environment to launch the transformation.

1. Context: Identify the needs or the requirements of the customers, stakeholders, and operators, the challenge of competitors, and the respect for compliance (for example, legislation and regulations).
2. Culture: Find the organization's culture, the community, and the nation where the organization is.
3. Vision: Tackle the problems of effectiveness, efficiency, economy, and quality of innovation.
4. Strategy: Define the possible content of the transformation.
5. Kick-off: Launch the project during a special meeting and notify all the stakeholders.
6. Governance: Define how to manage the project and set up the team.
7. Voice of the Customer (VoC): Listen to the VoC associated with the potential innovation and verify it.
8. Foster an organization-wide embrace of the transformation. The transition to robotic automation and AI is much more than an ICT project. It is a business transformation. A comprehensive communications campaign to all stakeholders is essential to obtain the buy-in and trust and collect operator insights on all affected processes.

> **HSBC**
> HSBC introduced a robot Pepper in its flagship Fifth Avenue branch in Manhattan (Srinivas & Wadhwani, 2019). The idea behind having a robot in the branch was not about replacing bank tellers. Pepper's

design was to make the banking experience more appealing. Pepper is programmed to answer customers' basic questions and direct them to the right adviser/personnel in the branch.

Discover

Agrawal et al. (2016) stated that all human activities have five high-level elements: data, prediction, judgment, action, and outcomes. AI can deal with the first two components of "data" and "prediction." In banking, especially mortgage advice, robotic process automation, and chatbots can support due diligence, credit checks, and read documents faster than humans. Machine learning enables robots and chatbots to respond to "what if" questions: There are natural limitations and weaknesses with robots and chatbots' data processing, such as biases. The third element of "judgment" poses more of a challenge to current AI capabilities. Judgment involves:

- Assessing all the facts connected with the customer.
- Recommending and advising on suitable financial products and services.
- Discussing the rewards and risks of such products

This assessment is more difficult for automated solutions as it involves evaluation, empathy, and lateral thinking if there needs to be a different solution. In complex cases, human judgment will become even more critical in future, especially in the financial services sector.

Macro Phase 2: "Discover." This stage includes generating ideas for potential development into a process, service, product, organization, or business model innovation.

9. Develop a baseline understanding of core processes. The first step in this journey involves understanding the most critical processes. This exercise will provide a focused approach (a roadmap) that will guide the improvement efforts.
10. Design with the goal of operator empowerment. The contribution of attended and unattended automation should aim primarily

at enhancing service and operator performance. It is essential to provide the staff a real-time, on-demand portal into any automated process that can support upselling and cross-selling and promote a host of operational challenges for the front office, back office, and shared services.
11. Invention: The creation of a new business model through an organization's creative process.
12. Selection: finding and evaluating a transformation to develop or adopt potentially.
13. Metrics: Translate the innovation and the VoC in Critical-to-Quality (CtQ) factors.
14. As-Is: Map the existing situation (services, products, processes, organization, or business models).

Design

A Deloitte study underlined that the collaboration between humans and automation should also extend to the entire financial institution. It is possible to (Srinivas & Wadhwani, 2021):

- Invest in-branch talent. With the banking experience in branches, financial institutions should continue to focus on branch operators training to ensure high-quality interactions with customers and create positive moments that matter. The Deloitte study underlined the need for "attentive and empathetic help customers with their complex queries and decisions."
- Blend the human touch with automation. One-third of the customers in the Deloitte survey said they would be open to using branches more if the financial institution would enhance its convenience. These enhancements include extending service hours through virtual remote services with a representative's help if needed to schedule a virtual video meeting. These options focus on how digital can drive close interactions with a banking representative, either remotely or in person. While these approaches are not new, they are not much used, although more financial institutions are experimenting with them.
- Accelerate the transition to a seamless omniaccess integration. The Deloitte survey demonstrated that consistent omniaccess experience

is essential or critical when selecting a primary financial institution. Reengineering future branches requires breaking the silos between physical and digital accesses and seamlessly allowing customers to move from different accesses.
- Provide a sense of community. Branch accesses should go beyond executing transactions and collecting information or advice. They should become an enjoyable experience. Nearly 31 percent in the Deloitte survey globally said they would be likely or very likely to increase visits to a branch if it resembled a café, where they could plug in, hang out, and work. Some financial institutions are experimenting with this very innovative approach.
- Embrace the human touch in digital accesses. Digital should not mean a lack of personal interactions. Banking should replicate the branch experience, especially responsiveness and empathy, in digital accesses in online banking, mobile apps, or ATMs.

Macro Phase 3: "Design." In this stage, there is a definition of the framework and the sequence of activities.

15. Identify which processes to automate. Bionic-driven tools are available to pinpoint business processes best suited to automation and provide the highest return on investment. First, financial institutions need to ensure systems to capture and analyze data to feed the bionic process audit. By combining the capabilities of experienced business analysts with intelligent bionic diagnostics, financial institutions can identify the business processes that will benefit most from automation and increase the likelihood of success. It is essential to assess the solution, once designed, for several aspects. There are models in this respect developed to enable transparent, audit-proof, and compliant solutions "by design," assessed and approved according to security, safety, legal, ethical or gender-relevant criteria. In Fig. 6.3, there is a schema of one of these models (Woitsch et al., 2020).
16. Lean: Define how to transform with the support of the team in workshops and meetings.
17. Kaizen Plan: Define the transformation intervention plan.
18. Architecture Design: Define the rules, policies, and process structure of the potential transformation.

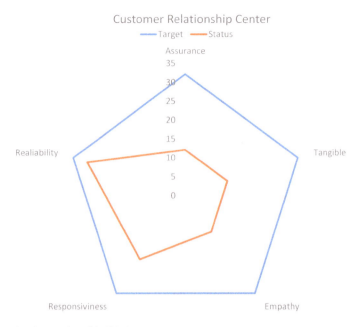

Fig. 6.3 Example of RATER assessment

HDFC

HDFC Bank is one of the Indian leading banks, which in 1994 received approval from the Reserve Bank of India (RBI) to set up a private sector bank. HDFC Bank has 5,485 branches and 14,533 ATMs spread across 2,866 cities and towns in India. It provides financial services distributed among three service lines: Retail Banking, Wholesale Banking, and Treasury. The bank net revenues (net interest income plus other income) grew to ₹ 23,760.8 crores for the period ended on the 31st of December 2020 from ₹ 20,842.2 crores for the quarter ended 31st December 2019 (HDFC Bank, 2021).

HDFC Bank has a clear mission to become the Indian number one financial service provider for retail and wholesale customers' segments. The central values that define HDFC Bank's way to do bank are operational excellence, customer focus, people, sustainability, and product leadership: all of them are qualities in line with the characteristics of bionic banking.

To achieve its goal, the bank has invested in the combination of ICT infrastructure and technology (ET Bureau, 2020).

HDFC Bank's value proposition bases its support on the sake of offering a high level of service personalization by an omniaccess distribution strategy.

Along with traditional accesses such as in-person banking and ATM services, HDFC relies on online distribution accesses as online banking also for Small-Medium Enterprises (SME) and innovative digital accesses, which are: mobile banking through smartphones, tablets, and innovative watch applications' phone banking through voice calls or Short Message Service SMS) and WhatsApp communications and even social media banking for instant chat. The latest innovation in customer relationships and communication access is the chatbot Eva for dedicated personal assistance. Eva is an AI software able to hold a conversation with persons since it understands customers' queries and knows how to reply in language. Eva chatbot is a primary channel that allows bankers to save time and effort to manage massive customer requests. Eva chatbot can also collect feedback about customer experience and provide analytics about, for example, the most requested service or the most frequent recurring issue. In this way, customer service can reduce the workflow and collect reliable information valuable for adjusting its offering.

In September 2020, HDFC Bank launched "Video KYC Facility" (KYC stands for Know Your Customer) to onboard bank accounts through the online banking web portal or mobile application. It is helpful to record the conversation with the bank operator to ensure transaction traceability and reliability. The banker is obliged to verify transactions' customer credentials such as identity card and One Time Password (OTP) code (HDFC Bank, 2020). This set of accesses and services demonstrate a customer-centric approach and human-digital operations excellence peculiar to bionic organizations (HDFC Bank, 2020).

HDFC Bank, an organization wherein digital technologies combine with person dimension, is on the right path to achieving a bionic transformation. According to the aspects discussed above, the characteristic of HDFC Bank is a sharp vision, an innovative distribution model, a customer-centric approach, technology and operational excellence, and financial and risk management concern.

Develop

Understanding Human Factors in Human-Automation Collaboration, the words "Human Factors" may have different meanings. For example, it may refer to "the human factor," a factor in a system's performance. This book relates to human factors as the differential factors that focus on humans' abilities, limitations, and characteristics. According to a blog post by S. Shorrock and Williams (2016), the development should include several types of factors:

- Cognitive abilities such as attention, working memory, and reasoning necessary to perform a task.
- Cognitive systems, such as the dual-process theory, imply that cognition may involve two independent but connected actors (De Neys, 2017).
- Types of performance such as knowledge-based, skill-based, and rule-based performance.
- Error types such as a lapse in judgment, reason's slips, defects in automation, and errors.
- Functions and qualities such as response times, accuracy, balance, and explainability can help in task performance.
- Subjective behaviors and non-technical skills such as situation awareness, decision-making, and teamwork that help enhance performance in HAC.
- Physical, cognitive, and emotional states such as stress, emotion, and fatigue may affect the performance of human operators.

It is necessary to understand these factors at a basic level to design and implement an effective collaboration system (Rajavenkatanarayanan, 2021). Human factors engineering is a branch of psychology that applies psychological principles in designing and developing products or procedures that involve a person and his/her working environment (Karwowski, 2005). Research in this domain aims to minimize human error, enhance safety, increase comfort, reduce workload, and at the same time increase productivity (Sadrfaridpour & Wang, 2017).

Macro Phase 4: "Develop." In this stage, an idea develops into a usable innovation.

19. Improve and stabilize core processes before automating. Critical processes should undergo a process-improvement and - stabilization period before being considered prime candidates for lean and bionic transformation. Organizations that skip this step often have to redo the work, consuming capital (both human and financial) alternatively possibly spent on initiatives that would have produced real value for the business.
20. Build the chosen solutions with the correct mix of automation and human collaboration.
21. Package surrounds the core solution with complementary products and services that form an integrated solution that a target adopter can effectively use for a given purpose.
22. Configure, which means deciding which solution features to use, whether as-is or with adaptations, how to integrate the technology with other solutions the organization already has in place, how related organizational elements (for example, structures, processes) will be changed, and how the organization will absorb and make use of the solutions.
23. Change management: Manage the changes.

Deconstruct

This transformation will generate new processes and roles (Goniwada, 2022). An example is automating the remaining manual work batch by batch, defining the individual customer's journey, and building and maintaining the ecosystem. Thanks to automation, all this is possible with a much smaller number of operators than today, mixed between new hires and retrained personnel. It is necessary to redesign processes to integrate the best of human talents with automation solutions. Financial institutions will have to adopt an agile way of working to make these changes effectively, with extensive training in the new processes and organizational culture.

Macro Phase 5: "Deconstruct" In this stage, the transformation should go at the maximum possible depth.

24. Build a Center of Excellence (CoE). It is essential to have a single, specialist business unit focused on managing, regulating, sustaining, and growing all process automation and optimization

activities to automate banking processes at scale including collaboration with human operators. CoE units should include business analysts in solutions and automation developers who can navigate the financial institution's entire automation journey.
25. Implement the bionic transformation.
26. Integrate cognitive tools to support the most complex scenarios. Intelligent self-service accesses can enable customers to interact with text- or voice-activated chatbots, which then communicate with back-end robots to execute tasks (including repetitive tasks associated with processing documents, but "reading" them as well). Real-time voice identification can seamlessly authenticate existing customers during chatbot interactions. This technology can also help detect and prevent fraud. Robots powered by AI engines in collaboration with human Subject Matter Experts (SMEs) can extract, organize, and interpret data to execute advanced tasks required in an increasingly data-driven industry and learn from human inputs.
27. Test (unit, system, integration, acceptance). Testing might include prototyping the innovation before implementing it on a large scale. When adequately executed, successful banking innovation should result in humans doing less, such as delivering the correct information and services at the right times. This way frees up precious bandwidth to pursue innovative growth strategies and find new ways to improve the customer experience.

Deploy

A key to effective and efficient innovation is commercializing new services quickly and economically while leveraging the benefits of collaborating between fintech organizations and traditional financial institutions (Marion & Friar, 2012). Opportunities include:

- Developing strong strategic partnerships with outside vendors.
- Using rapid prototyping resources to support agile development.
- Using short-run operators to test products and markets before building to volume.
- Using expert contractors to reduce fixed personnel costs.

Macro Phase 6: "Deploy." This stage includes the innovation implementation and the execution of the ancillary activities.

28. Deploy: Implement the chosen solution.
29. Document: Issue the documents related to the transformation.
30. Verify: Control the improvements and, if necessary, remediate faults and improve.
31. Internal and external benefits: Assess the benefits:—External: notice customers, shareholders, and operators' delight—Internal: assess the profitability, market share, internal improvements related to the new process.
32. Lessons Learned: Learn from the initiative with a specific session and documentation. Lessons learned are one of the most important and "value-added" aspects of a Project Management Lifecycle (PML) (Rückert et al., 2020). Rarely there is such a session at the end of a project. For lessons learned to be of value to any organization, it is necessary to do them regardless of time constraints (Walker, 2008). There is a need for some standardization approaching Lessons Learned. Concentration is on the cause-and-effect aspect of issues that arise during the project management life cycle and needs careful consideration.
33. Celebrate: Acknowledge the team's work.

Diffuse and Operations
High service quality results in better organizational performance and higher margins (Parasuraman et al., 1991). Even during economic downturns or pandemics (Fornell & Wernerfelt, 1987). Given the nature of services, there is no straightforward way to assess or measure the service quality per se. Quality is a multidimensional concept for Parasuraman et al. (1988). Service quality is the difference between the customers' expectations and their perceptions after the service (Parasuraman et al., 1988). The service quality work and SERVQUAL scale, developed by Parasuraman and his team, has some limitations as a helpful tool to measure service quality issues. A refined model which considers only five of them with RATER acronym: Reliability, Assurance, Tangibles, Empathy, and Responsiveness (see an example in Fig. 6.4) (Bicheno & Catherwood, 2005). The interpretation of the RATER dimensions in the case of a chatbot could be:

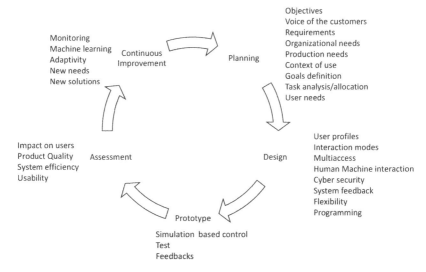

Fig. 6.4 Schema of a by design method

- Reliability. This dimension is based on the differences between accesses.
- Assurance. This dimension assesses the human-automation collaborations' ability to answer the customer questions or solve their problems and their competencies to provide trust, confidence, and security (Bicheno & Catherwood, 2005).
- Tangibles. This dimension includes the technical aspects of the human-automation collaborations service: the quality of the media used in the human-automation collaborations, the clarity and speed of the c response, and so on.
- Empathy. This dimension measures both the ways the chatbot is programmed to engage with the customer.
- Responsiveness. This dimension assesses the virtual agents' response to a particular request (for example, details on the payment due) and their ability to follow up.

Macro Phase 7: "Diffuse." In this stage, it is necessary to assemble and arrange the resources required to persuade and enable more organizations to adopt and use the transformation and diffuses or spreads across a population of potential customers.

34. Assimilation and continuous improvement happen when individuals and other units absorb the transformation into their daily routines and the work-life of the organization. Based on a German survey (Bauer et al., 2016), the top three considerations when implementing the human-automation collaboration process are: 1-operational efficiency, 2-innovation, and 3-ergonomics. From a methodological approach, lean principles are a leading approach to achieving operational efficiency, relying on a controlled level of automation, which leads to the possibility of performing incremental process improvements (also named *kaizen*), as an activity driven by operational workforce (Imai, 1986).
35. It may then be interesting to study how this incremental transformation can continue with new solutions introduction and the role played by the humans both in the design and the operation stages.
36. Appropriation involves managing intellectual property and the ecosystem of complementary products and services to protect the profits from vendors, customers, and imitators.
37. Transformation is implementing the technology and organization to take advantage of the new opportunities brought about by the innovation. Transformations can also happen at the market and organization levels.

Macro Phases 3, 4, and 5 should be done with an agile approach, doing several cycles (or springs in the agile terminology). The base of an agile approach is on iterative and incremental development, where requirements and solutions evolve through collaboration between self-organizing, cross-functional teams (Socha et al., 2013). It promotes adaptive planning, evolutionary development, and delivery, a time-boxed iterative approach, and encourages rapid and flexible responses to change.

Agile
The Agile Manifesto articulates on twelve principles (Beck et al., 2001). For the lean and bionic transformation, it is possible to customize them:

1. Pursue customer and organization satisfaction by rapid delivery of a valuable transformation.
2. Accept changing requirements, even late in the transformation project.
3. Deliver incremental working pieces of transformations and human-automation collaboration frequently (weeks rather than months).
4. Incremental working transformations and human-automation collaboration are the primary measures of progress.
5. Sustainable development should be able to maintain a constant pace.
6. Close, daily cooperation should take place between businesspeople and the transformation team.
7. In-person conversation is the best form of communication (co-location but also virtual teams).
8. Projects are built around motivated individuals who should be trusted.
9. Continuous attention to technical excellence, human resource management, and superior design are essential.
10. Simplicity, the art of maximizing the amount of work not yet done, is essential.
11. Teams should self-organize.
12. There should be a regular adaptation to the changing environment.

Figure 6.5 is a summary of the method.

Margaria and Steffen stressed the simplicity of the Agile approach (Margaria & Steffen, 2010). It is vital in implementing a transformation (Aaen, 2008). Brown also stressed how agile could foster innovation (Brown & Martin, 2015).

Innovation Acceptance Model

It is essential in introducing bionic banking to analyze a model to assess innovative solutions' acceptance: the Innovation Acceptance Model (IAM). The model improves the Technology Acceptance Model (TAM) (Chen, M. C. et al., 2016; Kim et al., 2016). Some studies have used this model to assess the acceptance of the internet and mobility innovations (Chen, M. C. et al., 2016; Kim et al., 2016) and supply chain (Kamble et al., 2019). Authors have applied TAM to innovative solutions for the banking sector (Tzanis, 2012) and built a generalized TAM

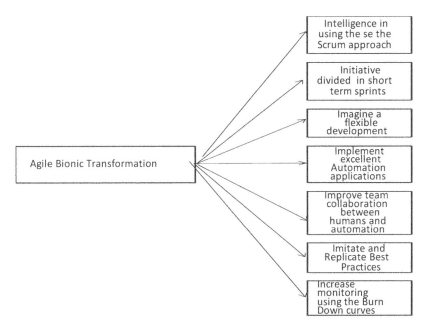

Fig. 6.5 Agile bionic transformation framework (7i)

(Technology Acceptance Model) (Nicoletti, 2017). TAM can also help introduce AI-based innovations (Bin et al., 2018).

IAM states that the critical determinants for the adoption and use of innovations are (Song, 2019):

- Perceived usefulness (PU) is how the decision-makers think a specific innovation allows their organization to improve its performance. The PU measures include increased performance, economics, productivity, efficiency, overall usefulness, time savings, and work productivity. Since the original TAM, perceived usefulness has been applied to many ICT applications to measure innovation performance for job, life, and study (Liu et al., 2011). Perceived usefulness is: "the degree to which a person believes that using a specific system will increase his or her job performance" (Davis & Botkin, 1994). On several occasions, perceived usefulness is a perceived relative advantage. For this reason, E. M. Rogers (2010) considers a similar

construct named "relative advantage," defined as "the way it is perceived as being better than its predecessor."
- Perceived ease of use (Peou) is how the decision-makers believe that an innovative solution requires little effort. The Peou measures include ease of control, simplicity, clarity, and flexibility.
- The definitions of Perceived trust are numerous. Gefen and Straub (2003) defined trust as "the expectation that other individuals or organizations with whom one interacts will not take undue advantage of a dependence upon them." The generation of trust has been considered a decisive factor in stimulating interaction with innovative solutions. Traditionally, trust has two essential components: a cognitive component that defines trust as "the belief that the other party's word or promise is reliable and the party will fulfill its obligations in an exchange relationship" (Dwyer et al., 1987; Schurr & Ozanne, 1985)' and a behavioral component which is a willingness or desire to follow a particular pattern of behavior, which determines the success rate of acceptance of the innovation (Liébana-Cabanillas et al., 2014).

In the case of organizations, small- and medium-sized enterprises, the IAM model can include:

- Other factors (Munoz-Leiva et al., 2017).
- The theory of planned behavior (Ajzen & Fishbein, 1980).
- The influence of several other potential factors (Bin et al., 2018).

IAM Model

A comprehensive model for IAM should include (Fig. 6.6) (Nicoletti, 2014; Schierz et al., 2010).

- Intention to use (IU) is the acceptance of innovation.
- ~~Perceived trust (PT) has a significant and direct effect on an organization's intention to adopt bionic banking.~~
- Attitude toward innovation (ATI) refers to the organization's favorable or unfavorable evaluation of the innovation (Ajzen & Fishbein, 1980) and to the feelings of favorableness or unavoidableness toward using the technology

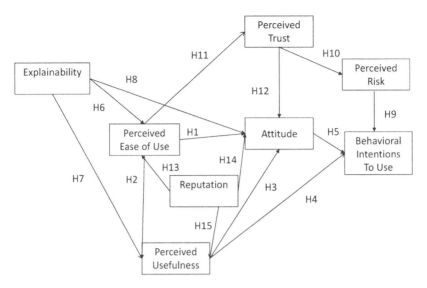

Fig. 6.6 Innovation acceptance model

- Perceived Risk constitutes a multidimensional construct built from several factors, the overall risk associated with adopting innovation (Munoz-Leiva et al., 2017).
- Explainability means to create a suite of HAC solutions that enables human customers to understand, appropriately trust, and effectively manage the emerging generation of artificially intelligent partners" (Gunning, 2017).
- Reputation is an aggregated value that is recommended by all the third-party recommendation agents. The aggregation can be weighted by the trustworthiness of the recommendation agents and the trustworthiness of the opinions (Chang et al., 2006).

In terms of relationships and referring to Fig. 6.6, it is possible to conclude that:

H1. The ease of use of the proposed customer automation positively impacts the customers' attitude toward it.
H2. The ease of use of the proposed solution has a positive impact on its perceived usefulness.

H3. Perceived usefulness has a positive effect on the attitude. Studies related to the impact of perceived usefulness in the field of innovative solutions present different results. Some studies support this construct's significant and positive effect on the intention to use (Pham & Afify, 2005), while others do not show significant results for this relationship (Li & Liu, 2014).
H4. Perceived usefulness has a positive effect on the intention of use of the proposed HAC (Fallis & Fuchs, 2019).
H5. Attitude has a positive effect on the intention to use (Gunning, 2017).
H6. Explainability has a positive effect on the ease of use of HAC.
H7. Explainability has a positive effect on the perceived usefulness of HAC.
H8. Explainability has a positive effect on attitudes toward HAC.
H9. The perceived risk of the proposed HAC harms customers' intention of using it.
H10. Perceived trust in the proposed solution harms customers' perceived risk toward it.
H11. Perceived trust in the proposed solution has a positive effect on its ease of use of it.
H12. Perceived trust in the proposed solution has a positive effect on customers' attitudes toward it.
H13. Reputation has a positive effect on perceived ease of use.
H14. Reputation has a positive effect on the customer attitude.
H15. Reputation has a positive effect on the perceived usefulness.

Conclusions

With advances in cognitive computing and automation, bionic banking will likely be dominant in the next generation of cognitive banking. This situation can primarily facilitate flexible servicing for mass personalization. Bionic banking enables human operators and automation to work for a common goal in a long-term bi-directional manner, achieving stepwise three unique cognitive teamwork skills:

- Inter-collaboration cognition. It enables real-time collaborative execution for shared banking activities concerning bi-directional empathy among automation states and human decisions.

- Temporal cooperation prediction. Predicting human-automation-customer interaction of sub-tasks/activities over time allows proactive automation action planning and intuitive human operation, achieving ahead-of-time and foreseeable cooperation,
- Self-organizing teamwork. Humans and automation decide how to organize themselves.

Assuming that there is a development for services currently rendered by humans, automation will take over at least parts of many tasks in the current banking processes (Decker et al., 2017). This situation brings about changes in the work of humans, who will now provide services with the support of automation. In case of a complete takeover of the entire service task, the change would make, in an extreme case, humans not working anymore and become unemployed. The possible outcome forecasted in this book is that with a proper design of the collaboration with automation, humans can provide their services more efficiently and better, reducing but not eliminating the percentage of jobs in this service segment.

Automation will likely put people with a low or a medium level of education under some pressure (Webb, 2019). In the meantime, it is essential to improve the collaboration between humans and automation.

It is possible to identify areas in which a bionic banking transformation makes sense today. The use of virtual robots is especially promising for tasks requiring a lot of effort, a complex daily rhythm, or a specific repetitiveness or burden for humans. The perspective of social work organizations takes account of availability and remuneration, the expectations of potential customers, the skills of current personnel, and the performance capability and purchase and maintenance costs of automated solutions.

This book indicates directions on how to use automation to augment human service capabilities. Criteria can be derived from both disciplinary perspectives, which enable an assessment of specific bionic transformation within their respective operational context. Analyzing these contexts makes it possible to develop performance criteria that make successful cooperation between humans and automation in a banking context very likely and beneficial if correctly transformed. The work science analysis of these cooperative services and the overall economic analysis allows interdisciplinary technology assessment to draw relevant conclusions. This situation can first result in direct recommendations for technological development, for example, optimizing the human–robot interface for a specific cooperative task. Secondly, there may be indications for legal regulations, for example, when it must be determined who or what is liable for damage in connection with a cooperatively rendered service.

Bionic banking transformation implemented using the approach described in this chapter can substantially improve the quality of the banking services, the standardization of work environments, the design of the human–robot interface, the level of professionality of the human service providers, and other aspects.

References

2010 ISO 9241-210, ergonomics of human-system interaction—Human-centered design for interactive systems.

Aaen, I. (2008). Essence: Facilitating agile innovation. In *Agile processes in software engineering and extreme programming* (pp. 1–10). Springer.

Agrawal, A., Gans, J., & Goldfarb, A. (2016). The simple economics of machine intelligence. *Harvard Business Review, 17*(1), 2–5.

Ajzen, I. (1991). The theory of planned behavior. *Organizational Behavior and Human Decision Processes, 50*(2), 179–211.

Ajzen, I., & Fishbein, M. (1980). *Attitude understanding and predicting social behavior*. Prentice-Hall.

Azim, T., Riva, O., & Nath, S. (2016, June). uLink: Enabling user-defined deep linking to app content. In *Proceedings of the 14th Annual International Conference on Mobile Systems, Applications, and Services* (pp. 305–318).

Barth, T. J., & Arnold, E. (1999). Artificial intelligence and administrative discretion: Implications for public administration. *The American Review of Public Administration, 29*(4), 332–351.

Bauer, W., Bender, M., Braun, M., Rally, P., & Scholtz, O. (2016). *Lightweight robots in manual assembly, best to start simply: examining companies' initial experiences with lightweight robots*. Fraunhofer Institut.

Beck, K., Beedle, M., van Bennekum, A., Cockburn, A., Cunningham, W., Fowler, M., ... & Thom, D. (2001). *Manifesto for agile software development*. www.agile.manifesto.org. Accessed 15 March 2022.

Bicheno, J., & Catherwood, P. (2005). Service quality concepts. *Six sigma and the quality toolbox* (pp. 132–150). PICSIE Books.

Bin, M. A., Pyeman, J. B., Ali, N. B., Abdul, N. B., & Khai, K. G. (2018). Determinants of supply chain finance adoption among Malaysian manufacturing financial institutions: A proposed conceptual framework. *International Journal of Education and Research, 6*(4), 237–248.

Bizer, C., Heath, T., & Berners-Lee, T. (2011). Linked data: The story so far. In *Semantic services, interoperability and web applications: Emerging concepts* (pp. 205–227). IGI Global.

Breazeal, C. (2001, September). Affective interaction between humans and robots. In *European conference on artificial life* (pp. 582–591). Springer.

Breuer, H. (2013). Lean venturing: Learning to create new business through exploration, elaboration, evaluation, experimentation, and evolution. *International Journal of Innovation Management, 17*(03), 1340013.

Brown, T. (2015). When everyone is doing design thinking, is it still a competitive advantage. *Harvard Business Review*, p. 27.

Brown, T., & Martin, R. (2015). Spotlight on the evolution of design thinking. *Harvard Business Review*, 56–85.

Bruckner, M., LaFleur, M., & Pitterle, I. (2017). *Frontier issues: The impact of the technological revolution on labour markets and income distribution*. Department of Economic & Social Affairs, UN.

Bullen, C. V., & Rockart, J. F. (1981). *A primer on critical success factors*. Sloan School of Business, MIT.

Chan, L. K., & Wu, M. L. (2002). Quality function deployment: A literature review. *European Journal of Operational Research, 143*(3), 463–497.

Chang, E., Hussain, F. K., & Dillon, T. (2006, October). Reputation ontology for reputation systems. In *OTM Confederated International Conferences "On the Move to Meaningful Internet Systems"* (pp. 1724–1733). Springer.

Chen, M. C., Chen, S. S., Yeh, H. M., & Tsaur, W. G. (2016). The critical factors influencing internet services finances satisfaction: An empirical study in Taiwan. *American Journal of Industrial and Business Management, 6*(6), 748–762.

Chiang, R. H., Grover, V., Liang, T. P., & Zhang, D. (2018). Strategic value of big data and business analytics. *Journal of Management Information Systems, 35*(2), 383–387.

Coelho, P. S., & Henseler, J. (2012). Creating customer loyalty through service customization. *European Journal of Marketing*.

Corvalán, J. G. (2019, April). Keynote: PROMETEA. Artificial intelligence to transform public organizations. In *2019 Sixth International Conference on eDemocracy & eGovernment (ICEDEG)* (p. 15). IEEE.

Davis, S., & Botkin, J. (1994). The coming of knowledge-based business. *Harvard Business Review, 72*(5), 165–170.

De Neys, W. (Ed.). (2017). *Dual process theory 2.0*. Routledge.

De Pace, F., Manuri, F., Sanna, A., & Fornaro, C. (2020). A systematic review of augmented reality interfaces for collaborative industrial robots. *Computers & Industrial Engineering, 149*, 106806.

Decker, M., Fischer, M., & Ott, I. (2017). Service robotics and human labor: A first technology assessment of substitution and cooperation. *Robotics and Autonomous Systems, 87*, 348–354.

Dwyer, F. R., Schurr, P. H., & Oh, S. (1987). Developing buyer-seller relationships. *Journal of Marketing, 51*(2), 11–27.

Eggers, W. D., Schatsky, D., & Viechnicki, P. (2017). *AI-augmented government: Using cognitive technologies to redesign public sector work.* Deloitte University Press.

Eraut, M. (1998). Concepts of competence. *Journal of Interprofessional Care, 12*(2), 127–139.

Erten, S. (2021). Chapter seven toward a new hybrid model. In M. Z. Çögenli (Ed.), *Digitalization in organizations* (p. 106). Google Books.

Essig, M. (2006). Electronic Insurance. Konzeption und Anwendung. In J. Zentes (Ed.), *Handbuch Handel* (pp. 735–758). Gabler.

ET Bureau. (2020, April). RBI announces more measures to deal with economic fallout of COVID-19. *The Economic Times.*

Ettlie, J. E., Bridges, W. P., & O'keefe, R. D. (1984). Organization strategy and structural differences for radical versus incremental innovation. *Management science, 30*(6), 682–695.

Ezer, N., Bruni, S., Cai, Y., Hepenstal, S. J., Miller, C. A., & Schmorrow, D. D. (2019, November). Trust engineering for human-AI teams. *Proceedings of the Human Factors and Ergonomics Society Annual Meeting, 63*(1), 322–326.

Fallis, J., & Fuchs, O. (2019). *Transforming banking with smart automation.* Nice and Bain & Company.

Fernández-Sanz, L., Gómez-Pérez, J., & Castillo-Martínez, A. (2017). e-Skills Match: A framework for mapping and integrating the main skills, knowledge and competence standards and models for ICT occupations. *Computer Standards & Interfaces, 51*, 30–42.

Fornell, C., & Wernerfelt, B. (1987). Defensive marketing strategy by consumer complaint management: A theoretical analysis. *Journal of Marketing, 24*(4), 337–346.

Freeman, C., & Perez, C. (1988). Structural crises of adjustment, business cycles and investment behaviour. *Technology, organizations and innovation: Theories, concepts and paradigms* (pp. 38–66).

Gefen, D., & Straub, D. (2003). Managing user trust in B2C e-services. *e-Service, 2*(2), 7–24.

Geissbauer, R., Weissbarth, R., & Wetzstein, J. (2016). *Banking 5.0: Are the organisation ready for the digital revolution?* PriceWaterhouseCoopers.

Goniwada, S. R. (2022). Enterprise cloud native automation. *Cloud native architecture and design* (pp. 523–553). Apress.

Gruber, M., De Leon, N., George, G., & Thompson, P. (2015). Managing by design: From the editors. *Academy of Management Journal, 58*(1), 1–7.

Gudem, M., Steinert, M., Welo, T., & Leifer, L. (2013). Redefining customer value in lean product development design projects. *Journal of Engineering, Design and Technology*.
Guilford, J. P. (1967). *The nature of human intelligence*. McGraw-Hill.
Gunning, D. (2017). Explainable artificial intelligence (XAI). *Defense Advanced Research Projects Agency (DARPA), and Web*, 2(2).
Halstrick, T. (2020). *Determining a bank's customer value proposition based on customer value dimensions* (Bachelor's thesis). University of Twente, Enschede, Netherlands.
HDFC Bank. (2020, September). *HDFC Bank launches Video KYC facility* [Press Release].
HDFC Bank. (2021, January). *Financial results (Indian Gaap) for the quarter and nine months ended December 31, 2020* [Press release].
Henderson, R. M., & Clark, K. B. (1990). Architectural innovation: The reconfiguration of existing product technologies and the failure of established firms. *Administrative Science Quarterly*, 9–30.
Kelley, T. (2001). Prototyping is the shorthand of innovation. *Design Management Journal (Former Series)*, 12(3), 35–42.
Iarovyi, S., Lastra, J. L. M., Haber, R., & del Toro, R. (2015, July). From artificial cognitive systems and open architectures to cognitive manufacturing systems. In *2015 IEEE 13th International Conference on Industrial Informatics (INDIN)* (pp. 1225–1232). IEEE.
Imai, M. (1986). *Kaizen* (Vol. 201). Random House Business Division.
Jacobides, M. G., Brusoni, S., & Candelon, F. (2021). *The evolutionary dynamics of the artificial intelligence ecosystem*. Evolution Academic Papers.
Jarrahi, M. H. (2018). Artificial intelligence and the future of work: Human—AI symbiosis in organizational decision making. *Business Horizons*.
Kagermann, H. (2014). von Industries 4.0 Chancen nutzen. In T. Bauernhansl, M. Ten Hompel, & B. Vogel-Heuser (Eds.), *Produktion industries 4.0. Automatisierung und Logistik* (pp. 603–614). Springer.
Kakati, M. (2003). Success criteria in high-tech new ventures. *Technovation*, 23(5), 447–457.
Kamble, S., Gunasekaran, A., & Arha, H. (2019). Understanding the Blockchain solution adoption in supply chains-Indian context. *International Journal of Production Research*, 57(7), 2009–2033.
Kanazawa, A., Kinugawa, J., & Kosuge, K. (2019). Adaptive motion planning for a collaborative robot based on prediction uncertainty to enhance human safety and work efficiency. *IEEE Transactions on Robotics*, 35, 817–832.
Karwowski, W. (2005). Ergonomics and human factors: The paradigms for science, engineering, design, technology and management of human-compatible systems. *Ergonomics*, 48(5), 436–463.

Kim, Y., Park, Y. J., & Choi, J. (2016). The adoption of mobile payment services for Fintech. *International Journal of Applied Engineering Research, 11*(2), 1058–1061.

Kollmann, T (2011). *E-Business: Grundlagen elektronischer Geschäftsprozesse in der net economy*. Gabler

Lee, J., Bagheri, B., & Kao, H. A. (2015). A cyber-physical systems architecture for industry 4.0-based manufacturing systems. *Manufacturing Letters, 3*, 18–23.

Lee, J., Kao, H. A., & Yang, S. (2014). Service innovation and smart analytics for industry 5.0 and big data environment. *Procedia CIRP, 16*, 3–8.

Li, H., & Liu, Y. (2014). Understanding post-adoption behaviors of e-service users in the context of online travel services. *Information & Management, 51*(8), 1043–1052.

Li, S., Wang, R., Zheng, P., & Wang, L. (2021). Towards proactive human–robot collaboration: A foreseeable cognitive manufacturing paradigm. *Journal of Manufacturing Systems, 60*, 547–552.

Li, S., Zheng, P., & Zheng, L. (2020). An AR-assisted deep learning-based approach for automatic inspection of aviation connectors. *IEEE Transactions on Industrial Informatics, 17*, 1721–1731.

Liébana-Cabanillas, F., Sánchez-Fernández, J., & Muñoz-Leiva, F. (2014). Antecedents of the adoption of the new mobile payment systems: The moderating effect of age. *Computers in Human Behavior, 35*, 464–478.

Liebau, D. (2016). *Design thinking in financial services*. Lightbulb Capital.

Liu, F., Tong, J., Mao, J., Bohn, R., Messina, J., Badger, L., & Leaf, D. (2011). NIST cloud computing reference architecture. *NIST Special Publication, 500*(2011), 1–28.

Liu, X., Zheng, L., Shuai, J., Zhang, R., & Li, Y. (2020). Data-driven and AR assisted intelligent collaborative assembly system for large-scale complex products. *Procedia CIRP, 93*, 1049–1054.

Lui, A., & Lamb, G. W. (2018). Artificial intelligence and augmented intelligence collaboration: Regaining trust and confidence in the financial sector. *Information & Communications Technology Law, 27*(3), 267–283.

Makridakis, S. (2017). The forthcoming artificial intelligence (AI) revolution: Its impact on society and firms. *Futures, 90*, 46–60.

Manyika, J., Chui, M., Miremadi, M., Bughin, J., & George, K. (2017). A future that works: AI, automation, employment, and productivity. *McKinsey Global Institute Research, Tech. Rep, 60*, 1–135.

Margaria, T., & Steffen, B. (2010). Simplicity as a driver for agile innovation. *Computer, 43*(6), 90–92.

Marion, T. J., & Friar, J. H. (2012). Managing global outsourcing to enhance lean innovation. *Research-Technology Management, 55*(5), 44–50.

Mehri, D. (2006). The darker side of lean: An insider's perspective on the realities of the Toyota production system. *Academy of Management Perspectives, 20*(2), 21–42.

Morais, R., Le, V., Venkatesh, S., Tran, T., 2021. Learning asynchronous and sparse human-object interaction in videos. *arXiv preprint* arXiv:2103.02758

Munoz-Leiva, F., Climent-Climent, S., & Liébana-Cabanillas, F. (2017). Determinants of intention to use the mobile banking apps: An extension of the classic TAM model. *Spanish Journal of Marketing-ESIC, 21*(1), 25–38.

Nash, K. (2015). CIO voices: Bank of America's Cathy Bessant says 'no' to innovation labs. *CIO Journal, The Wall Street Journal.*

Nicoletti, B. (2012). *Lean and digitize: An integrated approach to process improvement.* Gower Publishing. ISBN-10: 1409441946.

Nicoletti, B. (2014a). *Mobile banking.* Palgrave Macmillan.

Nicoletti, B. (2014b, June). Lean and digitized innovation. In *2014 International Conference on Engineering, Technology and Innovation (ICE)* (pp. 1–7). IEEE.

Nicoletti, B. (2017). *Future of FinTech.* Palgrave Macmillan.

Nicoletti, B. (2019). Digital transformation via open data in insurance. In A. L. Mention (Ed.), *Digital innovation harnessing the value of open data.* World Scientific.

Nicoletti, B. (2021). *Banking 5.0.* Springer.

Oosthuizen, R. M. (2021). The fourth industrial revolution: A resilience-based coping strategy for disruptive change. *Agile coping in the digital workplace* (pp. 11–34). Springer.

Owais, S. S., & Hussein, N. S. (2016). Extract five categories CPIVW from the 9V's characteristics of the big data. *International Journal of Advanced Computer Science and Applications, 7*(3), 254–258.

Oza, N., & Abrahamsson, P. (2009). *Building blocks of agile innovation.* Book Surge Publishing.

Parasuraman, A., Berry, L. L., & Zeithaml, V. A. (1991). Perceived service quality as a customer-based performance measure: An empirical examination of organizational barriers using an extended service quality model. *Human Resource Management, 30*(3), 335–364.

Parasuraman, A., Zeithaml, V. A., & Berry, L. L. (1988). SERVQUAL: A multiple-item scale for measuring consumer perceptions of service quality. *Journal of Retailing, 64*(1), 14–40.

Pham, D. T., & Afify, A. A. (2005). Machine-learning techniques and their applications in manufacturing. *Proceedings of the Institution of Mechanical Engineers, Part B: Journal of Engineering Manufacture, 219*(5), 395–412.

Pizzagalli, S. L., Kuts, V., & Otto, T. (2021, May). User-centered design for Human-Robot Collaboration systems. In *IOP Conference Series: Materials Science and Engineering,* 1140(1), 012011. IOP Publishing.

Poole, D., Mackworth, A., & Goebel, R. (1997). *Computational intelligence: A logical approach*. Oxford University Press.

Rajavenkatanarayanan, A. (2021). *Human factors analysis and monitoring to enhance human-robot collaboration* (Doctoral dissertation). The University of Texas at Arlington, Arlington, TX.

Ransbotham, S., Khodabandeh, S., Kiron, D., Candelon, F., Chu, M,. & LaFountain, B. (2020). Expanding AI's impact with organizational learning. *MIT Sloan Management Review*.

Realyvásquez-Vargas, A., Arredondo-Soto, K. C., García-Alcaraz, J. L., Márquez-Lobato, B. Y., & Cruz-García, J. (2019). Introduction and configuration of a collaborative robot in an assembly task as a means to decrease occupational risks and increase efficiency in a manufacturing company. *Robotics and Computer-Integrated Manufacturing, 57*, 315–328.

Reeves, M. (2020, July 2). A guide to building a more resilient business. *Harvard Business Review*.

Ries, E., & Euchner, J. (2013). What large companies can learn from start-ups. *Research-Technology Management, 56*(4), 12–16.

Rogers, E. M. (2010). *Diffusion of innovations*. Simon and Schuster.

Romani, J. C. C. (2009). *Strategies to promote the development of e-competencies in the next generation of professionals: European and international trends*.

Rückert, P., Tracht, K., Herfs, W., Roggendorf, S., Schubert, V., & Schneider, M. (2020). Consolidation of product lifecycle information within human-robot collaboration for assembly of multi-variant products. *Procedia Manufacturing, 49*, 217–221.

Sadrfaridpour, B., & Wang, Y. (2017). Collaborative assembly in hybrid manufacturing cells: An integrated framework for human–robot interaction. *IEEE Transactions on Automation Science and Engineering, 15*(3), 1178–1192.

Schierz, P. G., et al. (2010, May–June). Understanding customer acceptance of mobile payment services: An empirical analysis. *Electronic Commerce Research and Applications, 9*(3), 209–216.

Schlick, J., Stephan, P., Loskyll, M., & Lappe, D. (2014). Industries 4.0 in der praktischen Anwendung. In T. Bauernhansl, M. Ten Hompel, & B. Vogel-Heuser (Eds.), *Industrie 4.0 to Produktion, Automatisierung und Logistik: Anwendung. Technologien. Migration* (pp. 57–84). Springer.

Schmidt, R., Möhring, M., Härting, R. C., Reichstein, C., Neumaier, P., & Jozinović, P. (2015). Industry 5.0-potentials for creating smart products: Empirical research results. In *The International Conference on Business Information Systems* (pp. 16–27). Springer.

Schuh, G., Lenders, M., & Hieber, S. (2008, July 27–31). Lean innovation: Introducing value systems to product development. In *PICMET 2008 Proceedings*.

Schuh, G., Powerful, T., Wesch-Powerful, C., Weber, A. R., & Prote, J. P. (2014). Collaboration mechanisms to increase productivity in the context of industries 4. 0. *Procedia CIRP, 19*(2014), 51–56.

Schurr, P. H., & Ozanne, J. L. (1985). Influences on exchange processes: Buyers' preconceptions of a seller's trustworthiness and bargaining toughness. *Journal of Consumer Research, 11*(4), 939–953.

Sell, R., Leier, M., Rassolkin, A., & Ernits, J. P. (2018). Self-driving car ISEAUTO for research and education. In *Proceedings of 2018 19th International Conference on Research Education Mechatronics, REM 2018* (pp. 111–116).

Shorrock, S., & Williams, C. (2016). *Human factors and ergonomics in practice: Improving system performance and human well-being in the real world.* CRC Press.

Siota, J., Klueter T., Wyman, O. Staib, D., Taylor, S., & Ania, I. (2017). *Design thinking the new DNA of the financial sector—How banks can boost their growth through design thinking in an era of de-banking.* IESE Business School.

Smit, J. (2016). e-competency of practitioners: A grounded theory. In *SAIS 2016 Proceedings.*

Socha, D., Folsom, T. C., & Justice, J. (2013). Applying agile software principles and practices for fast automotive development. In *Proceedings of the FISITA 2012 World Automotive Congress* (pp. 1033–1045).

Song, Y. W. (2019). *User acceptance of an artificial intelligence (AI) virtual assistant: An extension of the solution acceptance mode* (Doctoral dissertation). The University of Texas at Austin, Austin, TX.

Srinivas, V., & Wadhwani, R. (2019). *Deloitte accelerating-digital-transformation-in-banking.*

Srinivas, V., & Wadhwani, R. (2021). *Recognizing the value of bank branches in a digital world findings from the global digital banking survey.* Deloitte Insights.

Sternberg, R. J. (1984). What should intelligence tests test? Implications of a triarchic theory of intelligence for intelligence testing. *Educational Researcher, 13*(1), 5–15.

Takeda, N., Shiomi, A., Kawai, K., & Ohiwa, H. (1993, January). Requirement analysis by the KJ editor. In *[1993] Proceedings of the IEEE International Symposium on Requirements Engineering* (pp. 98–101). IEEE.

Tambe, P., Hitt, L. M., Rock, D., & Brynjolfsson, E. (2019). *IT, AI and the growth of intangible capital.* Available at SSRN 3416289.

Temkin, A. (2017, April). Apply for a loan in less than 15 minutes. *The Times.*

Tomassetti, F. Rizzo, G., Glass, A., Hardy, L., Torchiano, M., & Morisio, M. (2011). Linked Data approach to the automation of the selection processes in systematic reviews. In *The Assessment and Evaluation in Software Engineering (EASE 2011), 15th Annual Conference* (pp. 31–350). EIT.

Tushman, M. L., & Nadler, D. A. (1980). Communication and technical roles in R&D laboratories: An information processing approach. *TIMS Studies in the Management Sciences, 15*(1), 91–112.

Tzanis, S. (2012). *Direct insurance: The determinants of success*. Dissertation of the University of St. Gallen, Switzerland.

Van Leeuwen, G., & Klomp, L. (2006). On the contribution of innovation to multi-factor productivity growth. *Economics of Innovation and New Solution, 15*(4–5), 367–390.

Van Weele, A. J. (2010). *Purchasing & supply chain management: Analysis, strategy, planning and practice*. Cengage Learning EMEA.

Walker, L. W. (2008). Learning lessons on lessons learned. In *PMI® Global Congress*.

Wang, L., Gao, R., Váncza, J., Krüger, J., Wang, X. V., Makris, S., & Chryssolouris, G. (2019). Symbiotic human-robot collaborative assembly. *CIRP Annals, 68*, 701–726.

Wang, L., Liu, S., Liu, H., & Wang, X. V. (2020). Overview of human-robot collaboration in manufacturing, In *Proceedings of 5th International Conference on the Industry 4.0 Model for Advanced Manufacturing* (pp. 15–58). Springer.

Wang, X. V., & Wang, L. (2021). A literature survey of the robotic technologies during the covid-19 pandemic. *Journal of Manufacturing Systems*.

Webb, M. (2019). *The impact of artificial intelligence on the labor market*. Available at SSRN 3482150.

Wessel, L., Baiyere, A., Ologeanu-Taddei, R., Cha, J., & Blegind-Jensen, T. (2021). Unpacking the difference between digital transformation and IT-enabled organizational transformation. *Journal of the Association for Information Systems, 22*(1), 102–129.

Wilson, K., & Doz, Y. L. (2011). Agile innovation: A footprint balancing distance and immersion. *California Management Review, 53*(2), 6–26.

Woitsch, R., Utz, W., Sumereder, A., Dieber, B., Breiling, B., Crompton, L., & Schumann, S. (2020). Collaborative model-based process assessment for trustworthy AI in robotic platforms. In *First International Conference on Society 5.0*.

Womack, J. P., & Jones, D. T. (2003). *Lean thinking banish waste and create wealth in your corporation* (2nd ed.). Simon & Schuster Inc.

Xu, W., Furie, D., Mahabhaleshwar, M., Suresh, B., & Chouhan, H. (2019). *Applications of an interaction, process, integration, and intelligence (IPII) design approach for ergonomics solutions*. Ergonomics.

Yamashina, H., Ito, T., & Kawada, H. (2002). Innovative product development process by integrating QFD and TRIZ. *International Journal of Production Research, 40*(5), 1031–1050.

Yao, B., Zhou, Z., Wang, L., Xu, W., Yan, J., & Liu, Q. (2018). A function block-based cyber-physical production system for physical human-robot interaction. *Journal of Manufacturing Systems, 48*, 12–23.

Young, M. M., Bullock, J. B., & Lecy, J. D. (2019). Artificial discretion as a tool of governance: A framework for understanding the impact of artificial intelligence on public administration. *Perspectives on Public Management and Governance, 2*(4), 301–313.

Zhang, J., Liu, H., Chang, Q., Wang, L., & Gao, R. X. (2020). Recurrent neural network for motion trajectory prediction in human-robot collaborative assembly. *CIRP Annals, 69*, 9–12.

Zheng, N. N., Liu, Z. Y., Ren, P. J., Ma, Y. Q., Chen, S. T., Yu, S. Y., ... & Wang, F. Y. (2017). Hybrid-augmented intelligence: Collaboration and cognition. *Frontiers of Information Technology & Electronic Engineering, 18*(2), 153–179.

Zheng, P., Wang, Z., Chen, C. H., & Khoo, L. P. (2019). A survey of smart product-service systems: Key aspects, challenges and future perspectives. *Advanced Engineering Informatics, 42*, 100973.

Zhu, B., Joseph, A., & Sastry, S. (2011, October). A taxonomy of cyber-attacks on SCADA systems. In *2011 International Conference on Internet of Things and 4th International Conference on Cyber, Physical and Social Computing* (pp. 380–388). IEEE.

CHAPTER 7

Bionic Banking Conclusions

Main Findings

Previous research applied the bionics discipline to the study of organization management. In the 1960s, scholars have conducted studies about organization bionics, which mainly aimed to develop new models about business age and organization life cycle. Further contributions in bionics appeared, dealing with the development of bionic operating systems, bio-inspired product design practices, and a significant transformation of the organization system-defined bionic enterprises.

Clay Carr's research cycle, published from 1989 to 1990, mentioned bionic organizations for the first time. In the first research in 1989, Carr distinguished three features of the bionic organization (Cherepanov et al., 2021):

- Critical agents in the processes include not only humans but computer systems.
- Any agent of activity or operator has access to massive storage of information and knowledge of the organization.
- All organization members, including computer systems, can interact with each other using standard methods.

Carr described modern organizations with digital assistants, chatbots, artificial intelligence, and messengers for communications. Considering such an organization as a bionic, he emphasized that computer systems become full-fledged collaborative process members.

In the early 2000s, there were mentions of bionic organizations using technologies in their processes (Cohen et al., 2002). After this research, there were no detailed mentions of bionic organization in scientific research and publications on economics, management, and related field researches. Further development of the bionic organization concept occurred in 2018–2019 in an article by Price Waterhouse Coopers (Everson et al., 2018). Boston Consulting Group conducted studies about bionic organizations and showed this business entity type (Hutchinson 2019). The main point of those publications is that digital technologies solutions such as artificial intelligence and big data can enhance human competencies and broaden organization capabilities rather than replacing them (Singh et al., 2019). Some BCG papers were also devoted to bionic banking (Walsh et al., 2015).

Past research does not provide an exhaustive framework about what bionic banking is and how it operates to grow exponentially. This book aimed to fill the research gap present in the organization bionics by answering the following research question:

Q0: *What is bionic banking, and how is it structured?*

And sub-questions:

Q1: *Which are the main characteristic elements of bionic banking?*
Q2: *What are the outcomes that bionic banking delivers into the market?*
Q3: *Which are the main components of the business model of bionic banking?*
Q4: *Is there evidence of the existence of bionic organizations?*
Q5: *How will bionic banking evolve in this time of crisis?*

Answering the first question:

Q0: *What is bionic banking, and how is it structured?*

The bionic organization is a hybrid entity where virtual robots and persons coexist as critical and essential pillars. These organizations are characterized by having completed a successful bionic transformation process and started a superior evolution to become bionic. The transformation toward bionics consists of achieving a balanced trade-off between people, who are flexible and unique, and automation that is exactly replicable but not so flexible and cannot rapidly react to unforeseen events.

Q1:   Which are the main characteristic elements of bionic banking?

The theory of bionic banking states that there is a need for an appropriate business model at the core of bionic banking. This business model requires a sharp vision and mission according to which it can define its objectives. Together with vision and mission, the two fundamental elements of bionic banking are automation—represented by the massive use of data analytics, AI, and robotic process automation—and persons who display digital capabilities and the ability to work within a dynamic organizational structure.

Q2:   What are the outcomes that bionic banking delivers into the market?

From the exploitation of the factors mentioned in answer to *Q1*, bionic banking has the opportunity to achieve a threefold outcome: agile operations, a superior customer experience, and relationship, a high degree of innovation in its value proposition, and often in business model composition. As discussed in the previous chapters, the bionic transformation is relevant since it boosts organizations to become market leaders. Nevertheless, empirical data demonstrates also that there is still limited awareness about the potential of becoming bionic.

Q3:   Which are the main components of the business model of bionic banking?

The study presents a bionic business model, structured from the twelve building blocks framework of the business model canvas introduced by Osterwalder and modified by the author of this book. It is essential to keep in mind that the coexistence of persons and automation reflects the "philosophy" at the base of a bionic organization. For this reason, it is a recurring element among the components.

Q4: Is there evidence of the existence of bionic banking?

There is minimal knowledge of the bionic banking opportunity and its benefits. Several case studies demonstrate how the human-automation collaboration in banking and insurance industries leads some organizations, such as Danske Bank, HDFC Bank, Banca Generali Private, and Ping An Insurance, to become leading organizations in a short term. These real-world examples provide empirical support to the research in evidence of bionic organizations' existence and success.

An exciting development is the presence of fintech organizations that are developing new and advanced solutions to support effective human-automation collaboration,

Q5: How will bionic banking evolve in this time of crisis?

In the critical scenario of the global crisis caused by the pandemic, organizations need to consider some new factors and include them in their daily operations for the post-pandemic phase: the "New Normal." It emerges that the elements to incorporate in the business model of bionic organizations after the pandemic are resilience, crisis management practices, remote modality, and cyber-security.

Future Research

The topics analyzed present some limitations due to the skepticism and resistance to change spread among organizations. Since most businesses are afraid about modifying the way, they currently operate and are discouraged by the size of the investments necessary to undergo this transformation, they tend not to recognize the potential of bionics. In addition to this resistance toward change, many small and medium-sized financial institutions are not ready for this superior evolution because they have not yet achieved a critical digitalization level. There is a criticism of bionic theory in some other cases because of the risk of job losses caused by automation in executing the business core operations.

Eventually, the book presents another limitation related to the qualitative and descriptive nature of the research: it lacks a mathematical and statistical foundation. Nevertheless, the empirical support provided by the case studies analyzed fully compensates for this lack.

In this regard, it is possible to identify further research suggestions, such as demonstrating the effectiveness of the bionic business model using a quantitative method. Future studies may focus on monitoring the complete conversion toward bionics of the organizations examined in this book, also beyond financial services.

REFERENCES

Cherepanov, V., Popov, E., & Simonova, V. (2021). Bionic organization as a stage of production enterprise development in a digital transformation process. In *E3S Web of Conferences* (Vol. 250, p. 03003). EDP Sciences.

Cohen, G. A., & Parkinson, J. S. (2002). *Perspectives on Business Innovation, 8*, 79–84.

Hutchinson, R., Aré, L., Rose, J., & Bailey, A. (2019). The bionic company. *Published November 7*.

Miles Everson, M. Sviokla, J-, & Barnes, K. (2018, October). Leading a Bionic Transformation, *strategy+business*.

Singh, S. K., & El-Kassar, A. N. (2019). Role of big data analytics in developing sustainable capabilities. *Journal of Cleaner Production, 213*, 1264–1273.

Walsh, I., Reinaud, A. de T'Serclaes, J. W., Reyero, B., Noakes, B. & Mönter, N. (2015, March). The Bionic Bank, *Boston Consulting Group Paper*.

Glossary

Accuracy. It is a quality parameter used in classification tasks. It measures the proportion of correctly identified results (true positives plus true negatives) over the entire population of cases under consideration.

Active Management. Most robo-advisors follow a passive approach. They follow indices as closely as possible. Some robo-advisors also apply active management in the sense that they try to outperform a given benchmark.

Agility. It is a metric to measure how quickly a solution responds to the customer's changes and resource load scales, distributing more and different resources to the activity.

Algorithms. They are an essential part of modern advanced applications. They are used for specific tasks, from recommending products and services to automate the investments online. Algorithms are connected directly into a digital exchange in stock markets, and trading happens without human intervention.[1] Pedro Domingos's (2015) definition is "An algorithm is a sequence of instructions telling a computer what to do." The algorithm's base is on three logical operations—AND, OR, and NOT. While these operations can chain together in complex ways, algorithms are built out of a simple rationale at the core.

Analytics. It is a discipline that deals with finding, interpreting, and communicating relevant models in data sets. Analytics analyzes data to

---

[1] www.bbc.com/news/solution-14841018. Accessed 25 July 2021.

produce insights by applying statistical formulas, computer programming, and operation research tools. It is beneficial in areas characterized by substantial amounts of recorded information. The goal is to guide the decision-making process considering the business context. The analytical flow includes descriptive analysis, diagnostic analysis, predictive analysis, and prescriptive measures.

App. It is short for application. It is a program or piece of software downloaded by a customer into a mobile device.

Application Programming Interfaces (API). They are programming interfaces that, by allowing the communication and sharing of data between applications, simplify the development of computer programs, supplying all the components developers then assemble. APIs also allow access to other applications in other systems in a bidirectional way.

Application. It is software that a user can run on ICT resources to achieve a specific function related to the user's or the organization's purposes. These ICT resources could be programmable logic controllers, standard computers, mobile devices, or the cloud.

Artificial Intelligence Bias and Human Bias. Like humans, artificial intelligence (AI) is prone to bias, not because it makes decisions based on illogical motivations, but because human errors can be latent in the machine learning process, from the training, the algorithm creation stage, up to the interpretation or completeness or correctness of the data and later interactions.

Asset Allocation. It is the distribution of assets in a portfolio to diversify the wealth of the investor. Typical asset classes include stocks, bonds, and cash. Other asset classes for robo-advisory may include real estate, commodities (gold), hedge funds, cryptocurrencies, and alternative investments.

Audit. It is the process by which an internal or external auditor independently verifies financial records, business processes, and information systems.

Augmented Intelligence or Artificial Intelligence (AI). It is a system that performs actions, reasoning, and behaviors that usually require the human being (visual perception, speech understanding, linguistic translation, learning, object management, decision-making ability, and so on).

Augmented Reality (AR). It is the solution that enriches the perception of reality by superimposing on the vision of natural environments information or virtual objects by using a unique visor.

Authentication. It is the verification of the identity of a customer or another person by a system or service.

Authorization. It is the procedure to check whether a customer or another person inside or outside the organization has the right to do a specific action, such as transferring funds or accessing sensitive data.

Automation. It is the automated handling of services or products. It is the percentage of requests to the partner handled without any human intervention.

Availability. It is the metric that measures the percentage, usually computed over a periodical (such as a month) basis and net of planned or unplanned service downtimes.

Banking as a Service (BaaS). It supplies complete banking processes, such as loans, payments, or deposit accounts, as a service. It uses an existing licensed bank's secure and regulated infrastructure with API-driven platforms (C. Skinner, 2014).

Banking. It is engaged in keeping or transferring money for savings and checking accounts, exchanging, issuing loans and credit, and other financial products.

Banks. It is an organization that accepts deposits, transfers money, and makes credit.

Behavioral Analysis. It is a type of analysis that uses data on people's behavior to understand their intentions and predict their actions. It is the bulk of customer data produced by e-commerce platforms, games, web, mobile applications, and the Internet of Things powers predictive behavioral analysis algorithms. This data allows marketers to target the right offers to the right microsegment at the right time.

Big Data Analytics. It examines large volumes of data of several types to find patterns, trends, correlations, and other helpful information to obtain insights that organizations can exploit to improve decision-making processes. Another definition is big data analytics is the science and engineering application of problem-solving, where the nature, size, and conformation of data make it challenging to use traditional analysis tools.

Big Data. It is any collection of large and complex data challenging to process using traditional data processing applications.[2] Big data has 9Vs characteristics: (Veracity, Variety, Velocity, Volume, Validity, Variability,

---

[2] Top Fintech Terms You Should Know—Trulioo: Global. www.trulioo.com/blog/top-fintech-terms-know/. Accessed 30 May 2021.

Volatility, Visualization, and Value). Big data technologies include data virtualization, data management and integration, and knowledge discovery and research.

Biometrics. It is the process by which a person's unique physical and other traits are detected and recorded by an electronic device or system to confirm identity.

Bionic Robo-Advisor. It is a robo-advisor that integrates a human advisor as well in their automatic process. The name bionic derives from the link of two approaches: the automation's strength by implementing an automatized process and a human for personal contact and empathy whenever necessary.

Bitcoin. It is a consensus network that enables a new payment system and completely digital money. It is the first decentralized peer-to-peer payment network powered by its users with no central authority or intermediaries.

Blockchain. It is a distributed database where consensus or mass collaboration proves trust. Each transaction is recorded continuously and sequentially on a public block creating a unique ongoing chain. Bitcoin transactions first used blockchain (M. Karajovic et al., 2017). Cryptocurrency transactions still use it. It runs like a distributed ledger where information, once entered, cannot be changed. There are several applications of blockchain solutions, including smart contracts and the recording of digital assets. It can record data: a digital ledger of transactions, agreements, contracts, or anything that needs to be registered independently and verified as having happened. Blockchain solutions run across several or even thousands of computers in some applications. Every time a new batch of transactions is encrypted, it is added to the ledger "chain" as a "block." Blockchain solutions are used in many applications, where data needs to be shared trustfully among organizations or persons.

Bot. It is a short form for a virtual robot. It can perform specific high volume, manual, and repeatable tasks that humans previously performed. Bot performs these tasks much faster than humans.

Business Intelligence (BI). It is a broad category of applications and solutions for collecting, storing, analyzing, retrieving, and supplying data to help customers make better organizational decisions. BI applications include decision support systems, querying and reporting, online analytical processing, statistical analysis, forecasting, and data mining. Analytics has generalized and extended business intelligence. The use of augmented intelligence (AI) in big data and business intelligence is essential. Organizations use machine learning algorithms to find trends and extract insights from substantial amounts of data to make critical decisions quickly or in real time.

Business Model Canvas (BMC). It is a strategic management and entrepreneurial tool. Osterwalder and Pigneur introduced the BMC to describe, design, challenge, invent, show, and pivot a business model (A. Osterwalder et al., 2010).

Business Model. It is a simplified representation of an organization and an abstraction of how its business and value creation make money. It describes the organization, cost structures, financial flows, value network, and organization's products compactly. The process of defining a business model is part of the business strategy.

Business-to-Customer (B2C). It refers to organizations that relate to individuals rather than other organizations.

Chatbot. It is an AI program. It simulates human conversations interactively, using pre-set sentences. It is used for assistance services (customer care) or marketing, such as social networks and instant messaging. More complex than speech-to-text programs, chatbots communicate with people using text (text chatbot) and voice (voicebot). Text chatbots have been used before voice bots, holding a verbal conversation, understanding language, and providing answers.

Cloud Computing. It is a computing capability that provides convenient and on-demand network access to a shared pool of configurable computing resources (F. Liu et al., 2011). These resources can be rapidly provisioned and released with minimal management effort or partner interaction. Cloud computing has six essential characteristics: pay-per-use, self-service, broad network access, resource pooling, flexibility, and measured service. In general terms, cloud computing enables four modes: Infrastructure as a Service (IaaS), Platform as a Service (PaaS), Software as a Service, and Business Process as a Service (BpaaS). It can be public, private, or hybrid,

Cloud. Short for cloud computing, it is a term that describes a network of remote servers that stores, manages, and processes data on the internet, cutting the need for a local server or personal computer (B. Nicoletti, 2013). Cloud computing solutions have developed rapidly. Cloud providers, for example, have incorporated features such as facial recognition of online photos and automatic translation of spoken language into their respective cloud services. The next stage of cloud evolution will be creating AI-based platforms that can be used by any type of business, regardless of size or solutions level. Many Platform-as-a-Service (PaaS) solutions have already begun to incorporate AI capabilities.

Cognition. It is the mental action of acquiring knowledge and understanding through thought, experience, and senses.

Cognitive Automation. It is an intelligent software to process substantial amounts of information. What distinguishes cognitive automation from robotic process automation (RPA) is the use of augmented intelligence.

Cognitive Computing (CC)-based hybrid-augmented intelligence. In general, it refers to new software and/or hardware that mimics the function of the human brain (N. N. Zhen et al., 2017). It improves the computer's capabilities of perception, reasoning, and decision-making. In that sense, it is a new framework of computing with more accurate models of how the human brain/mind senses, reasons, and responds to a stimulus, especially how to build causal models, intuitive reasoning models, and associative memories in an intelligent system.

Cognitive Computing. It is a system that learns at scale, reasons with purpose, and interacts with humans naturally. It is a mixture of computer science and cognitive science. A computer can solve problems and optimize human processes by self-teaching algorithms that use data mining, visual recognition, and natural language processing. It includes machine learning, natural language processing, natural language understanding, and computer vision.

Cognitive Robotic Process Automation (RPA). Cognitive RPA uses augmented intelligence solutions such as machine learning and natural language processing (NLP) to augment RPA capabilities and enhance the customer journey by incorporating unstructured tasks into process automation.

Collaborative robots (Cobots). They represent a natural evolution that can solve existing manufacturing and assembly challenges, as they allow for physical interaction with humans in a shared workspace (Colgate, J. E., 1996). They are designed to be easily reprogrammed even by non-experts to be repurposed for different roles in a continuously evolving workflow.

Compliance. It is respect for the internal and external compulsory rules of the organization or of the government.

Compound Annual Growth Rate (CAGR). It is a measure of the average growth over many periods.

Consensus. It is a mechanism that allows computer applications to agree on how to update the database. The modifications they have settled on are made unchangeable with the help of complex cryptography (*The Economist*, 2013).

Conversational Artificial Intelligence. It is a type of AI trained to interpret human (everyday) language and communicate with people. Equipped with advanced natural language processing (NLP) features, conversational AI is a logic that creates virtual conversations. An example of an application is the voice control devices present on voice bots.

Credibility. It expresses the believability, honesty, and trustworthiness of a person or an organization. It incorporates reputation, confidence, and general confidentiality.

Credit Risk Management. It is the practice of identifying and mitigating loss by understanding the limits of financial institutions' loss reserves at any given time to maximize adjusted returns (BIS, 2000).

Credit Scoring. It is used to evaluate the creditworthiness of a credit customer (T. P. Mpofu et al., 2014). Usually, it is a numerical value with specific creditworthiness associated with an individual or an organization. It describes the potential customers' ability to repay the credit. Credit scoring is based on several variables, such as income, personal and financial history, employment, and demographics (T. P. Mpofu et al., 2014).

Crisis. It is a situation formally declared as service interruption or the deterioration of one or more critical processes or as systemically essential because of incidents or disasters.

Critical Success Factors (CSFs). They are the limited number of satisfactory results that will ensure successful competitive performance for the individual, initiative, or organization (C. V. Bullen et al., 1981). CSFs are the key areas where "things must go right" to flourish and reach the organization's goals (L. Cooper, 2010).

Cryptocurrency. It is a medium of exchange using cryptography to secure transactions and control new units' creation.

Customer Journey. It is the entire sequence of touchpoints in a customer journey when interacting with an organization's offering, from initial awareness to buy to advocacy.

Customer Relationship Management (CRM). It is an information system for managing relationships with customers. It can control the relationship's life cycle with the customer, acquire new customers, customer proximity, and customer loyalty based on the organization's relationships. It lowers transaction costs between customers and the organization and integrates the processes of customer management.

Customer Value Proposition. They are the benefits a product or service holds for a customer. It is the reason why a customer might buy that product or service.

Customer. It is he/she who pays for the products, services, or activities. It is not necessarily the user of the product or the process or event. It can be external or internal to the organization. In the latter case, unless there is a system of internal prices, the internal customer does not pay for the product, the service, or the activity but uses it.

Cyber-Physical Services (CPS) Platform. It is the platform construct, the hardware, software, and communication systems with basic standardized CPS) mediation, interoperability, and quality of services for implementing and managing cyber-physical systems and their applications and their integration in value networks (R. A. Rojas, et al., 2020). CPS platform services are integral to domain-specific CPS application platforms with their basic functionality for implementing reliable operation and evolution of cyber-physical systems. They secure the cross-domain and cross-financial institution functionality and quality at the technological system level, for example, through Quality of Service (QoS)-capable communication, services for ICT security or self-diagnosis, self-healing, and reconfiguration.

Cyber-Security. It is the set of solutions and services aimed at protecting computers, other connected devices, equipment, and ICT systems from attacks of several types (malware, viruses, trojans, ransomware, and so on), to prevent losses, compromise of data and information, or other types of malicious actions.

Cyber-Physical Systems (Cps). They encompass embedded systems, production, logistics, engineering, coordination, management processes, and internet services that directly capture biological data using sensors and act on physical processes using actuators. They are connected using digital networks, use data and services available worldwide, and have multimodal person-robot interfaces. Cyber-physical systems are open socio-technical systems and enable several functions, services, and properties.

Data Analytics. It is an end-to-end process that involves cleaning, inspecting, and modeling data to find helpful and actionable information to support decision-making. In a B2C context, this process includes qualitative and quantitative methods used to derive insights on buying behaviors, trends, and patterns.

Data Breach. It is the intentional or unintentional release of secure information to an untrusted environment.

Data Science. It is a discipline that combines statistical systems and processes with computer science and information science to extrapolate insights through structured and/or unstructured data analysis. One of the most common data science applications (in AI and machine learning) is developing predictive tools.

Data. It is a set of quantitative or qualitative variables. A novel, a video, or a chart of accounts are all examples of data. Augmented intelligence (AI) needs data to train, learn, and act. The more it has access to correct data, the better its chances of success.

Decision Model. It is a set of rules used to understand and manage the logic that drives business decisions. It involves applying sophisticated algorithms to large volumes of data. Decision models can recommend a course of action and predict its outcome.

Decision Tree. It is both data representing a structure to support deciding and a method used for data mining and machine learning.

Deep Learning. It is a machine learning method whereby a system recognizes the patterns present in the data through the automatic learning of a hierarchy of features or characteristics (S. Raschka et al., 2020). Deep learning processes data through a "deep" succession of activation levels. Each level represents the data, and the following groups use features from the earlier level to make more complex representations. A category to which the data belongs maps the output of the final level. The goal of a deep learning algorithm is to make this final mapping correct. Superficial machine learning approaches rely on humans. Many feature engineering processes before the model can learn the relationships between features. In deep learning, on the other hand, the system gets the characteristics and their relationships simultaneously.

Design Thinking. It is a method to find practical and creative solutions to problems through an approach adopted by designers (R. Martin et al., 2009). Design thinking strategies have proven highly effective in the innovation sector because they allow organizations to develop creative thinking for customer needs.

Digital Assistant. It is an AI system capable of understanding voice commands and performing various tasks, for example, providing a customer support service.

Digital Banking. It is digitization (or moving online) of all the traditional banking activities and program services that were historically only available to customers physically inside a bank branch (A. Zujev, 2021). Any payment app or banking tool can adopt the term but lack the processes and customer-facing interface to complete banking tasks with minimal human attention.

Digital Financial Services (DFS). Financial products and services include payments, transfers, savings, credit, insurance, securities, financial planning, and account statements via digital solutions such as e-money, payment cards, and a regular financial institution account.[3]

Digital Transformation. It is a change in the business model, considering digital solutions. It is the social, cultural, and technological changes associated with digital solutions (C. Matt et al., 2015).

Disruptive Innovation. It is an innovation that completely changes how persons or organizations do something.[4] It describes innovations that unexpectedly improve products or services and change how things are done and the market. The mobile phone is an example of disruptive innovation.[5] It has completely changed how users connect to ICT services—disruptive innovation impacts persons, businesses, and society.

Distributed Ledger Solution (DLT). Distributed ledgers use independent computers (called nodes) to record, share, and synchronize transactions in their respective digital ledgers (instead of keeping data centralized as done traditionally).[6] Blockchain is a distributed ledger that organizes data into blocks, chained together in an append-only mode, once encrypted.

---

[3] G20 High-Level Principles for Digital Financial Inclusion. www.gpfi.org/publications/g20-high-level-principles-digital-financial-inclusion. Accessed 22 June 2021.

[4] Disruptive Innovation - Open Risk Manual. www.openriskmanual.org/wiki/Disruptive_Innovation. Accessed 20 May 2021.

[5] Disruptive Innovation. Open Risk Manual. www.openriskmanual.org/wiki/Disruptive_Innovation. Accessed 22 June 2021.

[6] Blockchain & Distributed Ledger Solution (DLT). www.worldbank.org/en/topic/financialsector/brief/blockchain-dlt. Accessed 22 June 2021.

Blockchain & Distributed Ledger Solution (DLT). www.worldbank.org/en/topic/financialsector/brief/blockchain-dlt. Accessed 22 June 2021.

Ease of use. It means easing the users' search, navigation, and connectivity, such as a service/website. It includes the system flexibility and user-friendliness in the offered services.

Ecosystem. It is a network of organizations, including partners, distributors, customers, competitors, government agencies, and others, to deliver a specific product or service through cooperation (C. Anitha et al., 2017). An ecosystem is an interconnected set of services that allow users to fulfill various needs in one integrated experience. Customer ecosystems tend to concentrate on requirements such as travel, health care, or housing. Business-to-business (B2B) ecosystems revolve around a specific function: marketing and sales, operations, procurement, or finance (T. Catlin, 2018). One of the main benefits of ecosystems is providing better solutions to those offered by the platform developer. In this sense, they can solve the problems of a sector but open new growth opportunities.

Efficiency. This dimension includes ease and speed of accessing and using, for example, e-banking service, and availability and functionality of the service that conveniently facilitates the timely completion of all the transactions.

Embedded Finance. It refers to non-financial organizations with value propositions that are significantly enhanced or even transformed through the associated financial products and services embedded within them (C. J. Yang, 2020).

Emerging Technologies. They are a set of technologies that are being generated and tested because of successive innovations. It is an essential part of the bionic transformation.

End-User. It is the end or final user of an application.

Equator Principles (Eps). They are a risk management framework adopted by financial institutions for determining, assessing, and managing environmental and social risks in projects.[7] The goal is to provide a minimum standard for due diligence and monitoring to support responsible risk decision-making. The Eps apply globally to all industry sectors and five financial products: (1) Project Finance Advisory Services, (2) Project Finance, (3) Project-Related Corporate Loans, (4) Bridge Loans, and (5) Project-Related Acquisition Finance and Refinance (D. Sarro, 2012).

---

[7] equator-principles.com/. Accessed 26 October 2021.

Exchange-Traded Fund (ETF). It is also called an index fund. It is an investment fund, which tries to minimize the tracking error compared to a given benchmark. It is used for passive investing and is part of many robo-advisory portfolios.

Fees. It is money charged for services. Examples of banking fees are fees associated with checking and savings accounts, such as if an overdraft occurs and the account owner has requested that the financial institution accepts overdrafts (M. Suiter, 2020).

Financial Institution (FI). It includes all organizations that supply financial services. Financial institutions operate at all scales, including large and small incumbent banks, brokerages, insurance organizations, or fintech organizations.

Financial Product. It is a financial instrument that allows for saving, spending, planning, or borrowing. For example, a credit card, Registered Retirement Savings Plan (RRSP) account, or a checking account are three examples of financial products.

Financial Service. It is an action or work that is done for a customer by their financial institution. An example of financial services includes managing and moving money between accounts. Financial services are not to be confused with a financial product. Financial services are what is done for a customer, while financial products are what a customer can use.

Fintech Organization. It is the emerging financial solution sector whose name is composed of "FINance" and "TECHnology." A fintech organization is an organization or digital service that automates the delivery and use of financial products and services. Fintech organizations are often quite different from traditional financial institutions in organizational structure and personnel and often consider themselves technology organizations. Some fintech organizations may offer similar services compared to traditional banks and interact directly with individual customers. Some fintech organizations only provide business-to-business solutions to other financial institutions.

General Artificial Intelligence. It is a form of artificial intelligence that can perform various human-made tasks in various environments.

General Data Protection Regulation (GDPR). It is an EU regulation that takes care of personal data protection and privacy in the European Union.

General-Purpose Technologies. The importance of general-purpose technologies lies in the overall impact on persons, businesses, and society and the wide range of complementary innovations they support. To date, the most powerful technologies are the engine, electricity, computers, and the internet. Augmented intelligence is another essential turning point in the development of this type of technology.

Goals. They are specific targets to be reached at a given time (C. V. Bullen et al., 1981). A goal is thus an operational transformation of one or more objectives.

Governance. It refers to the controls and processes that ensure a sector's effectiveness, efficiency, economics, and ethics.[8] The sector might refer to the entire organization or an organization unit, a process, or data.

High-Frequency Trading (HFT). It is an algorithmic trading solution. It is based on an infrastructure that minimizes network and other types of latencies using specific facilities as co-location, proximity hosting, or high-speed direct access and by a system determination of order initiation, generation, and execution without human intervention for trades or orders» (MiFid II, 2014).

Human-in-the-Loop (HITL). It is an expression that indicates the integration of a person in automatic learning processes to optimize outputs and increase accuracy. The tool is recognized as a best practice of machine learning.

Human-in-the-loop. Hybrid-augmented intelligence (HITL). It is an intelligent model that requires human interaction (N. N. Zhen et al., 2017). In this type of smart system, humans are always part of the system and consequently influence the outcome. Humans give different judgments if a computer gives a low confident result. HITL hybrid-augmented intelligence also readily addresses problems and requirements that machine learning may not quickly train or classify.

Human-Machine Interaction/Man-Machine Interaction (MMI)/Human-Computer Interaction (HCI). The computer science part deals with the user-friendly design of interactive systems and their human-robot interfaces. In addition to computer science findings, those from psychology, ergonomics, cognitive science, ergonomics, and design are used. Important sub-areas of human-robot interaction are, for example, usability engineering, interaction design, information design, and context analysis. The last aspect is vital for CPSs to ensure to adapt the interactions optimally to every situation.

---

[8] Governance. Open Risk Manual. www.openriskmanual.org/wiki/Governance. Accessed 30 May 2021.

Incident. It is an event that is not part of the standard operation of a service. It causes or may cause an interruption to or a reduction in the quality of service.

Inductive Reasoning. It is a process in which tests and datasets are used as the basis for reaching a specific conclusion. Given the evidence provided, the deduction may be probable since it is not inevitable.

Industry 4.0. It denotes the merge of ICT with automation, having at its base the internet solutions.

Information and Communication Technologies (ICT). It combines computers, storage, network, applications, and so on, which provides integrated and remote access to computer-based services.

Innovation. It describes when a new product (or service or idea or concept, or process) is brought to market and adopted by some customers. More broadly, innovation represents a novel idea that affects and creates impact.

Input. It is a resource introduced into the system or consumed in its operation, which helps get a result or output.

Integration. It is the process of combining components or systems into one integrated entity.

Intelligent Automation. It indicates an automation solution enhanced with cognitive abilities that allow programs and robots to learn, interpret, and respond.

Intelligent System. It is a machine integrated with a computer connected to the internet to collect and analyze data and communicate with other systems. It is a smart artificial system that can think and learn independently and adapt to current data.

Internet of Things (IoT). It is an expression that indicates an ever-expanding network of detection equipment such as sensors, cameras, and other devices connected via the internet and able to communicate and exchange information. It allows communication between objects over the internet, allowing data exchange, modified behavior based on input received instruction memory, and learning from the interactions.

Internet. It is a global computer network providing various information and communication facilities, consisting of interconnected networks using standardized communication protocols.

Interoperability. Independent, heterogeneous systems can work together (as far as possible) seamlessly to exchange information in an efficient and usable manner, cooperate, and provide services to users without the need for separate agreements between the systems.

Key Performance Indicators or Key Process Indicators. They are the metrics (or measures) used within corporations to measure one department's performance against another concerning revenue, sales, lead conversion, costs, customer support, and so on.

Know Your Customer (KYC). It is the process of an organization verifying its customers' identity and standing and the character of the business or transactions they generate. The term refers to the legal regulations which govern these activities.

Lean and Digitize. It is the method used to make the processes simultaneously streamlined and digitized, wherever it helps improve the processes (Nicoletti, 2012).

Lean Six Sigma. It is a complete, flexible, and highly structured method to achieve, maintain, and increase customer value (Dahlgaard-Park et al., 2006).

Machine Learning (ML). It is a set of algorithms used to make a system artificially intelligent. ML is a subcategory of AI. By collecting and classifying information, machine learning can identify types and patterns of data with few or no hard-coded rules.[9] It is a set of algorithms, or execution rules, to solve a problem(s) whose performance improves with experience (data) without hindsight. Machine learning is an interdisciplinary field that embraces information theory, control theory, statistics, and computer science. Banking uses machine learning for scoring, fraud detection, portfolio management, and risk assessment.

Management Process. It is a method to optimize the organization as a system, determine which processes need improvement and/or control, define priorities, and provide leadership to initiate and support improvement efforts. It is the management of the information obtained because of these processes.

Marketing. The American Marketing Association (AMA) defines marketing as the activity, set of institutions, and processes for creating, communicating, delivering, and exchanging offerings that add value for customers, partners, and society.[10]

Markets in Financial Instruments Directive (MiFID). It is a European directive to improve the visibility and efficiency of the European financial

---

[9] www.coursehero.com/file/43001568/Artificial-Intelligence-Sep2017pdf/. Accessed 22 June 2021.

[10] www.ama.org/the-definition-of-marketing/. Accessed 30 May 2021.

markets. It also decides standards for regulatory disclosures. Meanwhile, there is an updated regulation called MiFID 2.

Millennials (or Generation Y). It refers to the customer segment between 18 and 34 years. This segment is highly active on the web, social media, and mobile phones. Generation Y represents a quarter of the world population. It is a significant challenge for financial institutions to try and acquire this market, as they are the customers of the near future.

Mission. It is how to go ahead toward the vision.

Narrow Artificial Intelligence. It is an artificial intelligence application with an optimized model to perform a limited number of tasks. A concrete example could be that a chatbot assigned routine tasks that require accuracy and speed of execution, such as retrieving information from a banking database.

National Institute of Standards and Solution (NIST). It is a measurement standards laboratory part of the USA Department of Commerce non-regulatory agency. It also promotes the effective and secure use of cloud computing within organizations.

Natural Language Processing (NLP). It is the interaction in human language, including natural language understanding (NLU) (Sentimental Analysis, Conversational AI bots.) and natural language generation (NLG). It is a field of computer science aimed at understanding or generating human languages, both in the form of text and speech.

Natural Language Understanding (NLU). It is a sub-field of NLP aimed at building machines with a reading comprehension ability to allow humans to communicate with them naturally and receive proper answers.

Omniaccess. It is a generalization of omnichannel for access in general (S. Skinner, 2020).

Omnichannel. It is a cross-channel content strategy that organizations use to improve their user experience and drive better relationships across different accesses or contact points. The accesses' design and supporting resources can help communication synchronize the customer's information (Beaudon et al., 2019).

Operational Resilience. An organization's business operations can rapidly adapt and respond to internal or external dynamic changes—opportunities, demands, disruptions, or threats—and continue operations with limited impact to the business (Finextra, IBM, 2016).

Orchestration. It describes the setup and networking of software services to form a business process. It is possible to combine internal and external services. Each service realizes only one specific activity within the process. With conventional web services, a participant controls the process flow. In bionic banking, business processes will emerge *ad hoc*, and decisions made dynamically to control process flows. In this respect, the term orchestration is broader in this context than with conventional web services. It refers to the setting up of federated services used in several business processes simultaneously. They ensure their context for each software process.

Organization. It includes financial institutions, public or private institutions, central or local, department, or non-profit organizations.

Output. It is the result produced by a system or process. The final output is usually a product, a service, or an initiative.

Pandemic. It is an epidemic of disease that spreads across a vast region or globally.

Passive Robo-Advisor. In contrast to active portfolio management, passive management robo-advisor tries to track a given benchmark as closely as possible. The aim is to recreate, for example, an index returns as exact as possible and to avoid any deviations. Exchange-Traded Funds (ETFs) are a popular instrument for passively managed portfolios.[11]

Perceived Risk. It is a customer's subjective belief of suffering a loss in the pursuit of desired outcomes.

Perceived Use. It is an individual's perception that an innovative solution will enhance or improve his/her performance.

Personalization. It refers to providing individual designs to customers following their set of needs, wants, and preferences.

Platform. It is a group of technologies used as a base upon which to develop other applications, processes, or technologies. In this book, the term indicates any information and communication system or automation support.

Predictive Analytics. It combines data, statistical algorithms, and machine learning tools to identify the likelihood of future outcomes based on historical data and improve the predictions' reliability. It is the practice that uses historical data to predict future results. By combining

---

[11] Millennials do not trust us, investment advisers say. /www.theglobeandmail.com/globe-investor/advisers-view/millennials-an-elusive-target-for-investment-advisers/article25845221/. Accessed 20 March 2021.

mathematical models (or "predictive algorithms") with historical data, predictive analysis computes the values and probabilities of events. Machine learning-based predictive analytics have been around for some time. It recently lacked three crucial features to generating marketing value: scalability, speed, and explainability.

Problem. It is the cause that creates an incident. Incidents not resolved due to the lack of an available solution, and repeated incidents related to a known issue ("known problem/error"), pass through problem management. A workaround could remediate the problem before finding the root causes and resolving them.

Process Improvement. It is a continuous effort to learn the causes and effects to reduce complexity and variations and shorten times. The process gets better by removing incorrect root causes. Through the redesign of the process, it is possible to reduce the variations in common causes. It is a continuous effort to learn from the causes and effects, minimizing the complexity, variations, and cycle times. Eliminating or reducing the impact of the root causes improves the functions.

Process Management. It is a method to optimize the organization as a system, determine which processes need to be improved and/or controlled, define priorities, and encourage leadership to initiate and sustain process improvement efforts. It manages the information obtained in these processes.

Process. It is a set of interrelated activities that change inputs on results or outputs with a specific objective. Sometimes the process is identified with a system. It would be correct to regard it as a component of a system.[12]

Project Team. It is a group of persons from different fields (and in some cases, from various organizations) working for a certain period as a team to improve the process or reach goal.

Quality. It is not easily defined. Several variants are specified, at times specified by an adjective or specification added to the name. In general, quality is customer delight profitably for the organization.

Reference Architecture or Architecture Framework. It is a concept and method structure that forms a uniform basis for the description and specification of system architectures. The aim of reference architectures is, on the one hand, to create a standard structure and language

---

[12] Process - Open Risk Manual. www.openriskmanual.org/wiki/Process. Accessed 33 June 2021.

for architectural stories. On the other hand, they provide a method to get a detailed structural description.

Regtech Organization. It is a startup that uses solutions to help implement regulatory compliance (World Bank, 2018).

Reliability. It refers to the commitment to accessibility and accuracy of the services provided to the users.

Resilience. It is the capability to predict risks, limit impacts, and bounce back rapidly through survival, adaptability, evolution, and growth in the face of turbulent changes (Community and Regional Resilience Institute, 2013).

Responsiveness. It refers to the prompt responsiveness to the customers' inquiry, information retrieval, and navigation speed. It is a critical factor in assuring customers' delight.

Retail Banking. It is banking that takes place between individuals and their financial institutions (J. Pritchard, 2021). A retail financial institution offers customers essential banking services, including checking accounts, savings accounts, money transfers, and loans.

Risk. It is in financial terms as the chance that an outcome or investment's actual gains will differ from an expected outcome. Risks include the possibility of losing part or all an original investment.[13]

Robo-Advice. It is a digital investment advice tool that matches customers based on their personal preference for financial products.

Robo-Advisor. It is a financial service based on two components: investment advice and automatization through robots. The term robo-advice may include various levels of automatization. While algorithms typically provide the onboarding and risk profiling, the investment process can either be wholly rule-based or driven by a human advisor.

Robotic Process Automation (RPA). It is a solution that allows software or a virtual robot to implement applications to process transactions, manipulate data, generate responses, and communicate with other digital systems. In the financial sector, RPA can handle many repetitive tasks and processes.

Scalability. It is the ability of a system to scale up or down as needed. Augmented intelligence makes it possible to create models capable of

---

[13] www.investopedia.com/terms/r/risk.asp#:~:text=Risk%20is%20defined%20in%20fina ncial,all%20of%20an%20original%20investment.&text=In%20finance%2C%20standard%20d eviation%20is%20a%20common%20metric%20associated%20with%20risk. Accessed 22 June 2021.

handling vast amounts of data, supplying unparalleled real-time predictive performance and much more detailed, valuable insights from the decision point of view.

Securities and Exchange Commission (SEC). It is the USA Securities and Exchange Commission (SEC). It is a federal agency responsible for the regulation of markets and exchanges.

Security. It involves protection from any risk and fraud or financial loss.

Service. In computer science, it is the bundling of specialist functions of a program, in networks, providing an application on a server, and in telecommunications, data transmission. Services refer to the provision of services to meet a defined need. Services are also a product as the ones offered by financial institutions.

Sigma (σ). It is the eighteenth letter of the Greek alphabet. In statistics, it relates to the variance. It is a metric based on the number of defects that occur per million opportunities.

Six Sigma. It is a method and performance goal (R. G. Schroeder et al., 2008). A method is a structured approach to continuous process improvement. The goal is to measure a process's performance versus the target of several 3.4 defective parts per millions of opportunities.

Smart Application. It is a software program designed to perform certain functions directly for the user or, in some cases, for another application.

Smart Assistants. They are virtual assistants who process user requests in a dialogue system and perform tasks (O. Bendel, 2020). They can act audibly as voice assistants ("voice banking") and in text form as chatbots.

Smart Contracts. They are computer programs that automatically execute a contract or part of it. These contracts are automated and often blockchain based. They could save time and reduce costs in standard transactions. Smart contracts are computer protocols that ease, verify, or enforce a digital agreement. The idea is that these programs potentially replace notaries, lawyers, and financial institutions when handling standard legal and business transactions. Technically, it is a code stored on a blockchain solution, triggered by blockchain transactions, and reads and writes data in that blockchain database.

Smart Products. They are products capable of communicating with humans on a global network such as the internet.

Social Media. It is a platform that allows internet users to communicate and share user-generated content like knowledge, opinions, evaluations, impressions, and so on.

Software. It is the set of programs and other operational information used by a computer.

Standards. They are indications of voluntary or compulsory standardization.

Startup. It is a company that is in the first stage of its operations. Entrepreneurial founders launch these startups as they attempt to develop a product or service, they believe there is a demand.

Strategy. It is an essential component in the digital transformation process that includes the business model. It defines the impacts and opportunities of the business to create value-added services by using digital technology and data-based products and services (W. E. Deming, 1994).

Strong Artificial Intelligence. It is the idea that a computer program can function similarly to the human mind in terms of perception, beliefs, and other cognitive abilities associated with the human being.

System. It is a network of interacting components that cooperate to achieve specific goals.

Transaction. It is the action of executing a function or an application. An example of a transaction is executing a money order and processing authorization and clearing messages.

Trust. Two parties can define a positive relationship with proper authentication of the two parties.

Unbanked. It describes a person or group of people who do not have an account at any bank. Unbanked persons are either paid in cash or cash their paychecks rather than depositing them. Unbanked persons are often poor. Lack of a bank account often makes one ineligible to buy a house or take advantage of social services.

Underbanked. It is a person or business with poor access to mainstream financial services usually offered by retail banks. The underbanked is a distinct group from the unbanked, characterized by having no banking facilities.

Unstructured Data. It is information that does not have a predefined data model or is not organized by default. Unstructured data can be non-textual (e.g., JPEG images and MP3 files) and includes emails, videos, photos, audio files, word processing documents, presentations, and web pages. Unstructured data analytics tools, like natural language processing, conversation analytics, and video analytics, allow solutions to analyze the large volumes of unstructured data that organizations have access to.

User Interface (UI). It is a platform that allows a user to communicate with a computer that simulates a human conversation. Natural language processing (NLP) allows a conversational system to interact with users' feelings and context.

Validation. It is a method to provide specific personal information to prove ownership of the identity for identity verification.

Value Network. It is the sequence of activities that brings value to the customer (and indirectly to the organization). It is the process used to deliver a good or service. It is a set of activities and organizations needed to design, order, manufacture, and supply (or provide a given product or service in the case of a service). These activities cover the entire cycle of the product/service organization down to the end customer.

Value. It is the relationship between benefits and cost/damage of a product or service, as defined by the customer. In the case of a product/service, value measure is its ability to meet the customer's needs at a given price and at a given time.[14] The value perceived by the customer is all the features of the product/service that the customer considers necessary and valuable. Any activity that consumes resources (including time) and does not create value is a waste (*muda* in Japanese).

Virtual Agent. It is an augmented intelligence system that supplies a human-like user interface and executes transactions. Virtual agents can hold a conversation, intelligently answer questions, and nod as they speak.

Virtual Reality (VR). It is a solution that simulates reality, replacing it with a digital environment, whose input is made possible by unique accessories that allow an operator to interact within virtual reality (Acet16. M., 2020). Virtual reality applications create very engaging experiences seen and experienced by the user through a viewer. The user finds himself immersed in a 3D virtual environment of natural dimensions that breaks the barriers imposed by wearing it. To increase the feeling of reality, interactive handheld devices, such as motion trackers, respond to the user's physical movements.

Visibility. Artificial intelligence (AI) must be transparent in both the actions it performs and its decisions (T. van Nuenen et al., 2020). For this to happen, an AI application needs a capability that documents

---

[14] Value Proposition - Open Risk Manual. www.openriskmanual.org/wiki/Value_Proposition. Accessed 30 May 2021.

how it makes its decisions. Visibility means that there must be governance structures suitable to watch AI and, if necessary, to optimize its decision-making process and make it compliant with regulations.

Vision. It is the expression of what would represent a success for the organization. A vision defines the goal to implement to ensure that the organization supplies the creative tensions between the current reality and the vision. It is an expression of what would represent a success for the organization. The vision's goal is to produce a mental image for generating creative tensions between the current reality and the organization's future. To be valuable, the whole organization should know and accept the vision. Implementing the vision usually requires much effort and patience.

Voice of the Customer (VoC). It is the customer's voice, or the citizen's voice, in the case of public organizations.

Vulnerability. It consists of a system's intrinsic properties resulting in exposure to a risk that can produce damages.

Weak Artificial Intelligence. It is also known as restricted AI. It is an AI application in which the model performs a limited number of tasks. It applies to all routine tasks that require precision and speed of execution.

REFERENCES

———. (2007). *Encyclopedia Britannica 1*. London, UK.
———. (2015, April). Cyber-resilience in supply chains. *Technology Innovation Management Review*.
———. (2016, March). The blockchain in finance. Hype springs eternal. *The Economist*.
2010 ISO 9241-210, ergonomics of human-system interaction—Human-centered design for interactive systems.
Aaen, I. (2008). Essence: Facilitating agile innovation. In *Agile processes in software engineering and extreme programming* (pp. 1–10). Springer.
ACET16, M. (2020). The use of information and communication technologies (ICT) in the banking sector in Turkey. In *In Traders (2019): Academic studies in social, human and administrative sciences* (p. 27).
Adam, M., Wessel, M., & Benlian, A. (2020). AI-based chatbots in customer service and their effects on user compliance. *Electronic Markets*, 1–19.
Adamopoulou, E., & Moussiades, L. (2020). Chatbots: History, technology, and applications. *Machine Learning with Applications, 2*, 100006.
Agarwal, A., Singhal, C., & Thomas, R. (2021, March). *AI-powered decision making for the bank of the future*. McKinsey & Company.
Agrawal, A., Gans, J., & Goldfarb, A. (2016). The simple economics of machine intelligence. *Harvard Business Review, 17*(1), 2–5.
Ajzen, I. (1991). The theory of planned behavior. *Organizational Behavior and Human Decision Processes, 50*(2), 179–211.
Ajzen, I., & Fishbein, M. (1980). *Attitude understanding and predicting social behavior*. Prentice-Hall.

Aksin, O. Z., Armony, M., & Mehrotra, V. (2007). The modern CPC: A multidisciplinary perspective on operations management research. *Production and Operations Management*, 16(6), 665–688.

Akter, S., Michael, K., Uddin, M. R., McCarthy, G., & Rahman, M. (2020). Transforming business using digital innovations: The application of AI, blockchain, cloud and data analytics. *Annals of Operations Research*, 1–33.

Aldrich, H. E., & Wiedenmayer, G. (2019). From traits to rates: An ecological perspective on organizational foundings. In *Seminal ideas for the next twenty-five years of advances*. Emerald Publishing Limited.

Aldrich, H. E. (1979). *Organizations and environments*. Cornell University.

Alyoubi, B. A. (2015). Decision support system and knowledge-based strategic management. *Procedia Computer Science*, 65(2015), 278–284.

Andersen, B., & Fagerhaug, T. (2006). *Root cause analysis: Simplified tools and techniques*. ASQ Quality Press.

Anderson, W., Franke, M. R., Grebe, M., Leyh, M., & Rüessmann, M. (2020). *How bionic organizations translate digital maturity into performance*. Boston Consulting Group-BCG. Featured Insights.

Anitha, C., & Reddy, D. (2017, October). Evolution and emerging role of MFIs in Indian microfinance sector. *Sumedha Journal of Management*, 6(4), CMR College of Engineering & Solution, 87.

Aré, L., Bailey, A., Hutchinson, R., & Rose, J. (2019). *The bionic company*. Boston Consulting Group-BCG. Featured Insights.

Arner, D. W., Barberis, J. N., & Buckley, R. P. (2016). *The emergence of RegTech 2.0: From know your customer to know your data* (KPMG Paper).

Atanasova, P., Wright, D., & Augenstein, I. (2020). Generating label cohesive and well-formed adversarial claims. *arXiv preprint*:2009.08205.

Awotunde, J. B., Adeniyi, E. A., Ogundokun, R. O., & Ayo, F. E. (2021). Application of big data with Fintech in financial services. In *Fintech with artificial intelligence, big data, and blockchain* (pp. 107–139).

Azim, T., Riva, O., & Nath, S. (2016, June). uLink: Enabling user-defined deep linking to app content. In *Proceedings of the 14th Annual International Conference on Mobile Systems, Applications, and Services* (pp. 305–318).

Badhwar, R. (2021). AI code of ethics for cybersecurity. In *The CISO's next Frontier* (pp. 41–44). Springer.

Baesens, B., Van Vlasselaer, V., & Verbeke, W. (2015). *Fraud analytics using descriptive, predictive, and social network techniques: A guide to data science for fraud detection*. Wiley.

Barrelet, C. (2021). Eyes on the horizon. *Home, kpmg*.

Barth, T. J., & Arnold, E. (1999). Artificial intelligence and administrative discretion: Implications for public administration. *The American Review of Public Administration*, 29(4), 332–351.

Bauer, W., Bender, M., Braun, M., Rally, P., & Scholtz, O. (2016). *Lightweight robots in manual assembly, best to start simply: examining companies' initial experiences with lightweight robots*. Fraunhofer Institut.

Bawden, D., & Robinson, L. (2020). Information overload: An overview. In *Oxford encyclopedia of political decision making*. Oxford University Press.

Beaudon, G., & Soulier, E. (2019, February). Customer experience analytics in insurance: Trajectory, service interaction and contextual data. In *International Conference on Information Solution & Systems* (pp. 187–198). Springer.

Beck, K., Beedle, M., van Bennekum, A., Cockburn, A., Cunningham, W., Fowler, M., ... & Thom, D. (2001). *Manifesto for agile software development*. www.agile.manifesto.org. Accessed 15 March 2022.

Beckett, M., Elder, J., Ferri, G., et al. (2020). *Bionic revenue management in travel and tourism*. Boston Consulting Group-BCG. Featured Insights.

Bekkhus, R. (2016). Do KPIs used by CIOs decelerate digital business transformation? The case of ITIL. In *Digital Innovation, Technology, and Strategy Conference*.

Beltrán-Martín, I., Bou-Llusar, J. C., & Salvador-Gómez, A. (2021). HR flexibility and firm performance in professional service firms. *Journal of Management & Organization*, 1–22.

Bendel, O. (2020). Die Maschine an meiner Seite. In *Mensch-Roboter-Kollaboration* (1–14). Springer Gabler.

Bi, Y., Song, L., Yao, M., Wu, Z., Wang, J., & Xiao, J. (2020, July). DCDIR: A deep cross-domain recommendation system for cold start users in insurance domain. In *Proceedings of the 43rd International ACM SIGIR Conference on Research and Development in Information Retrieval* (pp. 1661–1664).

Bicheno, J., & Catherwood, P. (2005). *Service quality concepts. Six sigma and the quality toolbox* (pp. 132–150). PICSIE Books.

Bienhaus, F., & Haddud, A. (2018). Procurement 4.0: Factors influencing the digitization of procurement and supply chains. *Business Process Management Journal*, 24(4), 965–984.

Bin, M. A., Pyeman, J. B., Ali, N. B., Abdul, N. B., & Khai, K. G. (2018). Determinants of supply chain finance adoption among Malaysian manufacturing financial institutions: A proposed conceptual framework. *International Journal of Education and Research*, 6(4), 237–248.

BIS. (2000). *Principles for the management of credit risk*. BIS Book.

Bitter, P., & Uphues, S. (2017, September). Big data und die Versichertengemeinschaft—«Entsolidarisierung» durch Digitalisierung. *ABIDA-Dossier*.

Bizer, C., Heath, T., & Berners-Lee, T. (2011). Linked data: The story so far. In *Semantic services, interoperability and web applications: Emerging concepts* (pp. 205–227). IGI Global.

Bluerating. (2019, July). *Banca Generali, ora il consulente ha un'arma in più*. Bluerating.com.

Bouncken, R. B., Komorek, M., & Kraus, S. (2015). Crowdfunding: The current state of research. *International Business & Economics Research Journal (IBER), 14*(3), 407–416.

Bova, T. (2018). *Growth IQ: Get smarter about the choices that will make or break your business*. Penguin.

Brakman, S., Garretsen, H., & van Witteloostuijn, A. (2020). The turn from just-in-time to just-in-case globalization in and after times of Covid-19: An essay on the risk re-appraisal of borders and buffers. *Social Sciences & Humanities Open, 2*(1), 100034.

Breazeal, C. (2001, September). Affective interaction between humans and robots. In *European conference on artificial life* (pp. 582–591). Springer.

Breuer, H. (2013). Lean venturing: Learning to create new business through exploration, elaboration, evaluation, experimentation, and evolution. *International Journal of Innovation Management, 17*(03), 1340013.

Brown, T. (2015). When everyone is doing design thinking, is it still a competitive advantage. *Harvard Business Review*, p. 27.

Brown, T., & Martin, R. (2015). Spotlight on the evolution of design thinking. *Harvard Business Review*, 56–85.

Bruckner, M., LaFleur, M., & Pitterle, I. (2017). *Frontier issues: The impact of the technological revolution on labour markets and income distribution*. Department of Economic & Social Affairs, UN.

Brynjolfsson, E., & McAfee, A. (2014). *The second machine age: Work, progress, and prosperity in a time of brilliant technologies*. W. W. Norton.

Buheji, M., & Ahmed, D. (2020). *Planning for the 'new normal'*. Bahrain. CO Founder of the International Inspiration Economy Project.

Bullen, C. V., & Rockart, J. F. (1981). *A primer on critical success factors*. Sloan School of Business, MIT.

Calvert, P. (2017). Robots, the quiet workers, are you ready to take over? *Public Law Quarterly, 36*(2).

Capgemini Financial Services Analysis. (2021). *World Insurance Report 2021 executive interviews*.

Caprino, K. (2012, April). What you do not know will hurt you: The top 8 skills professionals need to master. *Forbes*.

Carletti, E., Claessens, S., Fatás, A., & Vives, X. (2020). *Post-Covid-19 world*. Centre for Economic Policy Research.

Carlzon, J. (1987). Putting the customer first: The key to service strategy. *McKinsey Quarterly, 3*, 38–51.

Carr, C. (1989). Software tools for empowering instructional developers. *Performance Improvement Quarterly, 28*(9), 44–46.

Carrozzi, L. (2009). *Procurement Management per la Protezione delle Infrastrutture Critiche*. Tesi Master in Procurement Management, Università di Tor Vergata, Rome, Italy.

Casey, K. (2019). *Robotic process automation (RPA) in 2020: 5 trends to watch.* Enterprisersproject.com.

Catlin, T., Lorenz, J., Nandan, J., Sharma. S., & Waschto, A. (2018, January). *Insurance beyond digital: The rise of ecosystems and platforms.* McKinsey Paper.

Çera, G., Belas, J., & Zapletalíková, E. (2019). Explaining business failure through determinist and voluntarist perspectives. *Serbian Journal of Management.*

Cerka, P., Grigiene, J., & Sirbikyte, G. (2015). Liability for damages caused by artificial intelligence. *Computer Law & Security Review, 31*(3), 376–389.

Cerka, P., Grigiene, J., & Sirbikyte, G. (2017). Is it possible to grant legal personality to artificial intelligence software systems? *Computer Law & Security Review, 33*(5), 685–699.

Chan, L. K., & Wu, M. L. (2002). Quality function deployment: A literature review. *European Journal of Operational Research, 143*(3), 463–497.

Chang, E., Hussain, F. K., & Dillon, T. (2006, October). Reputation ontology for reputation systems. In *OTM Confederated International Conferences "On the Move to Meaningful Internet Systems"* (pp. 1724–1733). Springer.

Chen, C. C., Huang, H. H., & Chen, H. H. (2021). *From opinion mining to financial argument mining.* Springer Nature.

Chen, M. C., Chen, S. S., Yeh, H. M., & Tsaur, W. G. (2016). The critical factors influencing internet services finances satisfaction: An empirical study in Taiwan. *American Journal of Industrial and Business Management, 6*(6), 748–762.

Chen, S. H. (2013). Devising appropriate service strategies for customers of different value: An integrated assessment model for the banking industry. *The International Journal of Human Resource Management, 24*(21), 3939–3956.

Chen, Z., Lu, M., Ming, X., Zhang, X., & Zhou, T. (2020). Explore and evaluate innovative value propositions for smart product service system: A novel graphics-based rough-fuzzy DEMATEL method. *Journal of Cleaner Production, 243,* 118672.

Cherepanov, V., Popov, E., & Simonova, V. (2021). Bionic organization as a stage of production enterprise development in a digital transformation process. In *E3S web of conferences* (Vol. 250, p. 03003). EDP Sciences.

Chiang, R. H., Grover, V., Liang, T. P., & Zhang, D. (2018). Strategic value of big data and business analytics. *Journal of Management Information Systems, 35*(2), 383–387.

Choi, R. Y., Coyner, A. S., Kalpathy-Cramer, J., Chiang, M. F., & Campbell, J. P. (2020). Introduction to machine learning, neural networks, and deep learning. *Translational Vision Science & Solution, 9*(2), 14–14.

Christodoulou, P., Zinonos, Z., Carayannis, E. G., Chatzichristofis, S. A., & Christodoulou, K. (2021). *Known unknowns in an era of technological and viral disruptions—Implications for theory, policy, and practice.*

et/11728/11735 Hephaestus Repository, Neapolis University, Paphos, Cyprus.

Chtourou, M. S., & Souiden, N. (2010). Rethinking the TAM model: Time to consider fun. *Journal of Consumer Marketing, 27*(4), 336–344.

Chu, P. Y., Lee, G. Y., & Chao, Y. (2012). Service quality, customer satisfaction, customer trust, and loyalty in an e-banking context. *Social Behavior and Personality, 40*(8), 1271–1283.

Clark, L., & Steadman, I. (2017, June). Remembering Alan Turing: From codebreaking to AI, Turing made the world what it is today. *Wired*.

Claudé, M., & Combe, D. (2018). *The roles of artificial intelligence and humans in decision making: Towards augmented humans? A focus on knowledge-intensive firms*.

Clegg, S. R., & Hardy, C. (1999). *Studying organization theory and method* (Vol. 1). Sage.

Clinard, M. B., & Cressey, D. R. (1954). Other people's money: A study in the social psychology of embezzlement. *American Sociological Review, 19*(3).

Close, K., Grebe, M., Schuuring, M., Rehberg, B., & Leybold, M. (2020). *Is your technology ready for the new digital reality?* Boston Consulting Group-BCG. Featured Insights, Boston.

Cocca, T. (2016). Potential and limitations of virtual advice in wealth management. *Journal of Financial Transformation, 44*(1), 45–57.

Cocheo, S. (2021, April). *Pandemic's acceleration of digital banking exposes Trouble Spots*. The Financial Brand.

Coelho, P. S., & Henseler, J. (2012). Creating customer loyalty through service customization. *European Journal of Marketing*.

Cohen, G. A., & Parkinson, J. S. (2002). *Perspectives on Business Innovation, 8*, 79–84.

Colgate, J. E., Wannasuphoprasit, W., & Peshkin, M. A. (1996). Cobots: Robots for collaboration with human operators. In *Proceedings of the 1996 ASME International Mechanical Engineering Congress and Exposition*.

Collie, F. (2021). *How banks are harnessing artificial intelligence*. IE Investment Executive.

Collis, J., & Hussey, R. (2014). *Business research: A practical guide for undergraduate and postgraduate students*. Palgrave Macmillan.

Columbus, L. (2020). The state of AI adoption in financial services. *Forbes*.

Community and Regional Resilience Institute (CARRI). (2013). *Definitions of community resilience: An analysis*. Meridian Institute.

Cooper, L. (2010). *CSF's, KPI's, metrics, outcomes and benefits*. ITSM Solutions.

Corvalán, J. G. (2019, April). Keynote: PROMETEA. Artificial intelligence to transform public organizations. In *2019 Sixth International Conference on eDemocracy & eGovernment (ICEDEG)* (p. 15). IEEE.

Costonis, M. (2018, August). *The future of capital markets: Embracing robo advice.* Accenture Post.
Cotton, D. L., Johnigan, S., & Givarz, L. (2016). *Fraud Risk Management Guide.* COSO, Committee of Sponsoring Organizations of the Treadway Commission.
Cui, L., Huang, S., Wei, F., Tan, C., Duan, C., & Zhou, M. (2017, July). Superagent: A customer service chatbot for e-commerce websites. In *Proceedings of ACL 2017, System Demonstrations* (pp. 97–102).
Cunha, P. R., Melo, P., & Sebastião, H. (2021). From bitcoin to central bank digital currencies: Making sense of the digital money revolution. *Future Internet, 13*(7), 165.
Dahlgaard-Park, S. M., Andersson, R., Eriksson, H., & Torstensson, H. (2006). Similarities and differences between TQM, six sigma and lean. *The TQM Magazine.*
Dane, E., Rockmann, K. W., & Pratt, M. G. (2012). When should I trust my gut? Linking domain expertise to intuitive decision-making effectiveness. *Organizational Behavior and Human Decision Processes, 119,* 187–194.
Danske Bank. (2020). *The essence of Danske Bank.*
Danske Bank. (2020, November). *Danske Bank wins international award for best open banking initiative* [Press release].
Darwin, C. (2004). *On the origin of species, 1859.* Routledge.
Davis, S., & Botkin, J. (1994). The coming of knowledge-based business. *Harvard Business Review, 72*(5), 165–170.
De Geus, A., (1997, March). The living company. *Harvard Business Review.*
De Neys, W. (Ed.). (2017). *Dual process theory 2.0.* Routledge.
De Pace, F., Manuri, F., Sanna, A., & Fornaro, C. (2020). A systematic review of augmented reality interfaces for collaborative industrial robots. *Computers & Industrial Engineering, 149,* 106806.
De Smet, A. Mysore, M., Reich, A., & Sternfels, B. (2021, July). *Return as a muscle: How lessons from COVID-19 can shape a robust operating model for hybrid and beyond.* McKinsey Paper.
De Véricourt, F., & Zhou, Y. P. (2005). Managing response time in a call-routing problem with service failure. *Operations Research, 53*(6), 968–981.
Decker, M., Fischer, M., & Ott, I. (2017). Service robotics and human labor: A first technology assessment of substitution and cooperation. *Robotics and Autonomous Systems, 87,* 348–354.
Deepmind. (2016, March). The Google DeepMind challenge match. *Deepmind.*
Dejoux, C., & Léon, E. (2018). *Métamorphose des managers* (1st ed.). Pearson.
Deloitte. (2020). *Beyond COVID-19: New opportunities for fintech companies.* Deloitte Center for Financial Services.
Deloitte Development LLC. (2020). *The social enterprise at work: Paradox as a path forward.* 2020. Deloitte Global Human Capital trends.

Deming, W. E. (1994). *The new economics for industry, government, education.* MIT Press.
Demirkan, H., Spohrer, J. C., & Welser, J. J. (2016). Digital innovation and strategic transformation. *IT Professional, 18*(6), 14–18.
Denning, P. J. (1986). Towards a science of expert systems. *IEEE Expert, 1*(2), 80–83.
Deutsche Bank. (2018). *How can mortgage lenders reap the benefits of the paperless revolution?* corporates.db.com.
Di Orio, G., Brito, G., Maló, P., Sadu, A., Wirtz, N., & Monti, A. (2020). A cyber-physical approach to resilience and robustness by design. *International Journal of Advanced Computer Science and Applications.*
Dignum, V. (2017). Responsible artificial intelligence: Designing AI for human values. *International Telecommunication Union Journal, 1*(1), 1–8.
DiNapoli, T. P. (n.d.). *Red flags for fraud* (S. J. Hancox, Ed.). Office of the State Controller.
Dirican, C. (2015). The impacts of robotics, artificial intelligence on business and economics. *Procedias—Social and Behavioral Sciences, 195*, 564–573.
Dirnberger, E., Freese, C., Hu, M., & Urban, M. (2020). *What lies beyond digital for insurance operations?* Boston Consulting Group-BCG. Featured Insights, Boston.12, 20.
Ditillo, A. (2004). Dealing with uncertainty in knowledge-intensive organizations: The role of management control systems as knowledge integration mechanisms. *Accounting, Organizations and Society, 29*, 401–421.
DMG Consulting. (2019). *DMG Consulting—I've heard there's some confusion about an order the Federal Communications Commission (FCC) released concerning automatic dialers calling cell phones. What's the issue?* DMG Consulting LLC, West Orange, NJ.
Domingos, P. (2015). *The master algorithm: How the quest for the ultimate learning machine will remake our world.* Basic Books.
Drucker, P. (1994, September–October). The theory of the business. *Harvard Business Review*, pp. 95–104.
Duchessi, P., O'Leary, D., & O'Keefe, R. (1993). A research perspective: Artificial intelligence, management and organizations. *Intelligent Systems in Accounting, Finance and Management, 2*, 151–159.
Dwyer, F. R., Schurr, P. H., & Oh, S. (1987). Developing buyer-seller relationships. *Journal of Marketing, 51*(2), 11–27.
Earle, R. H., Rosso, M. A., & Alexander, K. E. (2015). User preferences of software documentation genres. In *Proceedings of the 33rd Annual International Conference on the Design of Communication, 46.* ACM.
Ecommerce News. (2018, November). *Austrian app Jingle wants to boost local shopping.* Ecommerce News Europe.

Edwards, W. (1954). The theory of decision making. *Psychological Bulletin, 51*(4), 380–417.

Edwards. N. (2020, February). The digital side of deutsche bank that you have not heard about. *Forbes.*

Eggers, W. D., Schatsky, D., & Viechnicki, P. (2017). *AI-augmented government: Using cognitive technologies to redesign public sector work.* Deloitte University Press.

Eletter, S. F., Yaseen, S. G., & Elrefae, G. A. (2010). Neuro-based artificial intelligence model for loan decisions. *American Journal of Economics and Business Administration, 2*(1), 27.

Epstein, S. L. (2015). Wanted: Collaborative intelligence. *Artificial Intelligence, 221,* 36–45.

Eraut, M. (1998). Concepts of competence. *Journal of Interprofessional Care, 12*(2), 127–139.

Erlebach, J., Pauly, M., Du Croo De Jongh, L., & Strauß, M. (2020, November). *The sun is setting on traditional banking* (BCG Paper).

Erten, S. (2021). Chapter seven toward a new hybrid model. In M. Z. Çögenli (Ed.), *Digitalization in organizations* (p. 106). Google Books.

Essig, M. (2006). Electronic Insurance. Konzeption und Anwendung. In J. Zentes (Ed.), *Handbuch Handel* (pp. 735–758). Gabler.

ET Bureau. (2020, April). RBI announces more measures to deal with economic fallout of COVID-19. *The Economic Times.*

Ettlie, J. E., Bridges, W. P., & O'keefe, R. D. (1984). Organization strategy and structural differences for radical versus incremental innovation. *Management science, 30*(6), 682–695.

Everson, M., & Sviokla, J. (2018, Autumn). The bionic company. *Strategy+Business, 92* (Autumn).

EY Belgium. (2020, April). *Why remote working will be the new normal, even after the pandemic.* Multidisciplinary Professional Services Organization.

Ezer, N., Bruni, S., Cai, Y., Hepenstal, S. J., Miller, C. A., & Schmorrow, D. D. (2019, November). Trust engineering for human-AI teams. *Proceedings of the Human Factors and Ergonomics Society Annual Meeting, 63*(1), 322–326.

Fabeil, N. F., Pazim, K. H., & Langgat, J. (2020). The impact of Covid-19 pandemic crisis on micro-enterprises: Entrepreneurs' perspective on business continuity and recovery strategy. *Journal of Economics and Business, 3*(2).

Fåland, J. O., Stausland, K., Eide, L., Kulseth, S. S., & Hamre, V. G. (2020). *Johan Sverdrup 2025.* Equinor, Summer Internship, Stavanger, Norway.

Fallis, J., & Fuchs, O. (2019). *Transforming banking with smart automation.* Nice and Bain & Company.

Farooq, U., & Grudin, J. (2016). Human-computer integration. *ACM Interactions, 23*(6), 27–32.

Fenwick, M., & Vermeulen, E. P. (2020, March). Banking and regulatory responses to FinTech revisited-building the sustainable financial service 'ecosystems' of tomorrow. *Singapore Journal of Legal Studies*, 165–189.

Fernández-Sanz, L., Gómez-Pérez, J., & Castillo-Martínez, A. (2017). e-Skills Match: A framework for mapping and integrating the main skills, knowledge and competence standards and models for ICT occupations. *Computer Standards & Interfaces, 51*, 30–42.

Finextra IBM. (2016). *How to get ahead on operational resilience: Strategies for financial institutions*. Finextra Research Ltd.

Fintastico Team. (2019, June). *Banca Generali sempre più fintech con Ro4Ad*. Fintastico.

Fishburn, P. C. (1979). *Utility theory for decision making*. Krieger Publishing Company.

Fitzgerald, M., Kruschwitz, N., Bonnet, D., & Welch, M. (2014). Embracing digital technology: A new strategic imperative. *MIT Sloan Management Review, 55*(2), 1.

Fjeldstad, Ø. D., Snow, C. C., Miles, R. E., & Lettl, C. (2012). The architecture of collaboration. *Strategic Management Journal, 33*(6), 734–750.

Fluss, D. (2017). *The AI revolution in customer service*. DestinationCRM.

Fornell, C., & Wernerfelt, B. (1987). Defensive marketing strategy by consumer complaint management: A theoretical analysis. *Journal of Marketing, 24*(4), 337–346.

Freeman, C., & Perez, C. (1988). Structural crises of adjustment, business cycles and investment behaviour. *Technology, organizations and innovation: Theories, concepts and paradigms* (pp. 38–66).

Freese, C., Gard, J., Taglioni, G., et al. (2020). *The building blocks of bionic distribution in insurance*. Boston Consulting Group-BCG. Featured Insights, Boston. 7, 20.

Furong H., & Yanmei, X., (2001). *Enterprise bionics*. Enterprise Management Press.

Gakman, C. (2017). *Understanding FinTech categories*. The Ian Martin Group.

Galbraith, J. R. (2014). Organization design challenges resulting from Big Data. *Journal of Organization Design, 3*(1), 2–13.

Galily, Y. (2018). Artificial intelligence and sports journalism: Is it a sweeping change? *Technology in Society*

Gefen, D., & Straub, D. (2003). Managing user trust in B2C e-services. *e-Service, 2*(2), 7–24.

Geib, M., Reichold, A., Kolbe, L., & Brenner, W. (2005, January). Architecture for customer relationship management approaches in financial services. In *Proceedings of the 38th Annual Hawaii International Conference on System Sciences* (p. 240b). IEEE.

Geissbauer, R., Weissbarth, R., & Wetzstein, J. (2016). *Banking 5.0: Are the organisation ready for the digital revolution?* PriceWaterhouseCoopers.

Ghahroud, M. L., Jafari, F., & Maghsoodi, J. (2021). Review of the Fintech categories and the most famous Fintech startups. *Journal of FinTech and Artificial Intelligence, 1*(1), 7–7.

Ghazy, K., & Fedorova, A. (2021). Industry 4.0 and human resource management in the hotel business. *Human Progress, 7*(2), 1–1.

Godin, B. (2006). The knowledge-based economy: Conceptual framework or buzzword? *Journal of Technology Transfer, 31,* 17–30.

Goleman, D. (1996). *Emotional intelligence: Why it can matter more than IQ.* Bloomsbury Publishing.

Goniwada, S. R. (2022). Enterprise cloud native automation. *Cloud native architecture and design* (pp. 523–553). Apress.

Government Office for Science. (2015). *Artificial intelligence: Opportunities and implications for the future of decision making.* Government Office for Science.

Grant, R. M. (1996). Toward a knowledge-based theory of the firm. *Strategic Management Journal, 17* (Winter Special Issue), 109–122.

Grebe, M., Rüßmann, M., Leyh, M., Roman Franke, M., &, Anderson, W. (2020, November). *How bionic companies translate digital maturity into performance.* BCG Related Expertise.

Gruber, M., De Leon, N., George, G., & Thompson, P. (2015). Managing by design: From the editors. *Academy of Management Journal, 58*(1), 1–7.

Gudem, M., Steinert, M., Welo, T., & Leifer, L. (2013). Redefining customer value in lean product development design projects. *Journal of Engineering, Design and Technology.*

Guilford, J. P. (1967). *The nature of human intelligence.* McGraw-Hill.

Gulati, R. (2013). *Reorganize for resilience: Putting customers at the center of your business.* Harvard Business Review Press.

Gunning, D. (2017). Explainable artificial intelligence (XAI). *Defense Advanced Research Projects Agency (DARPA), and Web, 2*(2).

Guo, Y., & Liang, C. (2016). Blockchain application and outlook in the banking industry. *Financial Innovation, 2*(1), 1–12.

Gurkaynak, G., Yilmaz, I., & Haksever, G. (2016). Stifling artificial intelligence: Human perils. *Computer Law & Security Review, 32*(5), 749–758.

Haenen, A. M. (2017). *Robo-advisors for financial services: The effect of proactivity and human intervention on customer evaluation* (Master thesis). Eindhoven University of Technology, Eindhoven, Netherlands.

Hajli, N., Shanmugam, M., Papagiannidis, S., Zahay, D., & Richard, M. O. (2017). Branding co-creation with members of online brand communities. *Journal of Business Research, 70,* 136–144.

Halstrick, T. (2020). *Determining a bank's customer value proposition based on customer value dimensions* (Bachelor's thesis). University of Twente, Enschede, Netherlands.

Handfield, R. (2019). Shifts in buyer-seller relationships: A retrospective on. *Industrial Marketing Management, 83*, 194–206.

Härting, R. C., Reichstein, C., & Sochacki, R. (2019). Potential benefits of digital business models and its processes in the financial and insurance industry. In *Intelligent decision technologies 2019* (pp. 205–216). Springer Nature.

HDFC Bank. (2020, November). *HDFC Bank launches "Mooh Band Rakho" campaign to create awareness on cyber frauds* [Press Release].

HDFC Bank. (2020, September). *HDFC Bank launches Video KYC facility* [Press Release].

HDFC Bank. (2021, January). *Financial results (Indian Gaap) for the quarter and nine months ended December 31, 2020* [Press release].

Hendarmana, A. F., & Tjakraatmadja, J. H. (2012). Relationship among soft skills, hard skills, and innovativeness of knowledge workers in the knowledge economy era. *Procedia - Social and Behavioral Sciences, 52*, 35–44.

Henderson, R. M., & Clark, K. B. (1990). Architectural innovation: The reconfiguration of existing product technologies and the failure of established firms. *Administrative Science Quarterly*, 9–30.

Hengstler, M., Enkel, E., & Duelli, S. (2016). Applied artificial intelligence and trust—The case of autonomous vehicles and medical assistance devices. *Technological Forecasting & Social Change, 105*, 105–120.

Henry, T., Wampfeler, J., & Clarke, M. (2018). The hybrid advice model. *Automation*, 178.

Hess, T., Matt, C., Benlian, A., & Wiesböck, F. (2016). Options for formulating a digital transformation strategy. *MIS Quarterly Executive, 15*(2).

Hillmann, J., & Guenther, E. (2021). Organizational resilience: A valuable construct for management research? *International Journal of Management Reviews, 23*(1), 7–44.

Hi'ovská, K., & Koncz, P. (2012). Application of artificial intelligence and data mining techniques to financial markets. *Economic Studies & Analyses/Acta VSFS, 6*(1).

Hoffman, G., & Breazeal, C. (2004, September). Collaboration in human-robot teams. In *AIAA 1st Intelligent Systems Technical Conference Online Proceedings Conference Proceeding*.

Hofmann, P., Samp, C., & Urbach, N. (2020). Robotic process automation. *Electronic Markets, 30*(1), 99–106.

Holtel, S. (2016). Artificial intelligence creates a wicked problem for the enterprise. *Procedia Computer Science, 99*, 171–180.

Hosea, M. (2016, May). How brands are using artificial intelligence to enhance customer experience. *Marketing Week*.

Howland, D. (2018, June). *What b8ta has figured out about retail*. Retail Dive.

Hu, T. I., & Tracogna, A. (2020). Multichannel customer journeys and their determinants: Evidence from motor insurance. *Journal of Retailing and Consumer Services*, 54, 102022.

Huang, B., Huan, Y., Xu, L. D., Zheng, L., & Zou, Z. (2019). Automated trading systems statistical and machine learning methods and hardware implementation: A survey. *Enterprise Information Systems*, 13(1), 132–144.

Huang, M. H., & Rust, R. T. (2018). Artificial intelligence in service. *Journal of Service Research*, 21(2), 155–172.

Huang, S. Y., Lin, C. C., Chiu, A. A., & Yen, D. C. (2017). Fraud detection using fraud triangle risk factors. *Information Systems Frontiers*, 19(6), 1343–1356.

Human-Centered AI. (2019). Converge with global tech visionaries. *Insights*, 26, 42.

Hung, J. L., He, W., & Shen, J. (2020). Big data analytics for supply chain relationship in banking. *Industrial Marketing Management*, 86, 144–153.

Hutchinson, R., Aré, L., Rose, J., & Bailey, A. (2019). *The bionic company*. Published November 7.

Hızıroğlu, Z. H. (2021). *An empirical study on robotic process automation implementation: A case study on MetLife Investment Management Client Services Group* (Doctoral dissertation). University of Wales Trinity Saint David, Lampeter, UK.

Iansiti, M., & Lakhani, K. R. (2017). The truth about blockchain. *Harvard Business Review*, 95(1), 118–127.

Iarovyi, S., Lastra, J. L. M., Haber, R., & del Toro, R. (2015, July). From artificial cognitive systems and open architectures to cognitive manufacturing systems. In *2015 IEEE 13th International Conference on Industrial Informatics (INDIN)* (pp. 1225–1232). IEEE.

IEEE Corporate Advisory Group (2017). *2755-2017—Guide for Terms and Concepts in Intelligent Process Automation*. IEEE.

Imai, M. (1986). *Kaizen* (Vol. 201). Random House Business Division.

Injadat, M., Moubayed, A., Nassif, A. B., & Shami, A. (2021). Machine learning towards intelligent systems: Applications, challenges, and opportunities. *Artificial Intelligence Review*, 1–50.

International Trade Centre. (2020). *The pandemic: The great lockdown and its impact on small business*. International Trade Centre.

Interpol. (2020, August). *INTERPOL report shows alarming rate of cyberattacks during the pandemic* (Interpol Report).

Issantu, I. T. (2021). *User acceptance of logistics 4.0 and robotic warehouse solutions (RWS)* (Doctoral dissertation). Capella University, Minneapolis, MN.

Ivanov, S. H., & Webster, C. (2017, October 19–21). Adoption of robots, artificial intelligence and service automation by travel, tourism and hospitality companies-a cost-benefit analysis. Artificial Intelligence and Service Automation by Travel, Tourism and Hospitality Companies-A Cost-Benefit Analysis. *International Scientific Conference "Contemporary tourism-traditions and innovations"*. Sofia University, Bulgaria.

Jacobides, M. G., Brusoni, S., & Candelon, F. (2021). *The evolutionary dynamics of the artificial intelligence ecosystem*. Evolution Academic Papers.

Jarrahi, M. H. (2018). Artificial intelligence and the future of work: Human—AI symbiosis in organizational decision making. *Business Horizons*.

Jarrell, M. (2021). Artificial intelligence at square—Two use-cases. *Emerj*.

Jiali, Y., Wenming, L., & Yanmei, X. (2009). Evaluation of enterprise vitality and model of enterprise commercial age. In *International Conference on Management Science & Engineering*. IEEE, New York, NY.

Johnson, G., Whittington, R., Scholes, K., Angwin, D., & Regner, P. (2017). *Exploring strategy* (11th ed.). Pearson.

Johnston, R. (1995). The determinants of service quality: Satisfiers and dissatisfiers. *International Journal of Service Industry Management, 6*(5), 53.

Kagermann, H. (2014). von Industries 4.0 Chancen nutzen. In T. Bauernhansl, M. Ten Hompel, & B. Vogel-Heuser (Eds.), *Produktion industries 4.0. Automatisierung und Logistik* (pp. 603–614). Springer.

Kahneman, D. (2003). A perspective on judgement and choice. *American Psychologist, 58*(9), 697–720.

Kahneman, D., & Klein, G. (2009). Conditions for intuitive expertise. *American Psychologist, 64*(6), 515–526.

Kakati, M. (2003). Success criteria in high-tech new ventures. *Technovation, 23*(5), 447–457.

Kamble, S., Gunasekaran, A., & Arha, H. (2019). Understanding the Blockchain solution adoption in supply chains-Indian context. *International Journal of Production Research, 57*(7), 2009–2033.

Kamboj, S., Sarmah, B., Gupta, S., & Dwivedi, Y. (2018). Examining branding co-creation in brand communities on social media: Applying the paradigm of Stimulus-Organism-Response. *International Journal of Information Management, 39*, 169–185.

Kanazawa, A., Kinugawa, J., & Kosuge, K. (2019). Adaptive motion planning for a collaborative robot based on prediction uncertainty to enhance human safety and work efficiency. *IEEE Transactions on Robotics, 35*, 817–832.

Kaplan, J. M., Bailey, T., O'Halloran, D., Marcus, A., & Rezek, C. (2015). *Beyond cybersecurity: Protecting your digital business*. Wiley.

Karahanli, N. G., & Touma, J. (2021). *Digitalization of the customer experience in banking use of AI and SSTs in complex/sensitive tasks: Pre-collection* (thesis). KTH Royal Institute of Technology, Stockholm, Sweden.

Karajovic, M., Narula, H., Pandya, K. Patel, J., & Warring, I. (2017). *Blockchain: A manager's guide*. A report for OMIS 3710 Schulich School of Business York University Toronto, ON.

Karwowski, W. (2005). Ergonomics and human factors: The paradigms for science, engineering, design, technology and management of human-compatible systems. *Ergonomics, 48*(5), 436–463.

Kedziora, D., & Penttinen, E. (2021). Governance models for robotic process automation: The case of Nordea Bank. *Journal of Information Technology Teaching Cases, 11*(1), 20–29.

Kelley, T. (2001). Prototyping is the shorthand of innovation. *Design Management Journal (former Series), 12*(3), 35–42.

Khatik, R. K. (2021). Role of digital banking in strategic alliance and FinTech. *International Journal of Research and Analysis in Commerce and Management, 1*(1), 10–10.

Kim, Y., Park, Y. J., & Choi, J. (2016). The adoption of mobile payment services for Fintech. *International Journal of Applied Engineering Research, 11*(2), 1058–1061.

Kimura, R., Reeves, M., & Whitaker, K. (2019). The new logic of competition. *Boston Consulting Group, 3*, 19.

King, R. S. (2013). *BiLBIQ: A biologically inspired robot with walking and rolling locomotion*. Springer.

Klashanov, F. (2016). Artificial intelligence and organizing decision in construction. *Procedia Engineering, 165*(2016), 1016–1020.

Klein, G. (1998). A naturalistic decision-making perspective on studying intuitive decision making. *Journal of Applied Research in Memory and Cognition, 4*(2015), 164–171.

Kleindorfer, P. R., & Saad, G. H. (2005). Managing disruption risks in supply chains. *Production and Operations Management, 14*(1), 53–68.

Kobbacy, K. A. H. (2012). Application of artificial intelligence in maintenance modelling management. *IFAC Proceedings Volumes, 45*(31), 54–59.

Koch, V., Kuge, S., Geissbauer, R., & Schrauf, S. (2014). *Industry 5.0: Opportunities and challenges of the industrial Internet*. Strategy & PwC.

Kollmann, T (2011). *E-Business: Grundlagen elektronischer Geschäftsprozesse in der net economy*. Gabler

Kolodner, J. (2014). *Case-based reasoning*. Morgan Kaufmann.

Koole, G., & Mandelbaum, A. (2002). Queueing models of CPCs: An introduction. *Annals of Operations Research, 113*(1–4), 41–59.

Kopeć, W., Skibiński, M., Biele, C., Skorupska, K., Tkaczyk, D., Jaskulska, A., & Marasek, K. (2018). Hybrid approach to automation, RPA and machine learning: A method for the human-centered design of software robots. *arXiv preprint* arXiv:1811.02213.

Kornienko, A. A., Kornienko, A. V., Fofanov, O. V., & Chubik, M. P. (2015). Knowledge in artificial intelligence systems: Searching the strategies for application. *Procedia - Social and Behavioral Sciences, 166*(2015), 589–594.

Koskinen, K. U., & Vanharanta, H. (2002). The role of tacit knowledge in innovation processes of small technology companies. *International Journal of Production Economics, 80*(1), 57–64.

Kremer, M. (1993). The O-ring theory of economic development. *The Quarterly Journal of Economics, 108*(3), 551–575.

Krivkovich, A., White, O., Zac Townsend, Z., & Euart, J. (2020, December). *How US customers' attitudes to fintech are shifting during the pandemic*. McKinsey Paper.

Kumar, V., & Rajan, B. (2020). Customer lifetime value: What, how, and why. In *The Routledge companion to strategic marketing* (pp. 422–448). Routledge.

Kunreuther, H., & Heal, G. (2004). Interdependent security: The case of identical agents. *Journal of Risk and Uncertainty, 23*(2), 103–120.

Kuo, C. M., Chen, L. C., & Tseng, C. Y. (2017). Investigating an innovative service with hospitality robots. *International Journal of Contemporary Hospitality Management, 29*(5), 1305–1321.

Kuzhelko, K. (2021). *Losing their war: Using service-dominant logic to assess the market position of traditional Swedish banks*. Business and Economics, Luleå University of Technology, Luleå, Sweden.

Kwasniok, S., Kretz, J., & Kettnaker, F. (2021). Plattformentwicklungen im Versicherungsmarkt–Von Open Banking zu Open Finance. *Digitale Ökosysteme: Strategien, KI, Plattformen*, 437.

Laplante, P., & Kshetri, N. (2021). Open banking: Definition and description. *Computer, 54*(10), 122–128.

Laurent, A. (2017). *La guerre des intelligences*. JC Lattès.

Lee, I., & Shin, Y. J. (2020). Machine learning for enterprises: Applications, algorithm selection, and challenges. *Business Horizons, 63*(2), 157–170.

Lee, J., Kao, H. A., & Yang, S. (2014). Service innovation and smart analytics for industry 5.0 and big data environment. *Procedia CIRP, 16*, 3–8.

Lee, J., Bagheri, B., & Kao, H. A. (2015). A cyber-physical systems architecture for industry 4.0-based manufacturing systems. *Manufacturing Letters, 3*, 18–23.

Lehmann-Ortega, L., & Schoettl, J. M. (2005). *From buzzword to managerial tool: The role of business models in strategic innovation* (pp. 1–14). CLADEA, Santiago de Chile, Chile.

Leibowitz, S. (2018). *What's the difference between "attended" and "unattended" RPA bots?* Cloud Computing News.

Leno, V., Polyvyanyy, A., Dumas, M., La Rosa, M., & Maggi, F. (2021). Robotic process mining: Vision and challenges. *Business & Information Systems Engineering, 63*(3), 301–314.

Levanon, G. (2020, November). Remote work: The biggest legacy of the pandemic. *Forbes*.

Li, D., & Du, Y. (2017). *Artificial intelligence with uncertainty*. CRC Press.

Li, H., & Liu, Y. (2014). Understanding post-adoption behaviors of e-service users in the context of online travel services. *Information & Management*, *51*(8), 1043–1052.

Li, S., Wang, R., Zheng, P., & Wang, L. (2021). Towards proactive human–robot collaboration: A foreseeable cognitive manufacturing paradigm. *Journal of Manufacturing Systems*, *60*, 547–552.

Li, S., Zheng, P., & Zheng, L. (2020). An AR-assisted deep learning-based approach for automatic inspection of aviation connectors. *IEEE Transactions on Industrial Informatics*, *17*, 1721–1731.

Liébana-Cabanillas, F., Sánchez-Fernández, J., & Muñoz-Leiva, F. (2014). Antecedents of the adoption of the new mobile payment systems: The moderating effect of age. *Computers in Human Behavior*, *35*, 464–478.

Liebau, D. (2016). *Design thinking in financial services*. Lightbulb Capital.

Lihong, H., & Mengna, Z. (2014). The mathematical model of evaluation of enterprise activity. *In International Conference on Logistics Engineering, Management and Computer Science*. Atlantis Press, Paris, France.

Lihua, W., Wandui, M., Yu, L., et al. (2010). *Research on enterprise bionic and ERP application*. IEEE Publisher.

Liu, F., Tong, J., Mao, J., Bohn, R., Messina, J., Badger, L., & Leaf, D. (2011). NIST cloud computing reference architecture. *NIST Special Publication*, *500*(2011), 1–28.

Liu, L., Xu, Y., Huang, L., & Yao, X. (2013) Research on the improvement of business age model. In W. E. Wong & T. Ma (Eds.), *Emerging technologies for information systems, computing, and management*. Lecture notes in electrical engineering, 236 (pp. 1239–1250). Springer.

Liu, X., Zheng, L., Shuai, J., Zhang, R., & Li, Y. (2020). Data-driven and AR assisted intelligent collaborative assembly system for large-scale complex products. *Procedia CIRP*, *93*, 1049–1054.

Liu, Y., & Li, H. (2011). Exploring the impact of use context on mobile hedonic services adoption: An empirical study on mobile gaming in China. *Computers in Human Behavior*, *27*(2), 890–898.

Lohrmann, D. (2020, December). *2020: The year the pandemic crisis brought a cyber pandemic*. Government Technology.

Lu, Y. (2017). Industry 5.0: A survey on technologies, applications and open research issues. *Journal of Industrial Information Integration*, *6*, 1–10.

Lui, A., & Lamb, G. W. (2018). Artificial intelligence and augmented intelligence collaboration: Regaining trust and confidence in the financial sector. *Information & Communications Technology Law*, *27*(3), 267–283.

Lusinski, N. (2019, October). *9 of the most challenging things about working remotely, according to people who do it*. Business Insider.

Lutz, J. (2015). Committee of sponsoring organizations of the treadway commission: Internal control' integrated framework mit besonderer berücksichtigung der änderungen in der neuauflage 2013 - 2014.—14 Seiten Verzeichnisse, 84 Seiten Inhalt. Wien, Hochschule Mittweida - *University of Applied Sciences, Institut für Technologie- und Wissenstransfer, Masterarbeit*.

Ghobadian, A., Speller, S., & Jones, M. (1994). Service quality. Concepts and models. *International Journal of Quality and Reliability Management, 11*(9).

Ma, Y., & Liu, D. (2017). Introduction to the special issue on Crowdfunding and FinTech. *Financial Innovation, 3*(8).

Madan, R., Agrawal, R., & Matta, G. M. (2015). Relationship marketing strategies in the banking sector: A review. *International Journal of BRIC Business Research (IJBBR), 4*, 1–10.

Makridakis, S. (2017). The forthcoming artificial intelligence (AI) revolution: Its impact on society and firms. *Futures, 90*, 46–60.

Manyika, J., Chui, M., Miremadi, M., Bughin, J., & George, K. (2017). A future that works: AI, automation, employment, and productivity. *McKinsey Global Institute Research, Tech. Rep, 60*, 1–135.

Margaria, T., & Steffen, B. (2010). Simplicity as a driver for agile innovation. *Computer, 43*(6), 90–92.

Marion, T. J., & Friar, J. H. (2012). Managing global outsourcing to enhance lean innovation. *Research-Technology Management, 55*(5), 44–50.

Marr, B. (2017, December). 9 technology mega trends that will change the world in 2018. *Forbes*.

Marr, B. (2021, October). *AI and data at Dow Jones: Why humans are the machine behind AI*. Linkedin.com.

Martin, R., & Martin, R. L. (2009). *The design of business: Why design thinking is the next competitive advantage*. Harvard Business Press.

Martínez-López, F. J., & Casillas, J. (2013). Artificial intelligence-based systems applied in industrial marketing: An historical overview, current and future insights. *Industrial Marketing Management, 42*(2013), 489–495.

Maskey, S. (2018). *How artificial intelligence is helping financial institutions*. Forbes Technology Council.

Matt, C., Hess, T., & Benlian, A. (2015). Digital transformation strategies. *Business & Information Systems Engineering, 57*(5), 339–343.

Maurer, R. (2020, September). *Study finds productivity not deterred by shift to remote work*. SHRM.

Mazzone, D. M. (2014). *Digital or death: Digital transformation: The only choice for business to survive smash and conquer*. Smashbox Consulting Inc.

McCarthy, J., Minsky, M. L., Rochester, N., & Shannon C. E. (1955). *A proposal for the Dartmouth summer research project on artificial intelligence*.

McIntyre, A., et al. (2020). *Making digital banking more human*. Global Banking Customer Study an Accenture Paper.

McKinsey & Company. (2011). *Big Data: The next frontier for innovation, competition and productivity*.

McKinsey & Company (2017). *Artificial intelligence the next digital frontier*.

Mehri, D. (2006). The darker side of lean: An insider's perspective on the realities of the Toyota production system. *Academy of Management Perspectives, 20*(2), 21–42.

Mehrotra, A., & Menon, S. (2021, January). Second round of FinTech-trends and challenges. In *2021 2nd International Conference on Computation, Automation and Knowledge Management (ICCAKM)* (pp. 243–248). IEEE.

Mendling, J., Decker, G., Hull, R., Reijers, H. A., & Weber, I. (2018). How does machine learning, robotic process automation, and blockchains affect the human factor in business process management? *Communications of the Association for Information Systems, 43*(1), 19.

MiFid II. (2014). Directive 2014/65/Eu of the European Parliament and of the Council of 15 May 2014 on *Markets in Financial Instruments and Amending the Insurance Mediation Directive and Aifmd*. Article, 4(1)(39).

Miles Everson, M., Sviokla, J., & Barnes, K. (2018, October). Leading a bionic transformation *strategy+business*.

Miles, M. B., & Huberman, A. M. (1994). *Qualitative data analysis* (2nd ed.). Sage Publications.

Mitchell, V. W. (1993). *Handling customer complaint information: Why and how?* Management Decision.

Montani, S., & Anglano, C. (2008). Achieving self-healing in service delivery software systems by means of case-based reasoning. *Applied Intelligence, 28*(2), 139–152.

Morais, R., Le, V., Venkatesh, S., Tran, T., 2021. Learning asynchronous and sparse human-object interaction in videos. *arXiv preprint* arXiv:2103.02758

Morakanyane, R., Grace, A. A., & O'Reilly, P. (2017, June). Conceptualizing digital transformation in organizations: A systematic review of literature. In *Bled eConference* (p. 21).

Mpofu, T. P., & Mukosera, M. (2014). Credit scoring techniques: A survey. *International Journal of Science and Research, 3*(8).

Mukherjee, A., & Nath, P. (2003). A model of trust in online relationship banking. *International Journal of Bank Marketing*.

Mullen, A., et al. (2021, October). *Top strategic technology trends for 2022: Generative AI* (Gartner Paper).

Müller, R., Vette, M., & Geenen, A. (2017). Skill-based dynamic task allocation in human-robot-cooperation with the example of welding application. *Procedia Manufacturing, 11*, 13–21.

Munoz-Leiva, F., Climent-Climent, S., & Liébana-Cabanillas, F. (2017). Determinants of intention to use the mobile banking apps: An extension of the classic TAM model. *Spanish Journal of Marketing-ESIC, 21*(1), 25–38.

Murray, D. (2010). *Interaction design*. University of London International Programmes.

Nah, F. F. H., & Siau, K. (2020, July). Covid-19 pandemic–role of technology in transforming business to the new normal. In *International Conference on Human-Computer Interaction* (pp. 585–600). Springer.

Nash, K. (2015). CIO voices: Bank of America's Cathy Bessant says 'no' to innovation labs. *CIO Journal, The Wall Street Journal*.

Neff, G., & Nagy, P. (2016). Talking to bots: Symbiotic agency and the case of Tay. *International Journal of Communication*.

Nichols, C. (2020, February). *Why banks need to develop their own customer-facing technology*. Linkedin.

Nicholson, K. P., Pagowsky, N., & Seale, M. (2019). Just-in-time or just-in-case? Time, learning analytics, and the academic library. *Library Trends, 68*(1), 54–75.

Nicoletti, B. (2012). *Lean and digitize: An integrated approach to process improvement*. Gower Publishing. ISBN-10: 1409441946.

Nicoletti, B. (2013). *Cloud computing & financial services*. Palgrave Macmillan (also translated in Chinese).

Nicoletti, B. (2014a). *Mobile banking*. Palgrave Macmillan.

Nicoletti, B. (2014b, June). Lean and digitized innovation. In *2014 International Conference on Engineering, Technology and Innovation (ICE)* (pp. 1–7). IEEE.

Nicoletti, B. (2016). Resilience & outsourcing. *PMWORLD, 2*, 16.

Nicoletti, B. (2017). *Future of FinTech*. Palgrave Macmillan.

Nicoletti, B. (2019). Digital transformation via open data in insurance. In A. L. Mention (Ed.), *Digital innovation harnessing the value of open data*. World Scientific.

Nicoletti, B. (2021a). *Banking 5.0*. Springer.

Nicoletti, B. (2021b). Introduction. In Lechman, E., & Marszk, A. (Eds.), *The digital disruption of financial services: International perspectives*. Routledge.

Nikiforova, T. (2017). The place of robo-advisors in the UK independent financial advice market. Substitute or complement? *Substitute or Complement*.

Noble, E. (2020). The stages of industrial revolution and its impact on jobs. *The South African Institute of Chartered Accountants*.

Nofer, M., Gomber, P., Hinz, O., & Schiereck, D. (2017). Blockchain. *Business & Information SYSTEMS Engineering, 59*(3), 183–187.

Nonaka, I., & Takeuchi, H. (1995). *The knowledge-creating company: How Japanese companies create the dynamics of innovation*. Oxford University Press.

Noppen, P. V. (2019). *The qualitative impact of robotic process automation* (Master's thesis). Utrecht University, Utrecht, Netherlands.

Nott, B. (2018). *RPA use cases—Attended robots automation*.
Novet, J. (2021, March). *Microsoft's big email hack: What happened, who did it, and why it matters*. CNBC.
Nurmi, R. (1998). Knowledge-intensive organizations. *Business Horizons, 41*(3), 26–32.
Öger, M., Wecht, C., & Stalder, C. (2019). Hybrid business platforms-marketplaces of the future. *Marketing Review St. Gallen, 2*, 38–44.
Oliver, R. L., & Rust, R. T. (1997). Customer delight: Foundations, findings, and managerial insight. *Journal of Retailing, 73*(3), 311–336.
Olsher, D. J. (2015). New artificial intelligence tools for deep conflict resolution and humanitarian response. *Procedia Engineering, 107*, 282–292.
Omair, B., & Alturki, A. (2020). A systematic literature review of fraud detection metrics in business processes. *IEEE Access, 8*, 26893–26903.
Oosthuizen, R. M. (2021). The fourth industrial revolution: A resilience-based coping strategy for disruptive change. *Agile coping in the digital workplace* (pp. 11–34). Springer.
Osterwalder, A., Pigneur, Y., & Clark, T. (2010). *Business model generation*. Wiley.
Owais, S. S., & Hussein, N. S. (2016). Extract five categories CPIVW from the 9V's characteristics of the big data. *International Journal of Advanced Computer Science and Applications, 7*(3), 254–258.
Oza, N., & Abrahamsson, P. (2009). *Building blocks of agile innovation*. Book Surge Publishing.
Pan, Y. (2016). Heading toward Artificial Intelligence 2.0. *Engineering, 2*, 409–413.
Papadakis, V. M., Lioukas, S., & Chambers, D. (1998). Strategic decision-making processes: The role of management and context. *Strategic Management Journal, 19*, 115–147.
Parasuraman, A., Berry, L. L., & Zeithaml, V. A. (1991). Perceived service quality as a customer-based performance measure: An empirical examination of organizational barriers using an extended service quality model. *Human Resource Management, 30*(3), 335–364.
Parasuraman, A., Zeithaml, V. A., & Berry, L. L. (1985). A conceptual model of service quality and its implications for future research. *Journal of Marketing, 49*, 41–50.
Parasuraman, A., Zeithaml, V. A., & Berry, L. L. (1988). SERVQUAL: A multiple-item scale for measuring consumer perceptions of service quality. *Journal of Retailing, 64*(1), 14–40.
Paredes, D. (2018, July). *ANZ bank latest company to employ 'digital human'*. CIO.

Parker, H., & Appel, S. E. (2021). On the path to artificial intelligence: The effects of a robotics solution. In a Financial Services Firm. *The South African Journal of Industrial Engineering, 32*(2), 37–47.

Parry, K., & Cohen, M., & Bhattacharya, S. (2016). Rise of the machines: A critical consideration of automated leadership decision making in organizations. *Group and Organization Management, 41*(5), 571–594.

Penrose, E. T. (1952, December). Biological analogies in theory of the organization. *The American Economic Review, 42*(5), 804–819.

Peverelli, R., & de Feniks, R. (2019). *The four waves of Insurtech organization.* insurtechnews.com.

Pham, D. T., & Afify, A. A. (2005). Machine-learning techniques and their applications in manufacturing. *Proceedings of the Institution of Mechanical Engineers, Part B: Journal of Engineering Manufacture, 219*(5), 395–412.

Ping An Group. (2020, March). *Ping An life: Livestreaming channel + product reform blueprint to over one million agents across China.* Ping An.

Ping An Group. (n.d.). *Who we are.* Ping An.

Pizzagalli, S. L., Kuts, V., & Otto, T. (2021, May). User-centered design for Human Robot Collaboration systems. In *IOP Conference Series: Materials Science and Engineering*, 1140(1), 012011. IOP Publishing.

Pollari, I. (2021). Top Fintech Trends in H1'21. *KPMG.*

Pomerol, J. C. (1997). Artificial intelligence and human decision making. *European Journal of Operational Research, 99*(1997), 3–25.

Poole, D., Mackworth, A., & Goebel, R. (1997). *Computational intelligence: A logical approach.* Oxford University Press.

Prahalad, C. K., & Hamel, G. (1990). The core competence of the corporation. *Harvard Business Review, 68*(3), 79–91.

PriceWaterhouseCoopers. (2013). *Digitale Transformation – der gro€βte Wandel seit der Industriellen Revolution.* PriceWaterhouseCoopers.

Prieto, B., Plumbee, J., Vaughn, D., & Vaughn, J. (2015). *Resilience: Managing the risk of natural disaster.* Fluor.

Pritchard, J. (2021, May). *What is retail banking?* Thebalance.com.

PYMNTS. (2018). *Is AI's next evolution to digital humans?* PYMNTS.com.

Quanton. (2018). *Robotic process automation: Preparation and early-stage planning.* Quanton, Auckland, New Zealand.

Rajavenkatanarayanan, A. (2021). *Human factors analysis and monitoring to enhance human-robot collaboration* (Doctoral dissertation). The University of Texas at Arlington, Arlington, TX.

Ralston, P., & Blackhurst, J. (2020). Industry 4.0 and resilience in the supply chain: A driver of capability enhancement or capability loss? *International Journal of Production Research, 58*(16), 5006–5019.

Ransbotham, S., Khodabandeh, S., Kiron, D., Candelon, F., Chu, M,. & LaFountain, B. (2020). Expanding AI's impact with organizational learning. *MIT Sloan Management Review*.

Ransbotham, S., Kiron, D., Gerbert, P., & Reeves, M. (2017). Reshaping business with artificial intelligence: Closing the gap between ambition and action. *MIT Sloan Management Review*, 59(1).

Raschka, S., Patterson, J., & Nolet, C. (2020). Machine learning in python: Main developments and technology trends in data science, machine learning, and artificial intelligence. *Information*, 11(4), 193.

Rausch, J. (2021, February). *Personalization in financial services: An imperative to stay relevant*. pkglobal.com.

Realyvásquez-Vargas, A., Arredondo-Soto, K. C., García-Alcaraz, J. L., Márquez-Lobato, B. Y., & Cruz-García, J. (2019). Introduction and configuration of a collaborative robot in an assembly task as a means to decrease occupational risks and increase efficiency in a manufacturing company. *Robotics and Computer-Integrated Manufacturing*, 57, 315–328.

Reeves, M. (2020, July 2). A guide to building a more resilient business. *Harvard Business Review*.

Reid, M. (2017). Rethinking the fourth amendment in the age of supercomputers, artificial intelligence, and robots. *West Virginia Law Review*, 100.

Remane, G., Hanelt, A., Wiesboeck, F., & Kolbe, L. (2017). *Digital maturity in traditional industries—An exploratory analysis*.

Ries, E., & Euchner, J. (2013). What large companies can learn from start-ups. *Research-Technology Management*, 56(4), 12–16.

Rogers, E. M. (2010). *Diffusion of innovations*. Simon and Schuster.

Rojas, R. A., & Garcia, M. A. R. (2020). Implementation of industrial internet of things and cyber-physical systems in SMEs for distributed and service-oriented control. In *Industry 4.0 for SMEs* (pp. 73–103). Palgrave Macmillan.

Romani, J. C. C. (2009). *Strategies to promote the development of e-competencies in the next generation of professionals: European and international trends*.

Roth, R. R. (1983). The foundation of bionics. *Perspectives of biology and medicine*, 26(2)(Winter).

Rückert, P., Tracht, K., Herfs, W., Roggendorf, S., Schubert, V., & Schneider, M. (2020). Consolidation of product lifecycle information within human-robot collaboration for assembly of multi-variant products. *Procedia Manufacturing*, 49, 217–221.

Sadler-Smith, E., & Shefy, E. (2004). The intuitive executive: Understanding and applying 'gut feel' in decision-making. *Academy of Management Perspectives*, 18(4), 76–91.

Sadler-Smith, E., & Shefy, E. (2004, November). Understanding and applying 'gut feel' in decision-making. *The Academy of Management Executive (1993–2005), 18*(4).

Sadrfaridpour, B., & Wang, Y. (2017). Collaborative assembly in hybrid manufacturing cells: An integrated framework for human–robot interaction. *IEEE Transactions on Automation Science and Engineering, 15*(3), 1178–1192.

Salas, E., Rosen, M. A., & DiazGranados, D. (2010). Expertise-based intuition and decision-making in organizations. *Journal of Management, 36*(4), 941–973.

Samuels, M. (2019, July). Digital transformation: How one bank is using AI, big data and chatbots to create new services. *ZDNet*.

Sapriel, C. (2003). Effective crisis management: Tools and best practice for the new millennium. *Journal of Communication Management*.

Sarker, I. H. (2021). *Data science and analytics: An overview from data-driven smart computing, decision-making and applications perspective.*

Sarro, D. (2012). Do lenders make effective regulators? An assessment of the equator principles on project finance. *German Law Journal, 13*(12), 1525–1558.

Saunders, M., Lewis, P., & Thornhill, A. (1997). *Research methods for business students*. Pitman Publishing.

Savery, J. R., & Duffy, T. M. (1995). Problem based learning: An instructional model and its constructivist framework. *Educational Technology, 35*(5), 31–38.

Schierz, P. G., et al. (2010, May–June). Understanding customer acceptance of mobile payment services: An empirical analysis. *Electronic Commerce Research and Applications, 9*(3), 209–216.

Schlegel, D., & Kraus, P. (2021). Skills and competencies for digital transformation—A critical analysis in the context of robotic process automation. *International Journal of Organizational Analysis*.

Schlick, J., Stephan, P., Loskyll, M., & Lappe, D. (2014). Industries 4.0 in der praktischen Anwendung. In T. Bauernhansl, M. Ten Hompel, & B. Vogel-Heuser (Eds.), *Industrie 4.0 to Produktion, Automatisierung und Logistik: Anwendung. Technologien. Migration* (pp. 57–84). Springer.

Schmidt, R., Möhring, M., Härting, R. C., Reichstein, C., Neumaier, P., & Jozinović, P. (2015). Industry 5.0-potentials for creating smart products: Empirical research results. In *The International Conference on Business Information Systems* (pp. 16–27). Springer.

Schraft, R. D., Hägele, M., & Wegener, K. (2004). *Service-roboter-visionen*. Hanser Verlag.

Schroeder, R. G., Linderman, K., Liedtke, C., & Choo, A. S. (2008). Six Sigma: Definition and underlying theory. *Journal of Operations Management, 26*(4), 536–554.

Schuh, G., Powerful, T., Wesch-Powerful, C., Weber, A. R., & Prote, J. P. (2014). Collaboration mechanisms to increase productivity in the context of industries 4. 0. *Procedia CIRP, 19*(2014), 51–56.

Schuh, G., Lenders, M., & Hieber, S. (2008, July 27–31). Lean innovation: Introducing value systems to product development. In *PICMET 2008 Proceedings*.

Schurr, P. H., & Ozanne, J. L. (1985). Influences on exchange processes: Buyers' preconceptions of a seller's trustworthiness and bargaining toughness. *Journal of Consumer Research, 11*(4), 939–953.

Sebastian, I., Ross, J., Beath, C., Mocker, M., Moloney, K., & Fonstad, N. (2017, September). How big old organizations navigate digital transformation. *MIS Quarterly Executive, 16*(3).

Seiger, R., Huber, S., & Schlegel, T. (2018). Toward an execution system for self-healing workflows in cyber-physical systems. *Software & Systems Modeling, 17*(2), 551–572.

Sell, R., Leier, M., Rassolkin, A., & Ernits, J. P. (2018). Self-driving car ISEAUTO for research and education. In *Proceedings of 2018 19th International Conference on Research Education Mechatronics, REM 2018* (pp. 111–116).

Shevat, A. (2017). *Designing bots: Creating conversational experiences*. O'Reilly Media Inc.

Shorrock, S., & Williams, C. (2016). *Human factors and ergonomics in practice: Improving system performance and human well-being in the real world*. CRC Press.

Simon, H. A. (1997). *Models of bounded rationality. Empirically grounded economic reason* (Vol. 3). The MIT Press.

Simpson, A. (2017). *The innovation-friendly organization: How to cultivate new ideas and embrace the change they bring*. Springer.

Singh, S. K., & El-Kassar, A. N. (2019). Role of big data analytics in developing sustainable capabilities. *Journal of Cleaner Production, 213*, 1264–1273.

Siota, J., Klueter T., Wyman, O. Staib, D., Taylor, S., & Ania, I. (2017). *Design thinking the new DNA of the financial sector—How banks can boost their growth through design thinking in an era of de-banking*. IESE Business School.

Škavić, F. (2019). *The implementation of artificial intelligence and its future potential* (Doctoral dissertation). University of Zagreb, Faculty of Economics and Business, Department of Informatics.

Skinner, C. (2014). *Digital bank: Strategies to launch or become a digital bank*. Marshall Cavendish International Asia Pte Ltd.

Skinner, S. (2020, March). *Doing digital. Lessons from leaders*. Marshall Cavendish International Asia Pte Ltd.

Smit, J. (2016). e-competency of practitioners: A grounded theory. In *SAIS 2016 Proceedings*.

Smith, K. (2002). *What is the 'knowledge economy'? Knowledge intensity and distributed knowledge bases*. United Nations University, INTECH, Maastricht, Netherlands.

Snow, C. C., Fjeldstad, Ø. D., & Langer, A. M. (2017). Designing the digital organization. *Journal of Organization Design, 6,* 7.

Socha, D., Folsom, T. C., & Justice, J. (2013). Applying agile software principles and practices for fast automotive development. In *Proceedings of the FISITA 2012 World Automotive Congress* (pp. 1033–1045).

Somers, L., Dewit, I., & Baelus, C. (2018). Understanding product-service systems in a sharing economy context—A literature review. *Procedia Cirp, 73,* 173–178.

Song, Y. W. (2019). *User acceptance of an artificial intelligence (AI) virtual assistant: An extension of the solution acceptance mode* (Doctoral dissertation). The University of Texas at Austin, Austin, TX.

Srinivas, V., & Wadhwani, R. (2019). *Deloitte accelerating-digital-transformation-in-banking*.

Srinivas, V., & Wadhwani, R. (2021). *Recognizing the value of bank branches in a digital world findings from the global digital banking survey*. Deloitte Insights.

Stalidis G., Karapistolis D., & Vafeiadis A. (2015). Marketing decision support using artificial intelligence and knowledge modeling: Application to tourist destination management. In: *International Conference on Strategic Innovative Marketing, IC-SIM 2014*. Madrid, Spain September 1–4. *Procedia - Social and Behavioral Sciences, 175*(2015), 106–113.

Starbuck, W. H. (1992). Learning by knowledge-intensive organizations. *Journal of Management Studies, 29*(6), 713–740.

Staub, S., Karaman, E., Kayaa, S., Karapınar, H., & Güven, E. (2015). Artificial neural network and agility. *Procedia - Social and Behavioral Sciences, 195,* 1477–1485.

Sternberg, R. J. (1984). What should intelligence tests test? Implications of a triarchic theory of intelligence for intelligence testing. *Educational Researcher, 13*(1), 5–15.

Steyn, P. (2020). *Get educated for industry 4.0. Business Day Focus 4.0*. Cold Press Media (Pty) Ltd for Arena Holdings, Western Cape, South Africa.

Subroyen, L. (2020). *What is bionic banking? Business Day Focus 4.0*. Cold Press Media (Pty) Ltd for Arena Holdings.

Suiter, M. (2020). *Banking basics*. Federal Reserve Bank of St. Louis.

Susar, D., & Aquaro, V. (2019, April). Artificial intelligence: Opportunities and challenges for the public sector. In *Proceedings of the 12th International Conference on Theory and Practice of Electronic Governance* (pp. 418–426).

Susskind, R., & Susskind, D. (2015). *The future of the professions: How technology will transform the work of human experts* (1st ed.). Oxford University Press.

Swan, M. (2015). *Blockchain: Blueprint for a new economy*. Newton, MA.

Syed, R., Suriadi, S., Adams, M., Bandara, W., Leemans, S. J., Ouyang, C., & Reijers, H. A. (2020). Robotic process automation: Contemporary themes and challenges. *Computers in Industry*, *115*, 103162.

Taddeo, M., & Floridi, L. (2018). How AI can be a force for good. *Science*, *361*(6404), 751–752.

Takeda, N., Shiomi, A., Kawai, K., & Ohiwa, H. (1993, January). Requirement analysis by the KJ editor. In *[1993] Proceedings of the IEEE International Symposium on Requirements Engineering* (pp. 98–101). IEEE.

Tambe, P., Hitt, L. M., Rock, D., & Brynjolfsson, E. (2019). *IT, AI and the growth of intangible capital*. Available at SSRN 3416289.

Tang, Y. (2021). Corporate finance management in the age of artificial intelligence. *Journal of Frontiers of Society, Science and Technology*, *1*(10), 170–176.

Temkin, A. (2017, April). Apply for a loan in less than 15 minutes. *The Times*.

Teradata. (2018). *Danske Bank fights fraud with deep learning and AI*. Teradata Corporation, 10, 18.

Tharumarajah, A. (1996). Comparison of the bionic, fractal, and holonic manufacturing system concepts. *International Journal of Computer Integrated Manufacturing*, *9*(3), 217–226.

The European Commission' Science and Knowledge Service, Joint Research Centre. (2020). *Telework in the EU before and after the pandemic: Where we were, where we head to*. Science for policies brief. European Union.

Tierney, K., & Bruneau, M. (2007, May–June). Conceptualizing and measuring resilience: A key to disaster loss reduction. *TR News*, no. 250. pp. 14–16.

Tomassetti, F. Rizzo, G., Glass, A., Hardy, L., Torchiano, M., & Morisio, M. (2011). Linked Data approach to the automation of the selection processes in systematic reviews. In *The Assessment and Evaluation in Software Engineering (EASE 2011), 15th Annual Conference* (pp. 31–350). EIT.

Tomsett, D. (2011, August). *What does 'the new normal' mean for business anyway?* Forbes Technology Council.

Trang, N. T. K., Giang, N. M., Thuong, N. T., Trung, N. B. V., & Anh, N. K. (2020, July). Factors influence customers 'satisfaction toward online brand community: A case study of national economics university's online brand communities. In *Proceedings of the 12th NEU-KKU International Conference Socio-Economic and Environmental Issues in Development*.

Travia, G. (2021, March). *Robo Advisor: Cosa sono, come funzionano e la lista dei migliori*. Finaria.

Trivedi, N., Asamoah, D. A., & Doran, D. (2018). Keep the conversations going: engagement-based customer segmentation on online social service platforms. *Information Systems Frontiers*, *20*(2).

Turner, N., & Kutsch, E. (2015). Project resilience: Moving beyond traditional risk management. *PM World Journal*, *4*(11).

Tushman, M. L., & Nadler, D. A. (1980). Communication and technical roles in R&D laboratories: An information processing approach. *TIMS Studies in the Management Sciences, 15*(1), 91–112.

Tzanis, S. (2012). *Direct insurance: The determinants of success.* Dissertation of the University of St. Gallen, Switzerland.

Vakkuri, V., Kemell, K. K., Kultanen, J., & Abrahamsson, P. (2020). The current state of industrial practice in artificial intelligence ethics. *IEEE Software, 37*(4), 50–57.

van der Aalst, W., Bichler, M., & Heinzl, A. (2018). Robotic process automation. *Business & Information Systems Engineering, 60*(4).

van der Zant, T., Kouw, M., & Schomaker, L. (2013). Generative artificial intelligence. *Philosophy and theory of artificial intelligence* (pp. 107–120). Springer.

Van Leeuwen, G., & Klomp, L. (2006). On the contribution of innovation to multi-factor productivity growth. *Economics of Innovation and New Solution, 15*(4–5), 367–390.

van Nuenen, T., Ferrer, X., Such, J. M., & Cote, M. (2020). Visibility for whom? Assessing discriminatory artificial intelligence. *Computer, 53*(11), 36–44.

Van Weele, A. J. (2010). *Purchasing & supply chain management: Analysis, strategy, planning and practice.* Cengage Learning EMEA.

Verhoef, P. C., Broekhuizen, T., Bart, Y., Bhattacharya, A., Dong, J. Q., Fabian, N., & Haenlein, M. (2019). Digital transformation: A multidisciplinary reflection and research agenda. *Journal of Business Research.*

Villani, C. (2018). *Donner un sens à l'intelligence artificielle* (French Government report).

Villar, A. S., & Khan, N. (2021). Robotic process automation in banking industry: A case study on Deutsche Bank. *Journal of Banking and Financial Technology,* 1–16.

Vybornov, A., Miloslavskaya, N., & Tolstoy, A. (2020, September). Designing competency models for cybersecurity professionals for the banking sector. In *IFIP World Conference on Information Security Education* (pp. 81–95). Springer.

Wagner, P. W. (2017). Trends in expert system development: A longitudinal content analysis of over thirty years of expert system case studies. *Expert Systems with Applications, 76,* 86–96.

Walker, L. W. (2008). Learning lessons on lessons learned. In *PMI® Global Congress.*

Wall, L. D. (2018). Some financial regulatory implications of artificial intelligence. *Journal of Economics and Business, 100,* 55–63.

Walsh, I., Reinaud, A. de T'Serclaes, J. W., Reyero, B., Noakes, B., & Mönter, N. (2015, March). *The bionic bank.* Boston Consulting Group Paper.

Wang, L., Gao, R., Váncza, J., Krüger, J., Wang, X. V., Makris, S., & Chryssolouris, G. (2019). Symbiotic human-robot collaborative assembly. *CIRP Annals, 68*, 701–726.

Wang, L., Liu, S., Liu, H., & Wang, X. V. (2020). Overview of human-robot collaboration in manufacturing, In *Proceedings of 5th International Conference on the Industry 4.0 Model for Advanced Manufacturing* (pp. 15–58). Springer.

Wang, X. V., & Wang, L. (2021). A literature survey of the robotic technologies during the covid-19 pandemic. *Journal of Manufacturing Systems*.

Ward-Dutton, N. (2018). *From RPA to DPA: A strategic approach to automation* (Pegasystems paper).

Watson, W. T. (2017). *New horizon: How diverse growth strategies can advance digitisation in the insurance industry* (Willis Towers Watson's Report).

Wauters, M., & Vanhoucke, M. (2015). A comparative study of Artificial Intelligence methods for project duration forecasting. *Expert Systems with Applications, 46*(2015), 249–261.

Webb, M. (2019). *The impact of artificial intelligence on the labor market*. Available at SSRN 3482150.

Wessel, L., Baiyere, A., Ologeanu-Taddei, R., Cha, J., & Blegind-Jensen, T. (2021). Unpacking the difference between digital transformation and IT-enabled organizational transformation. *Journal of the Association for Information Systems, 22*(1), 102–129.

West, D. M., & Allen, J. R. (2018, April). *How artificial intelligence is transforming the world* (Report).

West, J., & Bhattacharya, M. (2016). Intelligent financial fraud detection: A comprehensive review. *Computers & Security, 57*, 47–66.

Westerman, G., Calméjane, C., Bonnet, D., Ferraris, P., & McAfee, A. (2011). Digital transformation: A roadmap for billion-dollar organizations. *MIT Center for Digital Business and Capgemini Consulting, 1*, 1–68.

Wilson, K., & Doz, Y. L. (2011). Agile innovation: A footprint balancing distance and immersion. *California Management Review, 53*(2), 6–26.

Winter, S. G. (1964, Spring). Economic natural selection and theory of the organization. *Yale Economic Essays, 4*, 1.

Woitsch, R., Utz, W., Sumereder, A., Dieber, B., Breiling, B., Crompton, L., & Schumann, S. (2020). Collaborative model-based process assessment for trustworthy AI in robotic platforms. In *First International Conference on Society 5.0*.

Wolf, R. A. (2016). Virtual currencies, M-payments & VAT: Ready for the future? *Bitcoin and mobile payments* (pp. 231–249). Palgrave Macmillan.

Womack, J. P., & Jones, D. T. (2003). *Lean thinking banish waste and create wealth in your corporation* (2nd ed.). Simon & Schuster Inc.

World Bank. (2018). *From spreadsheets to Suptech: Technology solutions for market conduct supervision*. World Bank.

Xu, W. (2019). Toward human-centered AI: A perspective from human-computer interaction. *Interactions, 26*(4), 42–46.

Xu, W., Furie, D., Mahabhaleshwar, M., Suresh, B., & Chouhan, H. (2019). Applications of an interaction, process, integration, and intelligence (IPII) design approach for ergonomics solutions. *Ergonomics, 62*(7), 954–980.

Xu, Y. M., Yu, J. L., & Li, W. M. (2009, September). Evaluation of enterprise vitality and model of enterprise commercial age. In *2009 International Conference on Management Science and Engineering* (pp. 569–574). IEEE.

Yamashina, H., Ito, T., & Kawada, H. (2002). Innovative product development process by integrating QFD and TRIZ. *International Journal of Production Research, 40*(5), 1031–1050.

Yang, C. J. (2020, May). *An introduction to embedded finance*. Medium.com.

Yao, B., Zhou, Z., Wang, L., Xu, W., Yan, J., & Liu, Q. (2018). A function block-based cyber-physical production system for physical human-robot interaction. *Journal of Manufacturing Systems, 48*, 12–23.

Yip, A. W., & Bocken, N. M. (2018). Sustainable business model archetypes for the banking industry. *Journal of Cleaner Production, 174*, 150–169.

Young, D., Woods, W., & Reeves, M. (2021). Optimize for both social and business value. *Winning the '20s* (pp. 83–94). De Gruyter.

Young, M. M., Bullock, J. B., & Lecy, J. D. (2019). Artificial discretion as a tool of governance: A framework for understanding the impact of artificial intelligence on public administration. *Perspectives on Public Management and Governance, 2*(4), 301–313.

Zeng, D. (2015, May). AI ethics: Science fiction meets technological reality. *IEEE Intelligent Systems, 30*(3), 2–5.

Zhang, A. X., Muller, M., & Wang, D. (2020). How do data science workers collaborate? Roles, workflows, and tools. *Proceedings of the ACM on Human-Computer Interaction, 4*(CSCW1), 1–23.

Zhang, J., Liu, H., Chang, Q., Wang, L., & Gao, R. X. (2020). Recurrent neural network for motion trajectory prediction in human-robot collaborative assembly. *CIRP Annals, 69*, 9–12.

Zheng, N. N., Liu, Z. Y., Ren, P. J., Ma, Y. Q., Chen, S. T., Yu, S. Y., ... & Wang, F. Y. (2017). Hybrid-augmented intelligence: Collaboration and cognition. *Frontiers of Information Technology & Electronic Engineering, 18*(2), 153–179.

Zheng, P., Wang, Z., Chen, C. H., & Khoo, L. P. (2019). A survey of smart product-service systems: Key aspects, challenges and future perspectives. *Advanced Engineering Informatics, 42*, 100973.

Zheng, Z., Xie, S., Dai, H. N., Chen, X., & Wang, H. (2018). Blockchain challenges and opportunities: A survey. *International Journal of Web and Grid Services, 14*(4), 352–375.

Zhou, Z., Xie, S. S., & Chen, D. (2011). *Fundamentals of digital manufacturing science*. Springer.

Zhu, B., Joseph, A., & Sastry, S. (2011, October). A taxonomy of cyber-attacks on SCADA systems. In *2011 International Conference on Internet of Things and 4th International Conference on Cyber, Physical and Social Computing* (pp. 380–388). IEEE.

Zimmer, J. C., Arsal, R. E., Al-Marzouq, M., & Grover, V. (2010). Investigating online information disclosure: Effects of information relevance, trust and risk. *Information & Management, 47*(2), 115–123.

Žitkienė, R., & Deksnys, M. (2018). Organizational agility conceptual model. *Montenegrin Journal of Economics, 14*(2), 115–129.

Zujev, A. (2021). *The road to true digital bank*. Ceo Insight.

Websites

www.hdfcbank.com/content/bbp/repositories/723fb80a-2dde-42a3-9793-7ae1be57c87f/?path=/Footer/About%20Us/News%20Room/Press%20Release/PDF/Press-Release-2021/Press%20Release_December%2020.pdf. Accessed 21 October 2021,

www.ibm.com/annualreport/2017/assets/downloads/IBM. Annual Report 2017.pdf Accessed 02 May 2021.

www.investmentexecutive.com/newspaper_/building-your-business-newspaper/how-banks-are-harnessing-artificial-intelligence/. Accessed 25 February 2021.

www.lulu.com/shop/robert-prieto/resilience-managing-the-risk-of-natural-disasters/paperback/product-22219550.html. Accessed 21 October 2021.

www.mckinsey.com/~/media/McKinsey/Industries/Advanced%20Electronics/Our%20Insights/How%20artificial%20intelligence%20can%20deliver%20real%20value%20to%20companies/MGI-Artificial-Intelligence-Discussion-paper.ashx. Accessed 29 March 2021.

www.mergermarket.com/info/new-horizons-how-diverse-growth-strategies-can-advance-digitalisation-insurance-industry. Accessed 30 May 2021.

www.resorgs.org.nz/Content/what-is-organisational-resilience.html. Accessed 1 January 2021.

www.strategyand.pwc.com/reports/insurance-4-digital-revolution. Accessed 20 March 2021.

Index

A
Academic and Research Institutions
  Fraunhofer Institute for
    Manufacturing Engineering
    and Automation, 92
  Henderson Institute, 150
  MIT, 51, 56, 150
  Stanford University, 51
  UC Berkeley, 51
America
  Latin America
    South America, 18
  United States of America
    American Marketing
      Association, 215
    IUSA Aerospace Division, 8
    New York, 77
    Ohio, Dayton, 8
    Oregon, Portland, 168
    USA Department of
      Commerce, 216
Asia
  Central Asia, 18
  China
    Shenzhen, 135
    Wuhan, 22
  India, 178
  Japan, 84
  Malaysia, 18
  North Asia, 18

C
Compliance
  Regulations
    Basel, 30
    California Customer Privacy
      Act (CCPA), 127
    General Data Protection
      Regulation (GDPR), 127
    Mifid II, 221
  Regulators
    National Institute of Standards
      and Solution (NIST), 224
Consultants and advisory
  Accenture, 133
  Bain, 149

Boston Consulting Group (BCG), 2, 24, 56, 69, 70, 107, 141, 150, 204
Capgemini, 77, 105, 142
Deloitte, 16, 101, 176, 177
Ernst & Young (EY), 27
Gartner, 103
KPMG, 69
Nice, 145
Price Waterhouse Coopers (PWC), 130, 204
Customer
  customer acquisition, 75, 124, 126
  customer experience (CX), 5, 25, 46, 49, 70, 74, 78, 80, 87, 98, 107, 108, 126, 131, 135, 141, 179, 182, 205
  customer relationships, 71, 73, 79, 82, 144, 151, 179
  Know Your Customer (KYC), 175
  prosumer, 50
  value
    customer lifetime value, 106, 107
    Innovative Value Proposition (IVP), 74
    product/service system, 75
    supply chain, 25, 29, 186

D
Distribution
  bancassurance, 164
  channel
    omnichannel, 78
  direct insurance, 1
  e-Commerce
    Amazon, 157
    Netflix, 157
  intermediaries
    agencies, 79
    bank, 159
    broker, 142
  Omnichannel, 78, 224
  relationships
    B2B, 140
    B2C, 213, 217

E
Europe
  Austria, 80, 134
  Denmark
    Copenhagen, 54
  European Union, 127
  Finland, 54
  Northern Europe, 55
  Norway, 54
  Portugal, 105
  United Kingdom
    Financial Conduct Authority (FCA), 88

F
fintech organizations
  Insurtech, 141
Function
  Bionic Transformation Steering Committee, 171
  data management
    data scientist, 91
    data & analytics, 91
  human resources (HR), 10, 30, 54, 88, 97, 144
  Information and communication technologies (ICT), 24–26, 50, 78, 89, 92, 94, 96, 100, 159, 162, 164, 167, 171, 174, 179, 187
  marketing
    pricing, 106, 128
  Mergers & Acquisition (M&A), 18
  operations, 13, 96, 164, 183
  risk management

underwriting, 19
sales, 78, 164

G
Generation
    Generation Y, 224
    Millennial, 133

I
Indicators
    Gross National Product (GDP), 22
    Key Behavioral Indicator, 83
    Key Performance Indicator, 74
    Net Promoter Score, 103
    RATER assessment, 183
    Return on Investment (ROI), 150, 177
    SERVQUAL, 183
Industry 5.0
    critical success factors
        clarity, 157, 158, 164
        cognition, 157, 158, 162
        collaboration, 38, 157–159, 161, 164
        competence, 157, 158, 161
        complementarity, 157, 158, 160
        confidence, 157, 158, 161
        connection, 38
        contribution, 157, 158, 162, 164
        creatural, 157, 158, 164
        customization, 157, 158, 162, 164
    industrial revolution, 6
Investment Vehicles
    Exchange-Traded Funds, 220, 225
    Initial Public Offer (IPO), 18
    Merger & Acquisition (M&A), 17
    options, 18

M
Models
    7D's, 171
    agile, 185, 186, 205
    bounded rationality, 11
    business model canvas, 3, 4, 65–68, 70, 74, 83, 84, 113, 115, 205
    business model innovation, 46, 61, 175
    Constructivism, 3
    design thinking, 167, 168
    Innovation Acceptance Model, 186, 188
    Innovative Product Development Process (IPDP), 166
    Interaction, Process, Integration, Intelligence (IPII), 166
    Know Your Customer (KYC), 179
    O-ring, 96
    Project Management Lifecycle (PML), 183
    Root Cause Analysis (RCA), 35
    Technology Acceptance Model, 186
    User Centered Design (UCD), 171

O
Organizations
    ecosystem, 9, 10, 13, 16, 56, 71, 96, 104, 105, 115, 130, 159, 160, 165, 181, 185
    financial institutions
        ANZ Bank, 102, 137
        Banca Generali Private, 139, 140, 206
        Bank of America, 138
        Bank of Australia, 136
        Barclays, 173
        Danske Bank, 54, 55, 206
        Deutsche Bank, 95, 137, 138
        HDFC Bank, 178, 179, 206
        HSBC, 174

JP Morgan, 129
NASDAQ, 18
NatWest Bank, 137
Paypal, 47
Rabobank, 126
Reserve Bank of India, 178
UBS, 140
Umpqua Bank, 168
Valhalla Bank, 131
fintech organizations
　Crowdfunding, 20, 76
　Fintech, 10, 14–21, 39, 50, 55, 71–73, 75, 77, 78, 83, 103, 106, 107, 114, 115, 123, 136, 140, 143, 182, 206
　Habito, 156
　Insurtech, 135
　Regtech, 21
　Square, 129, 130
industrial companies
　B8ta, 81
　General Electric, 12
　IDEO, 169
　Jingle, 80
　Moleskine, 169
　Unilever, 12
insurance companies
　Aflac, 84
　Colonial Life, 142, 143
　Metlife, 77, 78, 97
　Ping An, 135, 136, 206
　Zurich Insurance, 105–106
international organizations
　Financial Stability Board, 15
　IEEE, 52, 92
　International Trade Center, 22
　United Nations (UN), 142
　World Economic Forum, 15
　World Trade Organization, 22
media companies
　Dow Jones, 58, 59
　Forbes, 21, 135
　Fortune, 84, 135
　Technology Innovation Management Review, 30
social network companies
　Facebook, 50
technology companies
　Google, 50, 102, 157
　IBM, 27, 102
　Microsoft, 110
　Pega(system), 84

P
Pandemic
　coronavirus, 22
　lock down, 26
　lockdown, 5, 22, 25, 78, 142
　new normal, 3, 5, 8, 21–23, 25, 27, 28, 30, 39, 206
　remote working, 5, 23, 25–27
Persons
　Agrawal, A., 175
　Ahmed, D., 22
　Aldrich, H.E., 9, 10
　Buheji, M., 22
　Carr, C., 203
　Carrozzi, L., 30
　Dane, E., 57, 58
　Darwin, C., 10
　Davis, R., 169
　de Geus, A., 12
　Drucker, P., 66
　Eletter, S.F., 127
　Everson, M., 101, 204
　Fabeil, N.F., 23
　Furong, H., 12
　Gang. G.L., 12
　Henry, T., 126
　Jarrahi, M.H., 56–58, 87, 154
　Kremer, M., 96
　Kuo, C.M., 125

Lizhi, W., 12
Margaria, A., 186
Martin, I., 19
Maskey, S., 137
Mehri, D., 169
Nagy, 126
Nah, F.F.H., 23
Neff, G., 126
Nicoletti, B., 4, 10, 17, 18, 21, 35, 66, 90, 98, 107, 151, 162, 164–166, 170, 171, 187, 188
Osterwalder, A., 4, 66, 205
Parasuraman, A., 183
Penrose, E.T., 9
Peverelli, S., 15
Rogers, E.M., 187
Sadler-Smith, E., 58
Salim, R., 173
Shorrock, S., 180
Simon, H., 11
Steele, J., 8
Steffen, S., 186
Sviokla, J., 101
Turner, N.S., 30
Wang, L., 152, 153
West, D.M., 128, 137
Wiedenmayer, 9
Xu, Y.M., 12
Yip, A.W., 124
Profiles
  data scientist, 95, 98, 135, 164
  management
    Chief Digital Officer (CDO), 18
    Chief Executive Officer (CEO), 169
    Chief Information Officier (CISO), 97, 113
    head of content Management, 173
    risk manager, 130

Q
Quality
  agile management, 165
  critical success factors, 165
  Critical to Quality (CtQ), 176
  House of Quality, 165
  lean
    lean and digitize, 99
    lean principles, 165, 185
    Lean Product Development (LPD), 170
  Quality Function Deployment (QFD), 165
  Theory of Inventive Problem Solving (TRIZ), 165, 166
  Toyota Production System, 169
  Voice of the Customer, 174

R
Resilience
  business resilience, 27, 29
  cyber resilience, 30
  operational resilience, 17, 27

T
Technologies
  artificial intelligence
    chatbot, 76, 77, 80, 81, 87, 113, 114, 125, 126, 135–139, 174, 175, 179, 182–184, 203
    cognitive, 51, 154, 182
    explainability, 158, 189
    machine learning, 23, 82, 89, 90, 93, 98–100, 114, 126, 128–131, 136, 162, 175
    natural language processing, 131
    neural networks, 99, 127
    optical character recognition, 95, 96

predictive analysis, 28, 89
voicebot, 126
automation, 101
   human-automation collaboration, 8, 21, 23, 45, 51, 54, 86, 101, 103, 129, 133, 150, 152–156, 159, 165, 169, 170, 172, 180, 185, 186, 189, 206
   human–robot collaboration, 86, 152, 153
   human–robot interaction, 13
   intelligent automation (IA), 28, 58, 95, 149, 150, 174
   Pepper, 174
   Robotics, human–robot interface, 192
   Robotics, robo-advisor, 113, 131
   Robotics, virtual robots, 80
Augmented Reality, 210
cloud computing
   Business Process as a Service (BpaaS), 213
   Infrastructure-as-a-Service (IaaS), 90
   Platform-as-a-Service (PaaS), 90
   Software-as-a-Service (SaaS), 90
data management
   big data analytics, 50, 132, 152, 162
   business intelligence, 82, 91
   Connection Modes, Application Programming Interface (API), 210
   Connection Modes, Web service, 225
   data-driven, 53, 82, 91, 93, 102, 182
   linked data, 165

distributed ledger protocol
   blockchain, 19, 24, 51, 135
   Smart Contract, 228
information and communication technology
   Customer Relationship Management (CRM), 53, 142
   Enterprise Resource Planning (ERP), 25
   Straight Through Processing (STP), 84
network
   Internet, Internet of Things (IoT), 23, 51, 222
   Mobility, instant Messaging, 213
   Mobility, mobile, 218
   Virtual Private Network (VPN), 26
operating systems, 7, 90, 91, 203
Proof of Concept, 126
security
   cybersecurity, 5, 23, 39, 89, 109, 110, 113
   DDos attack, 110
   hacker, 109, 110
   malware, 109
   One Time Password (OTP), 179
   Phishing, 110
   ransomware, 109
   trojans, 216
   virus, 161
SMACIT, 50
telecommunication
   Interactive Voice Response (IVR), 129
   Short Message Services (SMS), 179
transformation

bionic transformation, 1, 3–6, 32, 45–47, 49, 55, 59, 61, 65, 66, 68, 71–73, 88, 100, 123, 136, 143, 144, 150, 157, 164, 167, 169–171, 174, 179, 181, 182, 185, 191, 205

digital transformation, 3, 4, 13, 46, 47, 50, 87, 97–99

V

Virtual Currencies
  Bitcoin, 212
  stablecoins, 18